The United States Marines
in North China, 1894–1942

The United States Marines in North China, 1894–1942

by Chester M. Biggs, Jr.

McFarland & Company, Inc., Publishers

Jefferson, North Carolina, and London

Library of Congress Cataloguing-in-Publication Data

Biggs, Chester M., 1921–
    The United States marines in North China, 1894–1942 / by
Chester M. Biggs, Jr.
        p.   cm.
    Includes index.

    ISBN 0-7864-1488-X (softcover: 50# alkaline paper)

    1. China—History—20th century.   2. United States.
    Marine Corps—History—20th century.   I. Title.
    DS774.B47   2003
    327.73051'09'041—dc21   2003006021

British Library cataloguing data are available

On the front cover: The 39th Company (Artillery) in front of the
Chien Men Pagoda on the Tartar Wall, ca. 1925 (*Marine Corps University Archives, Quantico, Virginia*)—and see page 141

Manufactured in the United States of America

McFarland & Company, Inc., Publishers
    Box 611, Jefferson, North Carolina 28640
    www.mcfarlandpub.com

To my wife, Betty,
to whom I owe so much.

Table of Contents

Preface   1

Introduction   5

   1. Early Military Operations in North China   7

   2. Early Marine Legation Guards   11

   3. The Boxer Rebellion of 1900   15

   4. The Marine Legation Guard in Peking — 1900   26

   5. Seymour's Relief Column   34

   6. Major Waller's Column   40

   7. The Capture of Tien-Tsin   47

   8. The Siege of the Legations at Peking   63

   9. The Relief of Peking   118

  10. Marines Return to Peking   137

  11. The End of an Era — The Old China Marine   168

Epilogue   210

Appendix A: Chronology   211

Appendix B: The Legation Guard at Peking, 1900   220

Appendix C: Reports of Colonel Robert J. Meade and Major
   L.W.T. Waller (as Reported by the *New York Times,*
   August 18, 1900)   222

Appendix D: The Letter Sir Claude MacDonald
Received from "Prince Ching and Others"   228

Appendix E: U.S. Marines Who Received the
Medal of Honor During the Boxer Rebellion   230

Appendix F: Marine Officers Receiving a Brevet
Commission During the Boxer Rebellion   232

Appendix G: Appreciation from the American
Missionaries for the Marine Legation Guard   234

Appendix H: Letters to Major Waller from British Officers
Commending the Marines' Action at Tien-Tsin   236

Appendix I: Operation Reports of the U.S. Marines in the
Relief of the Besieged Legation Quarter at Peking   238

Appendix J: Roster of Marine Personnel in North China
on December 8, 1941   246

Appendix K: Knights of the Round Table Roster   250

Notes   253

Bibliography   265

Index   269

Preface

In this book I have attempted to collect, as far as possible, the facts, movements and accomplishments of the United States Marine Corps in North China during the years 1894 through 1942.

In some cases the Marines operated with other military forces. I have referred to the U.S. Army, U.S. Navy and foreign troops only when necessary to make the narrative intelligible. This was necessary, not to minimize the accomplishments of these troops, but to keep the book a manageable size.

Throughout this book I have used the word "Marine" to signify the United States Marines. Marines from other countries are prefixed by their nationality: British Royal Marines, Japanese Marines, etc.

Like most foreign troops stationed in China, the Marines' mission was to protect the embassy, consulates, missionaries, tourists, and other American citizens doing business in China. Usually, they did not do any physical defending; the mere visible presence of the Marines protected the Americans' interest in China. There were, however, exceptions to this. The major exception was the struggle during the Boxer Rebellion of 1900, which not only involved the United States Armed Forces but most of the major European powers as well. During the Boxer Rebellion, the Marines distinguished themselves on many occasions.

During these years, the Marines saw China as it will never be again. The victories of the Opium Wars and the Boxer Rebellion gave the white race a certain standing, certain prerogatives and privileges that they, as well as the Chinese, looked upon as a natural order of existence. While this lordly way of life was not morally right, it was that way during this period.

1

Throughout this book the spelling of Chinese towns and cities varies because the spellings changed over time. For example, early in the 1900s many Chinese cities' names were hyphenated: Tien-Tsen, Yang-fang. Later, they were spelled without the hyphen. Peking, now universally known as "Beijing," has been spelled and known by many names: Pekin, Peking, and Peiping, as well as Beijing. Because the spelling of the names was sometimes significant in Chinese history, I changed the spelling as the century progressed.

Chinese history and politics fill volumes of books. For some three hundred years internal strife, famines and floods weakened the Chinese government. Taking advantage of this, through treaties or sometimes by military force, foreign powers imposed upon China terms that not only exploited China but also made the Chinese people second-class citizens within their own country. Again, while this may not have been right, that's the way it was.

In this book I do not condone the foreign powers' actions. I briefly relate only enough to explain and, perhaps, justify in the eyes of the Western European Powers, including Japan, their right to station troops in China to protect their citizens and their trade.

Generally speaking, the reader will find little or nothing of the interplay of Chinese politics with the Marines' operations in China.

When local disturbances in China threatened Americans, Marines landed, not to quell the civil unrest but to protect the Americans and their property. The Marines had little interest in the cause of the disturbance. Once the Chinese government restored order and Americans were no longer threatened, the Marines were withdrawn.

In the cases of the Boxer Rebellion of 1901 and the landing of the Third Marine Brigade in 1927, however, I felt the reader should have a better understanding of the political situation that landed Marines in China.

Because of the magnitude of the Boxer Rebellion, I have devoted Chapter 3 to briefly explaining why and how the Boxer Rebellion developed and the position the Chinese Government took when confronted with it.

Scattered throughout Chapter 10 are brief explanations of the situations arising in China that caused the United States to feel justified in landing Marines on Chinese soil. Perhaps these brief explanations will help the reader understand why a military presence was necessary.

Because the Boxer Rebellion was complicated, with several operations going on at once, I have tried to make the reader's task a little easier by separating the various operations into independent chapters. Anyone interested in the continuity of the various operations is referred to the chronology in Appendix A.

To avoid confusion, all time is based on the twenty-four hour military clock. One o'clock in the morning is 0100 hours, while twelve o'clock midnight is 2400 hours.

In researching material for this book I found that dates for some events vary as much as two or three days. This may seem strange, especially since people who actually participated in the events wrote some of the accounts. While trying to be historically correct, I have found it necessary to select dates that are chronological so that the narrative has continuity. The same can be said of other facts. It has also been necessary to select the facts that seem to be the most consistent throughout the research material.

An excellent example of such a conflict is the arrival of the relief column at Peking, the attack on the city and the entrance into the Legation Quarter. A legation diarist recorded August 14 as the date of the relief column's arrival and entrance into the Legation Quarter. Military records indicate the relief column arrived at Peking late in the afternoon of August 14. The attack commenced during the early morning hours of August 15, and British and American troops entered the Legation Quarter during the afternoon. For continuity, in the reporting of the siege of the legations in Peking in Chapter 8, I have used August 14. However, in Chapter 9, "The Relief of Peking," and the chronology, I have let stand August 15 for the same reason.

The title of Chapter 11, "The End of an Era — The Old China Marine," is not to imply that Marines did not serve in China after 1942; they did. At the end of World War II, the First and Sixth Marine Divisions of the III Amphibious Corps (IIIAC) occupied North China for several years. Their mission was to disarm and repatriate the defeated Japanese soldiers and civilians in North China. In addition, the Marines were to keep order until the Nationalist Government led by Generalissimo Chiang Kai-Shek could assume control of North China.

In the writer's opinion, these were a new breed of Marines. They operated in division strength with supporting air wings. It was not the same world as it was before World War II.

Before World War II, the Marines serving in the Far East were usually in small detachments of a hundred men or so, and sometimes fewer than that. Armed with a rifle and bayonet and sometimes machine guns and 3-inch naval field pieces, and at times reinforced by "bluejackets" (sailors), they accomplished their assigned missions. These Marines were from an era that no longer exists. Therefore, I feel justified in choosing the title I did for Chapter 11.

Among those who have assisted me in the preparation of this book are Richard A. Long, Curator of Special Projects at the Marine Corps Museum for over 30 years, and later head of the Oral History Unit, Marine Corps Historical Center, retired; the National Archives; and the staff of the Marine Corps Historical Center, all located in Washington, D.C.; the staff of the Marine Corps University Archives, Quantico, Virginia, and the Library Staff of the Cumberland County Library, Fayetteville, North Carolina.

Special thanks are in order for the Library Staff at Southeastern Community College, Whiteville, North Carolina, especially Kay Houser, who secured through inter-library loan much needed reference material.

I am grateful for important assistance from Joe K. Marshall, MSgt., USMC, Ret., now deceased, and Frank P. Prater, former Marine, who provided me with material from their private papers that cover the years 1930 through 1941.

Grateful acknowledgment is made to Shanna Nicole Mishue, my granddaughter, who simplified the mysteries of my computer.

Of special significance are the maps provided by my grandson, Walker O. "Scott" Biggs, Jr. He deserves special thanks. From rough sketches, and other material I provided, he was able to produce the maps that illustrate this book.

Jack G. Biggs, my brother, executed the task of reviewing, correcting and commenting on the initial draft. To him, I give thanks.

I must also acknowledge the encouragement and support my wife, Betty, gave while I gathered the material and wrote the book.

Chester M. Biggs, Jr.
MSgt., USMC, Ret.
Spring 2003

Introduction

Western Europe's interest in China (Cathay) really began during the Crusades. Starting shortly before 1100 and lasting until almost 1300, the Crusades were a series of seven Christian military expeditions to recapture the Holy Lands from the Muslims. For religious reasons thousands of men fought in these Crusades to restore the Holy Lands to Christian control.

However, not all took part for religious reasons. Some, such as the Normans, hoped to win glory, wealth and new lands. Merchants from the Italian cities of Genoa and Venice joined the Crusades in search of new markets.

The Crusades to the Holy Lands acquainted Western Europe with a way of life and technology that was superior to anything they had ever known. They acquired new tastes in food and clothing. They learned to build better ships and draw better maps. Above all, the Crusades brought progress, profit and a new way of life to Western Europe. This knowledge prepared Europe for expansion into world trade during the Renaissance.

Marco Polo lived and traveled extensively in China from about 1275 to 1292. Returning to Italy, he told of the highly civilized and rich country called Cathay. While some branded his adventures as fabrications, others, with knowledge gained in the Crusades, accepted the tales as valid and began seeking ways to reach this fabulous land of Cathay.

Emerging from the period known as the Dark Ages, the Europeans were ready for changes. Using their new knowledge of the Far East and the technology gained during the Crusades, Europeans sought new routes to Cathay, and the source of spices and other riches they had become accustomed to during the Crusades.

In 1498, Vasco da Gama, a Portuguese explorer, became the first European to sail around Africa and reach India. After that, trade spread quickly to the Orient.

While most of the European nations sought trade with the Far East, Portugal and Britain were the first nations that exploited the riches of China. The Portuguese arrived in China in about 1557. They first settled in the province of Macao and paid China for the use of the land. After 1857, the Chinese recognized Macao as Portuguese territory.

English traders arrived in China at Canton in 1627. At that time, Canton was the only port open to European commercial trading. By the early 1800s, powerful European nations had built vast colonial empires in the Far East. These nations ruled about one third of Asia and controlled all trade between Asia and the West.

Early in the 1840s, Great Britain declared war on China. The primary reason for the so-called "Opium War" was to expand British trade and gain what was to be later known as "extraterritorial rights." In 1842, the Treaty of Nanking gave Great Britain trading rights at the ports of Amoy, Canton, Foochows, Ningpo and Shanghai. Britain also gained Hong Kong as a colony. Since these rights were not extended to other European nations, the treaties became known as the "Unequal Treaties." Other European nations complained that the Treaty of Nanking gave Britain complete control of the trade between China and the West.

The United States had its first brush with the Chinese in 1844 on Whampoa Island, off Canton. An American trader became embroiled in a Chinese riot. On June 19, the USS *St. Louis* arrived and landed a contingent of Marines augmented by a party of sailors. The landing party pushed its way to the trader's compound, dispersed the Chinese, and remained on guard until the American consul at Macao settled the dispute. As a result of this action, the Treaty of Whampoa was signed. This treaty was negotiated, not imposed by force, and involved China in no territorial concessions. It did, however, permit the United States to trade freely in China.

To counter the British "Unequal Treaties," Secretary of State John Hays negotiated an agreement with the Western Powers that became known as the "Open Door Policy." Under this policy, the Western Powers agreed to permit their merchants and investors to trade freely in China.[1]

Trade with the European Powers invariably turned into exploitation of China through the seizures of land, power, and in some cases, military aggression. Consequently, at times, the Chinese lashed out at all foreigners. The conflicts that ensured had to be settled at diplomatic levels. Therefore, it was not long before foreign ministers and ambassadors moved northward to Peking, the capital. This move met resistance from the Chinese officials.

1

Early Military Operations in North China

Tien-Tsin is located some 85 miles southeast of Peking near the mouth of the Pei-Ho River. Before the early 1400s, Tien-Tsin was a typical Chinese village. Around 1421, Emperor Yung Lo, of the Ming Dynasty, made it into a garrison town to protect Peking, which became his capital in 1431. The first walls were built around Tien-Tsin in 1423.

Translated, the characters of "Tien-Tsin" mean "Heavenly Ford." In 1655, when the first Dutch Ambassador traveled to Peking and passed through the town, it was called Tiencienwey, which also meant "The Heavenly Ford."

In 1860, the Chinese made Tien-Tsin an open port to foreign trade. The Chinese emperor did not permit foreign businessmen to live in the rich capital of Peking. European traders doing business in northern China settled in Tien-Tsin (later Tientsin). Further, the traders were not permitted to reside in the city of Tien-Tsin. Therefore, areas were assigned to them along the banks of the Pei-Ho River outside the walled city. Each of the major European powers were assigned specific areas known as concessions—the British Concession, the French Concession, the Japanese Concession. The United States did not have a concession.

Consequently, Tien-Tsin became an important center for foreign trade in North China. Eventually railroads from Tangku, a shallow water seaport situated at the mouth of the Pei-Ho River, connected Tien-Tsin with Peking.

After 1655, foreigners flocked to North China in large numbers. In 1793, the British government sent Lord McCartney to Tien-Tsin to negotiate trade treaties. Following him were Lord Amherst in 1816 and Karl Gutzlaff, a German missionary, in 1831.

In 1858, following the Opium War in South China, the French and British began the first foreign military operation in North China. Lord Elgin and Baron Gros were in command of an expeditionary force that bombarded the Taku Forts at the mouth of the Pei-Ho River. After two hours and a quarter of bombardment, the forts were captured. The British and French forces came up the Pei-Ho River without further resistance. Because of the successful invasion, the Treaty of Tien-Tsin was signed. The treaty contained the following clauses:

> Foreigners were permitted to reside in Peking.
> Foreigners were permitted to travel for business and pleasure in the interior of China, provided they carried passports.
> Foreigners in China were placed under their own laws.
> The Christian religion was to be tolerated.
> The tariff was to be revised and ten ports were to be opened to foreign trade. [Tien-Tsin was not included.]

These rights were some of the treaty rights, which later became known as "extraterritorial rights" which gave foreigners almost unlimited access to China.

The following year, 1859, the British government instructed their ambassador to go to Peking. He tried to enter the Pei-Ho River but found his passage barred. Obtaining the assistance of eighteen gunboats of the British Naval Forces, he tried again, unsuccessfully, to force a passage. This operation ended with four gunboats sunk, 89 men killed and 354 wounded.

This failed operation resulted in a major invasion of China by British and French forces.

The March on Peking, 1860

In 1860, Lord Elgin and Baron Gros were again put in command of an expeditionary force of 10,000 British and 6,000 French with orders to determine why the ambassadors could not go to Peking. The invading force landed some ten miles from Tangku, marched around to the rear and captured the city. This operation cost the invading forces 330 killed. The force then advanced on Tien-Tsin.

At Tien-Tsin, the allied army was unopposed. The Chinese commissioners convinced the commanders of the allied forces they would negotiate a peace.

Both sides agreed that the preliminaries should take place at Tungchow, a town about ten miles from Peking. Escorted by a small number of troops, forty British officials and as many Frenchmen were sent forward to Tungchow. After a period of unsuccessful parlaying, the allied negotiators were tricked into an ambush and captured. A few of the troops managed to cut their way out and return to the allied army.

General Montauban led a troop of Sikh cavalry to the rescue, and had little difficulty in gaining entrance to Tung-chow. When he arrived, the prisoners had disappeared. A later newspaper account said, "The Chinese officials professed complete ignorance as to their whereabouts, but later it was ascertained that the unfortunate Europeans had been bound with green withes, tumbled into carts, and taken to the Summer Palace, where they were viewed by the Emperor and the ladies of his Court. Later they were sent to Pekin [*sic*], put in cages for awhile and then tortured, some of them put to death, exactly as were the Japanese prisoners at Port Arthur."[1] Only thirteen of the negotiators returned alive.

When Lord Elgin and Baron Gros learned their flag of truce had been violated, they advanced on Peking from the north. The Summer Palace was captured and looted. From the Summer Palace, the allied forces advanced on Peking. Before the force reached Peking, the Chinese government capitulated, sending out the bodies of the dead and 13 survivors of the negotiating party. Included in the capitulation was a 500,000-tael indemnity. Because of the violation of the negotiating party, the allied commanders were not fully appeased. Lord Elgin ordered the Summer Palace burned and a few days later the allied forces entered the walled city of Peking without resistance. The expeditionary force decided how the East would meet the West in diplomacy and trade in the years to come.

The United States' Foreign Policy

Following the march on Peking, people from European countries and Japan came to China to partake in the rich trade and resources. This almost invariably turned into the exploitation of China though foreign seizure of land and power, and even military aggression. Therefore, the Chinese frequently lashed out at all foreigners. Many times this put American nationals and diplomatic missions in jeopardy.

The United States did not participate in any of the foregoing operations in North China, primarily because of its Open Door Policy. The United States' foreign policy at the time was to respect China's sovereignty and not to interfere or engage in conflict with the Chinese. At the same time, the United States was committed to protecting American interests in China, which included missionaries. It might be noted here that an article in the Treaty of Tien-Tsin in 1858 guaranteed the toleration of Christian religion in China. The Chinese people resented this provision and from time to time protested in civil unrest. Trying to balance the rights of Americans and the government policy proved to be diplomatically difficult. This was the reason Marines were used later in an attempt to implement the contradictory government policies.

Historically, the landing of Marines on foreign soil was not considered an act of war by the State Department, whereas army troops landing would probably be considered an overt act of war and result in such. Further, except for the legation guard at Peking, Marines were not bound to cooperate with foreign troops in China. (The sole exception to this policy was the terms of the Protocol of 1901, which obligated the Marine legation guards to support the allied powers in the defense of the Legation Quarter in Peking.)

The Marine Corps also had a record of dependability and a speedy reaction time, and, when Marines were called to intervene in diplomatic situations, it did not cause public alarm in the United States. Therefore, whenever a military presence was needed ashore in pre–1940 China, the State Department preferred Marines to soldiers.

The years following the British and French march on Peking were marked with civil and political unrest in China. Therefore, American nationals and diplomatic missions were frequently in danger. Diplomacy at such times was not possible. During these times when it was diplomatically difficult to safeguard United States interests, Marines were sent to China to help restore normalcy.

While Marines landed in Shanghai in 1854, Shanghai and Hong Kong in 1855, Canton in 1856, Shanghai again in 1859, and New Chwang, Tung Chow Foo and Shanghai in 1866 to protect American diplomatic missions and interests, it was not until 1894 that Marines went ashore in North China.

2

Early Marine Legation Guards

During the Sino-Japanese War of 1894, conditions in China became more unsettled than usual. As the Japanese forces advanced on Peking, anti-foreign riots broke out. The American Minister in Peking, Colonel Charles Denby, requested protection of a Marine guard.

Rear Admiral Charles C. Carpenter, commander of the Asiatic Squadron, was ordered to provide Marines to give protection to American interests in North China. The USS *Baltimore*, flagship of the squadron, was dispatched to Chefoo, China, with orders to put the ship's Marines at the disposal of Minister Denby for the protection of the Legation. On December 4, 1894, the Marines of the *Baltimore*, under the command of Captain George F. Elliott, were assigned to provide that protection.[1]

They were transferred to the small steamer *Yiksang* at Chefoo and proceeded to Taku. Going ashore at the river port Tangku, the detachment traveled in open railroad cars to Tien-Tsin. Unprotected from the cold, the detachment arrived in Tien-Tsin half frozen.

Captain Elliott and his Marines reported on board the USS *Monocacy*, which was lying at anchor in the Pei-Ho River. Because the Emperor had issued an edict forbidding foreign troops from entering Peking, the Marine detachment could proceed no further. And although the need for a Legation guard was imminent, the New Year of 1895 found the Marines still waiting in Tien-Tsin.

Despite the Emperor's edict, Admiral Carpenter ordered Captain Elliott to go unescorted to Peking to confer with Minister Denby, and arrange for the quartering of the Marine guard, if one was needed. He was

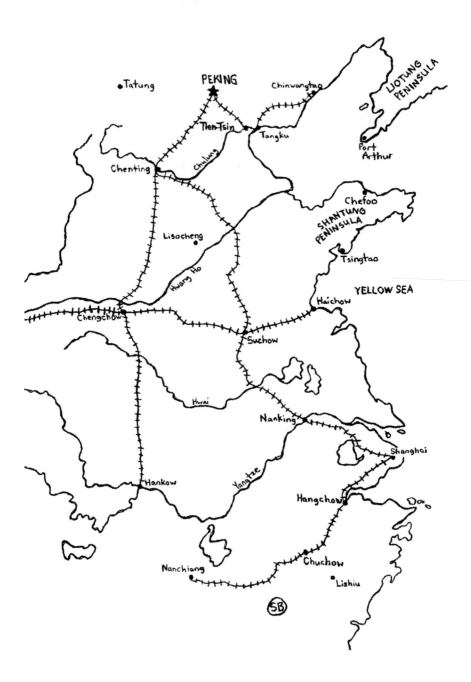

Map 1. Eastern China

further instructed to learn the intention of the missionaries should Japan invade China.

Because both Japanese and Chinese troops were active in the area, the Chinese army had stopped all rail traffic between Tien-Tsin and Peking. Captain Elliott was not intimidated. Securing a horse, he made the eighty-mile journey to Peking in two days.

In Peking, Elliott not only completed his assigned mission, but also acted as military attaché for Colonel Denby's audience with the Emperor when Prince Lung asked the Colonel to help settle the war with Japan. Peace negotiations between the two nations commenced a few days later and Captain Elliott returned to the *Monocacy* at Tien-Tsin. Later the captain and his detachment rejoined the *Baltimore* at Nagasaki, Japan. The Marines had been ashore nearly six months.

Marine Legation Guard of 1898

Because of civil unrest in China, on September 30, 1898, the American, British, French, German, Italian and Russian ministers at the Legation Quarter in Peking called their respective governments for guards.

On October 7, 25 British Marines with machine guns, 30 Germans Marines, and 30 Russian Marines and 30 mounted Russian Cossacks, escorted by Chinese officials, marched up Legation Street in Peking to their corresponding Legations.

Almost a month later, on November 4, Lieutenant Robert McN. Dutton in command of eighteen Marines taken from the USS *Boston,* the USS *Raleigh,* and the USS *Baltimore* were escorted by Chinese officials through the streets of the ancient capital and into the American Legation. The Marines were hand-picked for this special duty.

The Marines were quartered in four rooms at the minister's house. Lieutenant Dutton's quarters was one room in an adjoining office building.

Later Mrs. Sara Conger, minister E.H. Conger's wife, wrote: "Marines are guarding us day and night. They perform their duties with promptness, and there is much about their obedience to the law and order that I greatly admire."[2]

On Thanksgiving Day, November 24, all Americans in Peking spent the day with Minister Conger and his wife. Before setting down to Thanksgiving dinner, Minister Conger informed his guests that one of the Marines had smallpox.

Since the Americans frequently encountered the disease while moving about the city, the dinner continued. The Marine, however, was moved to the Nan T'ang Catholic Hospital. The following day, November 25, the remaining Marines were moved to separate quarters outside the Legation Compound, but connected to it. Despite all medical efforts, on December 26, the Marine died. He was buried with military honors on December 27, in the British Cemetery just outside the city.

On their departure from the Legation in March 1899, Mrs. Conger wrote in her diary: "The American Marines, our first guards, arrived in Peking in November 1898, and remained until March 1899. These men were in every way an honor to our country and an honor to themselves. They were trusted to go out into the city, and they never abused that liberty. When they left Peking, Mr. Conger wrote them a strong letter of recommendation to Admiral Dewy in Manila. Upon their departure, Mr. Conger stepped in front of them, spoke a few words of good cheer and good-bye, and shook hands with each man. They gave three cheers for the American Minister and three cheers for the American Legation at Peking, then again three cheers for the foreign citizens at Peking. They carried away with them the good will and respect, not only of their countrymen, but of the community."[3]

She added, apparently as an afterthought, "They were pleased as it is not common thing for a foreign minister to show such attention to men in the ranks."[4]

A week after the Marine guard was assigned to the Legation at Peking, a guard of 30 Marines from the same vessels was stationed at the America Consulate in Tien-Tsin. The Marines were under the command of Lieutenant John Gibson, U.S. Navy. Both detachments were fully equipped with supplies, weapons, including a Gatling gun, and adequate ammunition.

By March 1899, the civil unrest had subsided. No longer being needed, the Marines returned to their ships on March 15. The other legation guards were also withdrawn.

3

The Boxer Rebellion of 1900

The *I Ho Ch'uan* or Fist of Righteous Harmony, commonly known as the "Boxers," was originally a semi-religious guild founded during the reign of Chia Ch'ing (1796–1820). Nominally, it was formed to revive the worship of ancient heroes. The real purpose, however, was to unite the people for mutual defense.

The name of the society implied that they were ready to support the cause of peace and righteousness, if necessary, by force. Fearing the society, the Chia Ch'ing Reign condemned it by imperial edict. For nearly a century, the society was dormant. During the late 1800s, the Society awakened from its slumber. Political activists became alarmed by the territorial aggression of the European Powers in China and the tyrannical ways they treated the Chinese.

The Boxer Rebellion was not a rebellion against the Manchu Dynasty but a war to rid China of foreign missionaries. Although the rebellion started in 1898, the seeds for the rebellion were actually sown in 1858. It was during that year that Lord Elgin and Baron Gros led a European military expeditionary force into North China and captured the Taku Forts near the mouth of the Pei-Ho River. Proceeding up river, the international force captured and occupied Tien-Tsin. Consequently, the Treaty of Tien-Tsin was negotiated between the European powers and the Chinese government. One of the principal terms of the treaty stated that the Christian religion would be tolerated in China. If the teaching of Christianity had been confined to the treaty ports where the Chinese people were more tolerant of the Europeans and their customs, probably nothing much would have happened. That, however, was not the case. With the signing of the treaty, thousands of missionaries poured into China and spread to the interior where the Chinese people viewed them and their customs with suspicion. The missionaries pursued a policy that in some cases aggressively forced Christianity upon the Chinese.

There were many other reasons for the Chinese to hate the foreigners, but the their religion was the chief one. While the average Chinese citizen might not have understood that the European Powers were exploiting their country, they could be reached through their religion. Religion gave political reactionaries such as Tung Fu Hsiang a powerful argument with which to persuade his ignorant followers to exterminate alike the foreigners and their Chinese converts.

In the teaching of Christianity, the Boxers saw the teaching of a doctrine which turned the Chinese away from Chinese customs and religion. They wanted to restore the old religion, the old freedoms, the old habit of thought and life endeared to the people by experience of centuries.

The initial thrust was against the Roman Catholic Church. The Roman Catholic Church had grown large and powerful. Catholic bishops and priests began to assume the style and power of great mandarins and their government supported all their actions. Once Chinese citizens converted to Christianity, they came under the protection of the church. They ceased to be subject to the law and authority of the national government and were judged by the church. Unless a Christian convert, a Chinese citizen could not appear before the church court.

For fear of intervention by foreign military forces, no magistrate dared to condemn a Christian convert, even for open breach of common law. Consequently, in the Chinese eyes, honest men were deprived of justice in the Chinese courts.

To restore China to the Chinese, the Boxers claimed their crusade was based on no human design, but on a divine command, and would be supported by divine assistance. In proof of this claim they professed to work miracles, and actually performed strange feats that convinced both the ignorant peasant and the more educated.

Revived from its century slumber in 1898 by political activists, the society "rapidly attracted multitudes of men, both young and old, who formed into small bands of gymnasts. Each band was conducted by a 'demonized' leader, who by the selection of an epileptic patient or by the aid of hypnotism, caused a 'medium' to display wild or unnatural symptoms or to utter wild and strange speech, this serving as a basis for the claim of this society to spiritual power."[1]

Another account explains, "Their gymnastic exercises, from which they derived their name, were taught them, and they were promised that when they attained perfection they would be given service under the Empress with good pay and rapid promotion. The exercise consisted of bowing low to the ground, striking the forehead onto the earth three times each toward the east, and then the south, then throwing themselves upon their backs and lying motionless for several minutes, after which they would throw themselves from side to side a number of times, and finally rising, go through a number of posturings, as through warding off blows and making passes at an enemy."[2]

The followers were assured immunity from death or physical injury, their bodies being spiritually protected from sword cuts and bullets. Further, the youngest child would be a match for a grown man of the uninitiated.

"They were told among other things, that at the time of their uprising a myriad of regiments of angelic soldiers would descend from the skies to assist them in their righteous war against the foreigners."[3]

"Upon completion of their training they were given red turbans, a red sash to cross their chest, and a red *tae tzio*, wide tape, to tie in their trousers at the ankles."[4]

It was not only the common folks and the village ne'er-do-wells who joined the Boxer crusade, but the better class of farmers who shared this superstitious belief. Later, it was the ne'er-do-wells who prematurely set the Empress Dowager's plans into motion.

Strange as it may seem, the Boxers never forced themselves on a village. The requests to join, in most cases, came from the gentry and the headmen of the village.

Another cause which aided the Boxers in their recruitment was the drought of 1899. The harvest was scanty and food was scarce. Spiritually, many Chinese believed that such natural calamities were punishments sent to avenge some evil in the nation. Knowing this, the leaders of the movement did not fail to use it to their advantage. They proclaimed that the drought was due to the presence of the foreigners and to the influence of the foreign doctrines. Once these Christians were expelled from China, all would be well again.

Until the gods provided them with abundance in the future, the activists promised their followers that the loot from the Christians their present means of support.

"The society claimed to be purely patriotic in purpose. Its contentions were [that] the teaching of the Christians was not only subversive of the ancient faith of China, but their results were destructive of the Chinese system of government. Therefore, it was regarded as a patriotic duty to prevent the spread of Christianity."[5]

Gymnastic exercises and drills were soon taking place in hundreds of villages. Rooted in religious traditionalism and peasant unrest, and inflamed by floods and famine, the Boxer movement spread rapidly throughout North China.

In 1900, when the Chinese government demobilized over one-third of its army, many veterans joined the movement. Many of these disgruntled veterans brought their weapons with them. By the spring of that year, the Boxers had added vast numbers to their ranks and were not only armed with broadswords and spears, but in some cases with firearms.

The feelings against the Catholic Church were intensified in 1899 when the Catholics purchased a temple in the village of Li Lien Yuan and replaced it with a church. The Boxers' first outbreak in the Chihli Province took place on the night of December 31, 1899 against this mission. A large number of Boxers attacked the mission, burned the chapel, and killed and mutilated two Chinese converts. The district magistrates, in sympathy with the Boxers, did not act. One magistrate who tried to act was removed from office without explanation.

As the civil unrest continued, the Chinese had difficulty in making a distinction between the Catholic Church and the Protestant Church. To the Chinese all foreigners were Christians and all Christians were to be judged alike. Consequently, what began as an anti–Catholic movement became an anti–Christian and finally an anti-foreign movement.

Hundreds of Chinese families were rendered homeless, many were killed, and the Boxers, unchecked, looted, burned, robbed and killed until they were beyond control. In December 1899, in one district alone, the homes of two hundred families were looted and burned, all property confiscated, and the Chinese Christians forced to flee without food or sufficient clothing in the midst of an unusually cold winter. According to the *New York Times,* "Some were captured and held for ransom, others were taken to temples and forced to kneel before heathen idols, but most of them were taken in by missionaries and given such aid and protection as was possible."[6]

The Governor of Shantung, Yu Hsien, was anti-foreign. He saw the Boxer movement as a way to wreak vengeance on the foreigners that were his bitter enemy. He encouraged the Boxers, supported them with his influence and praised their actions as patriotic and religious. The magistrates naturally followed his lead. Consequently, the movement spread rapidly throughout Shantung Province.

Because of the Chinese government's indecisive policy, there was a popular feeling among the foreign ministers in Peking that the rebellion had its origin in Peking and the Chinese Court was collaborating with the

Boxers. In fact, their suspicions were correct. The Boxer headquarters was located in the palace of Prince Taun in Peking. From his palace emissaries were sent first to Shantung and afterwards throughout Chihli to organize new companies of Boxers as well as cooperate with existing secret societies. In every city, town and village visited, the headmen were consulted, and the young men and boys enrolled in the society.

The foreign ministers at the Legations in Peking knew the Boxers were at the center of the civil unrest that was developing throughout North China. It was, however, difficult to get an official statement from the Chinese concerning the Boxers' identity. "In London Sir Halladay Macartney, counselor and English Secretary to the Chinese Lega-

The only know authentic unposed photograph of Boxers. Their armbands, turbans and clubs identify them. (Marine Corps University Archives, Quantico, Virginia.)

tion in London, reported that the 'Boxers' is a new organization and its members hate all white [people]."[7]

In the United States, a news correspondent for the *New York Times* reported in an article dated May 31, 1900:

> Wu Ting Fang, the Chinese Minister to Washington, appears to be uninformed about the character or even the existence of the organization of the Boxers in China.
>
> When the Minister's attention was directed to newspaper dispatches concerning the Boxers, he commented that the writers of the dispatches not knowing China may [have] exaggerated the movement. Further, [he said], "I heard nothing from my Government on the subject, and I cannot judge its proportions from newspaper dispatches.

It seems to me to be a local disturbance, which does not involve any broad international question. I know nothing of what the disturbance is. I know nothing of what the 'Boxers' are."

When asked, "What does the term (Boxer) signify in China?" he replied: "I presume that the name comes from athletics; men who box are athletes. I see by the Chinese papers that the organization is called 'Yee [sic] Ho Chuan,' which signifies righteousness, harmony, and fists. This probably means what you would call being in training as athletes are developing their strength in the interest of harmony and righteousness. It is a new order to me."[8]

To complicate matters, the Chinese Court in Peking was a bed of intrigue with much in-fighting. Around January 24, 1900, an heir to the throne had been proclaimed in the person of P'u Chun, a boy of fourteen, the son of Taun, a previously unknown prince. This announcement heralded the dethronement of Kwang Hsu and the appointment of Empress Dowager Tzu Hsi as Regent. The Empress Dowager dominated the court. The heir apparent's father, Prince Taun, headed the Boxer movement.

The Chinese officials were fully aware of the terror the Boxers were imposing on the missionaries and Chinese Christians. Although the Chinese government spoke openly against the Boxers, surreptitiously it encouraged the Governor of Shantung Province to aid the Boxers in their organization. The Peking government privately spoke of the Boxers as "patriots," a sort of militia formed to prevent the encroachment of the Germans in Shantung. Despite petitions from both the Chinese converts and the missionaries, the pillaging and rioting went on unchecked and became an open rebellion.

American Minister Conger acted promptly on all complaints received from American missionaries. However, despite ready acquiescence and polite letters from the Chinese Tsung Li Yamen (Foreign Office), nothing was done to put down the rebellion.

The severity of the situation was recognized when the Rev. Brooks, a prominent British missionary, was murdered. Brooks was on a short journey when he fell in with a party of Boxers who kidnapped and decapitated him.

In response to the Rev. Brooks' execution, Minister Conger wrote: "This has finally aroused the authorities here to the extreme gravity of the situation, and a special edict has been telegraphed Gen. Yuan, Military Governor, to forthwith arrest and punish the offenders and also to punish all derelict officials, and he promised prompt and energetic compliance."[9]

Later two men who actually murdered Brooks were executed, but Yu Hien, the man responsible for his death, was allowed to escape. While this was unsatisfactory to the British government, they were in no position to make an issue of the incident. The Chinese government, however, could no longer ignore the rebellious Boxers.

Later, Conger telegraphed the missionaries: "Tsung Li Yamen has peremptorily ordered Governor to dispatch soldiers, use every means to suppress rioters, and afford protection."[10] Nine days later he secured a promise that they would take "vigorous action" in Shen Chou.

Despite these edicts and promises, Chinese officials took little action against the Boxers. When the missionaries asked for troops for protection, Minister Conger telegraphed that "Yamen sent instructions to send troops, but no troops were sent, nor was there any reason to think that such orders were ever issued."[11]

Early in December 1899, the Chinese government, believing the disturbances might bring intervention of European military forces, removed Yu Hsien, the Shantung Governor who had encouraged and given aid to the Boxers, from office. He was replaced by General Yuan Shih K'ai.

Although General Hsien was supposed to be in disgrace for his failure to suppress the rioters, he was received by the Court in Peking with honor. The Empress Dowager presented him with a scroll written by her own hand, a mark of high favor.

Gen. Yuan Shih K'ai perceived that the Boxer movement, if allowed to continue, would end in the ruining of his country. Acting accordingly, he established some degree of order in the Shantung Province. The province remained peaceful when the Boxers in Chihli rose in force. By December 1899, however, the general had not gained full control and the outlook for the province was again darkening.

On January 13, 1900, the court published an edict that urged the officials to be careful in dealing with the Boxers to avoid confounding the innocent with the guilty. This edict was all that was necessary for the officials to favor the anti-foreign movement and to hold their hands and do nothing. The edict was intended to have that effect. Judging from the results, it seemed to be the policy of the government to annoy and harass the missionaries to induce them to quit the country.

Many officials, in sympathy with the Boxers, were content with parlaying with the rioters, asking them as a favor to refrain from drilling. If the Boxers refused, the matter was dropped entirely. Many of the officials denied the presence of Boxers in their districts. This fact made it impossible for foreign ministers to ask for troops for protection, since, according to the officials, there was no need for them.

The following from a 1900 article in the *New York Times* is a typical example of Chinese government and diplomacy of the time.

The methods adopted by the local officials are illustrated by the act of the Hsia Chin Magistrate, who, on one occasion found a large force assembled to plunder on the border of his district. He requested them to cross the river into Chihli, and to facilitate this gave them an abundance of bread cakes, as he had done to another army of Boxers in his own city a month before. The Boxers gladly crossed the river, but when the Magistrate had departed to report that he had met and dispersed the bandits, they returned to resume their plundering in his own country. This is a fair sample of Chinese government and diplomacy. In a later instance, this same Magistrate replied to the Foreign Bureau, [Tsung Li Yamen] when complained of by Americans, that he appeared with an army and routed the Boxers, the fact being that he forbade the troops to fire a shot.

The P'ing Yuen Magistrate, whose district is alive with rebellion, went last month to a large market town, a Boxer centre, [sic] and had the head men sign a paper declaring that there were no Boxers there, he promising that previous offenses should be condoned. This document was only one of many similar ones sent in to the Government, other Magistrates having followed the worthy example of this one, thus relieving themselves of responsibility and excusing their inaction.[12]

Reports such as these made it difficult, if not impossible, to get justice from the Chinese government in Peking.

On January 31, 1900, almost no Boxer leaders had been arrested, and the officials were still inactive. An imperial edict issued in May 1900 warned officials not to confuse the patriots who were drilling for national defense with rioters, and to be cautious in awarding punishment.

Despite the lack of protection from the Chinese officials, the missionaries protected and aided the Chinese converts that came to them. The Roman Catholic Bishop at Chi Nan Fu reported that he had some 5,000 refugees in his care. This was indicative of the task the missionaries faced in caring for the Chinese converts that became refugees because of their religious beliefs.

Believing the sympathies of the government were with them, the Boxers adopted as a motto "Exalt the Dynasty and Extirpate the Foreigners."

Placards which were widely circulated read:

THE UNIVERSAL SOCIETY

You are personally invited to meet on the
Seventh day of the ninth moon.
Elevate the Manchus.
Kill the foreigners.
Unless this summons is obeyed, you will lose
Your heads.[13]

The time set by the Empress Dowager for the uprising was fixed for the Chinese ninth moon, seventeenth day, being two days after the annual "harvest festival," or *pa yueh chieh.* According to the Gregorian calender, this would probably be during the fall months.[14]

Emboldened by the government's feeble efforts of restraint, the Boxers moved northward toward Peking. Vast numbers drilled daily within thirty miles of Tien-Tsin. Although some Boxers had been killed, the lack of spiritual protection was attributed to their lack of faith. The spirit of defiance had not diminished, and open threats were heard that in the spring vast armies of Boxers would march on Tien-Tsin to join General Tung Fu Hsiang, who they believed was waiting for them. Thereafter, they would march on Peking. Then, "Every foreign devil will be swept into the sea and China will be saved."

At this point, the Boxers were primarily armed with broadswords, spears and a few firearms. Because of this armament during the early days of the rebellion, many missionaries spoke of the society not as Boxers but as Broadswords.

The Boxers felt that the government intended to give arms and ammunition to all grown men. With these arms, they would be able to carry out their threat of eliminating all foreigners from China soil.

The Empress Dowager, believing in soothsayers and the like, probably believed the story that regiments of angelic soldiers would descend from the sky to aid the Boxers in their righteous war against the foreigners, as well as the possibility of their own invulnerability to foreign bullets. In the early part of May 1900, she consulted the Chinese planchette to read her destiny.[15] According to an account by Robert Coltman:

> Two blind men, holding the instrument under a silk screen, wrote in the prepared sand underneath the following message from the spiritual world:

> > "Ta Chieh Lin T'ou
> > Hung Hsieh Hung Liu
> > Pai Ku Ch'ung Ch'ung
> > Chin Tsai Chin Ch'in
> > Tan Kan
> > T'ieh Ma Tung His Tscu
> > Shui Shih Shui Fei
> > Ts'ai pai shiu."

The interpretation of this read in English:

> > "The millennium is at hand
> > Blood will flow like a deluge

> Bleaching bones everywhere
> Will this autumn time be seen.
> Moreover, the iron horse
> Will move from east to west;
> Who's right and who's wrong
> Will then be clearly established."[16]

Coltman explains, "The millennium is used by the Chinese as a critical period in a cycle of years. The iron horse is supposed to mean war. The Empress understood this to mean that in the war, which she intended to commence, it would be clearly shown by her success that she was right."[17]

At first, the Chinese government in Peking made feeble efforts to restrain the Boxers. In an article published in the *London Daily Mail* on May 31, 1900, a dispatch from Shanghai dated May 30 reported: "Yesterday the Chinese Government issued an edict prohibiting the 'Boxers' organization under the penalty of death.

"The edict, which was signed by the Emperor [*sic*], was couched in equivocal terms, and promulgated more as an excuse than in condemnation of the movement."

In some cases, when government troops attempted to stop the burning, looting and murders, the Court at Peking censured their officers.

While the Chinese Court in Peking gave lip service to the foreign ministers' protests and the petitions of the missionaries and Chinese converts, covertly plans were laid to support the Boxers.

Some ministers in the Chinese court opposed the Empress Dowager's policies. Several members of the Tsung Li Yamen, like Prince Chia Ching and Liao Shou Heng, tried to persuade her to abandon her plans. They were promptly dismissed from the court. Of the others remaining in the Tsung Li Yamen, no one dared to question her dealing with the foreigners for fear they would also be dismissed.

A few days before the siege of Peking commenced, the Empress Dowager appointed Prince Tuan as head of the yamen in place of Prince Chia Ch'ing. At the same time Chi Shui and Na T'ung, two fire-eating foreigner-haters, were given seats in the yamen.

Gradually, the Court in Peking lost control of the Boxer movement. On May 28, heavy fighting took place between imperial troops and the Boxers at Lai Shin Hi Sien near Tien-Tsin. During the fighting, rail traffic between Tien-Tsin and Peking was interrupted. However, after the indecisive battle, travel was restored. About the same time Boxers attacked and burned a mission station at Lau Tson, forty miles southwest of Peking, and murdered the missionary in charge.

By the end of May, Boxers began to appear openly in the streets of

Peking. Those who fixed the date of open rebellion for the ninth moon did not anticipate the premature explosion of the movement. The Boxers completely spoiled all the Empress Dowager's plans by their eagerness to obtain loot. According to Coltman, "Being promised the spoils of the foreigners after the completed uprising in the eighth [*sic*] moon they regarded the property of the Christians and their teachers as already mortgaged to them, and, fearful lest the government troops would acquire some of it, they commenced the campaign themselves before the appointed time."[18]

By this time the Boxers were in Peking and it was said that they were in league with Tung Fu Hsiang, the general whose Kansu braves had caused so much trouble eighteen months earlier that Marine guards were brought into the city to protect the legations against attack.

On May 28, 1900, the Boxers turned their attacks against the Belgian-built railroad between Peking and Paotingfu. The next day they attacked Fengtai, a railway junction below Peking. The whole railroad station, workshops and locomotive sheds were gutted, and much of the rolling stock was destroyed, including the imperial palace car. After looting the railroad station, the rioters burned large godowns (Chinese warehouses) full of valuable merchandise. The damage was estimated as 500,000 taels. Neighboring villagers joining in the attack showed the movement was not confined to the Boxers.

The situation had reached a point where the Peking government could no longer control the populace nor afford protection to the foreigners. All missionary work had ceased and most of the missionaries had been forced to leave their missions and take refuge in Tien-Tsin, Peking or one of the treaty ports. The Boxer Rebellion had begun.

This detailed explanation illustrates the Boxer movement was more that a local uprising. Revived by political activists after almost 100 years of dormancy and supported by religious fanatics, the Boxer movement was eventually sanctioned by the Chinese government. Supporting the Boxers with the army, the Chinese government finally declared war on eight major world powers. It would take more than a handful of Marines and sailors from the eight foreign powers concerned to settle the matter.

4

The Marine Legation Guard in Peking — 1900

During the spring of 1900, the Boxer movement spread northward toward Peking. In the remote villages in the Chihli Province, they attacked European missionaries and Chinese Christians— massacres and pillaging were daily occurrences. The refugees from the interior fled to Tien-Tsin and Peking.

By late spring, Boxers were rioting and drilling in the streets of Peking. Despite the massacre of Europeans and the stream of refugees seeking safety in Peking and Tien-Tsin, some of the foreign ministers of the European Powers, as well as missionaries and businessmen who had lived in China for many years, regarded the Boxer movement as civil unrest that occurred each spring.

It is known that Mr. E. H. Conger, the American Minister, was concerned with the situation. He had acted promptly on all complaints received from American missionaries. Despite ready acquiescence and polite letters from the Chinese Tsung Li Yamen (Foreign Office), nothing was done to put down the rebellion.

The *New York Times* reported that in response to earlier dispatches, "The United States State Department instructed Conger to inform the Chinese Government that the United States expected China to stamp out the Boxer society, and to provide proper guarantees for the maintenance of life and property of Americans in China, all now threatened by the operations of the Boxers."[1]

There were no instructions, however, as to the course of action that the United States intended to pursue in case the Chinese government ignored or failed to observe the warning conveyed in the communication. The newspaper article explained, "The United States recognized, however, the right of a nation to deal with its own subjects at its pleasure, there were reasonable grounds for foreign intervention, which would include the participation of United States warships and even troops, if such should be necessary."[2]

Further, "Conger was specifically instructed that he must act on his own responsibility, and, while his course might be parallel to that followed by the other Ministers ... in Peking, he must under no circumstances join with them in concert."[3]

Anticipating the need for naval support, Conger requested Admiral Watson, United States Asiatic Squadron, to send a warship to a point as near Peking as possible.

The USS *Wheeling* was dispatched from Manila to Taku, which lies at the mouth of the Pei-Ho River. The *Wheeling*, with her light draft, could easily ascend the river as far as Tien-Tsin, one of the storm centers of the rebellion and a point giving access by rail to Peking. It was over this route that Marines were sent to Peking from one of the United States' warships in 1898.

On 28 May 1900, emboldened by the Chinese government's feeble effort at restraint, the Boxers attacked and destroyed several stations on the Belgian railroad between Peking and Paotingfu. The following day they attacked the Peking–Tien-Tsin railroad junction at Fengtai, and destroyed the railroad shops, telegraph lines and communication centers.

On May 28, thoroughly alarmed by these attacks, the foreign ministers in Peking telegraphed their governments for troops to guard the Legation Quarter. Earlier, Mr. Conger had telegraphed for legation guards.

In answer to these belated requests, the Asiatic Squadrons of the foreign powers operating in the Far East set their courses for North China. The USS *Newark* was the first United States ship to reach Taku Bar, the Yellow Sea roadstead forty miles down the Pei-Ho River from Tien-Tsin. Arriving on 27 May, the *Newark* carried a double complement of Marines.

On 24 May, the USS *Oregon*, lying at anchor at Nagasaki, Japan, received a signal to transfer 25 Marines and one officer to the *Newark* for duty ashore in North China. Captain John T. Myers, known as "Handsome Jack" by his peers, was named commanding officer of the Marine detachment.

At Taku, Myers, senior to Captain Newt H. Hall, commanding the *Newark*'s Marines, combined the two detachments and took command. The combined Marine detachment was made up of captains Myers and Hall, 48 eight enlisted Marines, Assistant Surgeon T.M. Lippett, USN, Hospital

Bluejacket (sailors) Colt Machine gun crew and Marine legation guard, Peking, China, 1900. (Marine Corps University Archives, Quantico, Virginia.)

Apprentice R. Stanley, and four bluejackets (sailors) to service the 3-inch landing gun and the Colt machine gun that accompanied them.

On May 29, Myers' detachment disembarked and proceeded to Tangku, inside the river bar. Three hours after Myers' departure, four naval officers and 60 seamen joined the Marines at Tangku.

Under orders from Rear Admiral Louis Kempff, USN, Senior Squadron Commander of the United States Naval Forces Asiatic Station, "grand old Captain Bowman H. McCalla"[4] took command of the combined naval force.

At Tangku, Chinese officials refused to transport the naval force by rail to Tien-Tsin. McCalla was not intimidated by the Chinese refusal. Commandeering a steam tug and several junks, he dispatched his troops up the Pei-Ho River to Tien-Tsin.

McCalla, accompanied by Paymaster H.E. Jewett, USN, proceeded by rail to Tien-Tsin. Arriving at about 1830 hours, he secured quarters for his troops in the American Mission and the adjoining Temperance Hall. (Considering the purpose of the hall, billeting Marines there was somewhat amusing.) Finally at 2300 hours the detachment arrived in Tien-Tsin where they were met by the foreign colony with a band and escorted to their quarters.

Herbert Hoover, a young 25 year old American engineer and future 31st president of the United States, later wrote: "I do not remember a more satisfying musical performance than the bugles of the American Marines [sic] entering the settlement playing "'There'll Be a Hot Time in the Old Town Tonight.'"[5]

Although there were 25 British Royal Marines already in Tien-Tsin guarding the British Concession, McCalla's detachment was the first of the foreign legation guards to arrive. Their prompt arrival doubtless prevented an attack on the foreign settlement by thousands of Boxers who surrounded the concessions.

It was obvious from the urgent telegraph messages received from the foreign legations in Peking that the legation guards must move to Peking promptly. Although the Chinese government in Peking had authorized the exact number of legation guards, Chinese railroad officials refused to permit the guards to travel to Peking. After considerable pressure was brought to bear (including a threat by the British to hang the stationmaster) the officials relented and a train for Peking was authorized.

On 31 May, the first train departed with McCalla, Captains Myers and Hall, Surgeon Lippett, the 48 enlisted Marines, five sailors and the better of the Colt machine guns on board. The 3-inch naval gun was left behind. Captain Myers ordered the Marines to leave their personal baggage behind. In its place, they took 20,000 rounds of rifle ammunition, which averaged about 372 rounds per man, and 8,000 rounds for the Colt machine gun.

In addition to this train, one other followed carrying 79 British

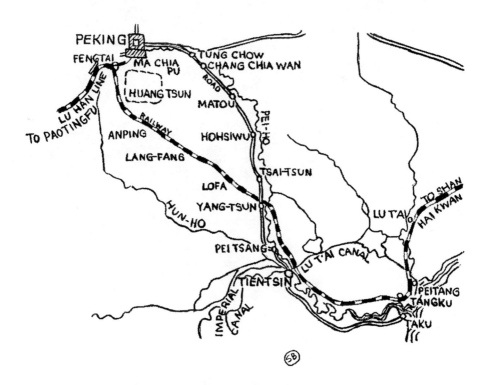

Map 2. The Tangku–Tient-Tsin–Peking Railroad.

Marines, 75 French sailors, 72 Russian sailors, 51 German Marines, 39 Italian sailors, 30 Austrian Marines and a 23-man Japanese Special Naval Landing Force. In her diary, Mrs. Conger noted that the German Marines and Italian sailors did not arrive with the first contingent of legation guards, but arrived on a later train.[6]

In addition to the individual weapons, which were mainly rifles and the American Marines' Colt machine gun, the soon to be legation guard also had one Italian one-pounder, an Austrian Mannlicher machine gun, and one old British Nordenfelt machine gun. Later the Nordenfelt proved to be not very useful; it jammed after firing four rounds and the mechanism had to be cleared before further use.

In the confusion of entraining, the Russians loaded a thousand rounds for their field gun on board the train, but they forgot the field gun and left it at the station in Tien-Tsin.

Captain Bowman H. McCalla, USN, prior to leaving the American Legation on June 3, 1900, and returning to Tien-Tsin. To the right is the Colt machine gun that played a vital part in the later defense of the Legation Quarter. (Marine Corps University Archives, Quantico, Virginia.)

The force totaled 22 officers and 423 enlisted men. The foreign legation guards had no overall commander. Each nationality was under control of its respective minister.

Expecting an early arrival of the legation guards, the foreign population of Peking gathered at the railroad station to greet them. Further, Peking carts were brought to provide transportation of their baggage to the Legation Quarter. After a long delay and the arrival of no legation guards, the foreign population returned to the Legation Quarter.

Finally, word came that the guards would arrive at about 2000 hours in the evening. Arrangements had to be made to keep the city gates open after 1800 hours so that the guards could enter the Legation Quarter once they reached Peking. At the designated hour, a delegation from the Legation Quarter, with carts to transport baggage, again gathered at the railroad station to greet the guards.

American officers at the American Legation on June 3, 1900. Left to right: Captain McCalla's aide Wood (rank not known), Captain Newt Hall, Captain Bowman H. McCalla, USN, Captain Poole, Captain Lippett, surgeon, USN, Captain John Myers. The man in the background (second from right) is believed to be Minister E.H. Conger. Picture taken by Mrs. (Anna Graham) Morgan S. Woodward, guest of United States Minister Conger. (Marine Corps University Archives, Quantico, Virginia.)

Marine legation guards who participated in the defense of the foreign legations during the 55 day siege by the Boxers in 1900. (Marine Corps University Archives, Quantico, Virginia.)

Mr. Herbert Squires, First Secretary of the American Legation and a former army officer, greeted Captain McCalla and the American guard. There was much excitement at the station as to which nationality should lead the guards into the Legation Quarter. As one account explained, "Captain McCalla who came up with the fifty Marines [*sic*] hurried his men at the double-quick to get it, and our troops were the first to march up Legation Street."[7]

On arrival at the Peking railway station, the guard was not only met by the Legation Quarter delegation, but also by thousands of silent, sullen Chinese who lined the street leading into the Quarter.

The Marines marched through this densely packed, muttering mass of Chinese while Bluejackets followed dragging the high-wheeled Colt machine gun, which would prove to be invaluable in the days to come.

Before the arrival of the American guards, Mr. Squires had arranged for them to be billeted in a Russian compound adjoining the American Legation. For access to the legation compound, a gate was cut through the compound wall.

Captain McCalla spent 1 June in conference with Minister Conger. On 2 June, he took the eleven o'clock train back to Tien-Tsin to rejoin his ship, the *Newark.* On 5 June, the railroad between Tien-Tsin and Peking ceased running and on 10 June, the telegraph lines were severed. The Legation Quarter at Peking was cut off and under siege.

For the next fifty-five days, the legation guards guarded, patrolled, built barricades and did their best to keep the Boxers out of the Legation Quarter.

5

Seymour's Relief Column

It soon became evident that the situation in North China would require more than a handful of legation guards. Accordingly, ships from the major European powers began to gather at the Taku Roadstead in the Yellow Sea. Further, troops from these nations were rushed to Taku as reinforcements. The admirals in command of these squadrons not only were to support the foreign ministers in Peking but were also given additional powers, which they could use at their discretion.

Conditions grew worse in Peking. With no train or telegraph service, as far as the European powers were concerned, Peking was isolated from the world.

During the interval Captain McCalla's contingent of 60 bluejackets (sailors) and four naval officers was joined by another 50 bluejackets and a couple squads of Marines under a first sergeant. The international force in Tien-Tsin now numbered some 2,500 men.

Vice Admiral Sir Edward Seymour, Royal Navy (RN), with the British fleet at Taku, received a telegram from British Minister Sir Claude MacDonald concerning the affairs in Peking. "Situation extremely grave," he wrote, "unless arrangements are made for immediate advance on Peking it will be too late."[1]

In answer to the telegram, Seymour left Taku with a battalion of British Marines for Tien-Tsin. On arrival, he assembled an international force to march to Peking to raise the siege. The relieving column was made up of about 900 British, 500 French, 200 Germans, 200 Russians, 120 Americans, 100 Italians, 25 Austrians, and 200 Japanese. Later, an additional 65 Frenchmen joined the column. This relief column totaled some 2,300 men. Seymour, being the senior officer present, became *de facto* commander in chief. McCalla was named second in command and a Russian colonel became chief of staff.

In Peking, the foreign ministers had previously petitioned the Chinese Imperial Government to increase the legation guard. The Imperial Government, which by now openly sided with the Boxers, refused.

Once the relief column was organized, and to give the appearance it was sanctioned by the Chinese government, Seymour petitioned the General of Chihli, Yu Lu, for permission to depart Tien-Tsin. Although not authorized to do so by the Imperial Government in Peking, General Yu Lu granted permission for the column to proceed.

On June 9, the allied forces met in a council of war to plan the joint operation. The council could not agree on anything. It was at a stalemate.

Finally, after a long period of indecision, crusty old Captain Bowman McCalla, USN, stood up, faced the council and proclaimed, "I don't care what the rest of you do. I have 112 men here. I'm going tomorrow morning to the rescue of my own flesh and blood in Peking. I'll be damned if I sit here 90 miles away and just wait."[2]

McCalla's remark broke the stalemate. On June 10, the relief column got underway. A detachment of allied forces was left behind to garrison the foreign concessions at Tien-Tsin.

Despite the fact the railroad had to be repaired and General Niehs' army of Imperial troops and an unknown number of Boxers stood between the column and Peking, Seymour expected to reach Peking within 24 hours. Consequently, many European officers packed full dress uniforms. They fully expected to formally celebrate their arrival in the city and the lifting of the siege. When Seymour's column was forced withdraw from Lang-Fang, all this baggage had to be abandoned.

The first train moved out of the Tien-Tsin station during the early morning hours of June 10. A six-pounder gun mounted on a flat car headed the lead train of the relief expedition. British and American Marines were in the vanguard. Four other trains loaded with troops, three days' rations, ammunition, and material to repair the railroad followed. The five-train column moved north repairing the railroad as it advanced.

The most essential man on the first train was an American sailor who had been a section hand before entering the navy. He was the only man in the relief column who could set a fishplate and spike down a rail.

Although the column met strong resistance at Peitsang, it was able to advance without too much delay. The column finally reached Yang-Tsun, where the railroad crossed the Pei-Ho River. Advancing had been slow; the railroad had to be repaired all the way. Seymour was fortunate in one respect; the railroad bridge crossing the river had not been destroyed.

The Advance Train of the Seymour Column. The lead train of the relief expedition was headed by a six-pound gun mounted on a flat car. American and British Marines were used as ground support for the advance. (Marine Corps University Archives, Quantico, Virginia.)

Further, General Niehs' Imperial troops who guarded the crossing offered little resistance.

As the column advanced, it not only had to repair the railroad, but it met stubborn resistance from both the Boxers and Imperial Army troops. As a result, garrison troops had to be left at strategic points along the line of march.

Reaching Lang-Fang on 12 June, Seymour was 65 miles from Tien-Tsin and 25 miles from Peking. At Lang-Fang the Boxers attacked with great determination but were repulsed with the loss of only 5 Italian Marines. On 14 June the column could not get beyond Anting because of stubborn resistance and extensive destruction of the railroad beyond Anting.

On the afternoon of 14 June, the Boxers attacked the garrison at Lofa Station. Reinforcements were sent back and the enemy driven off. Two British seamen were wounded during the engagement. At Anping the column's advance was decisively checked.

On June 15, Seymour sent a supply train to Tien-Tsin for material to repair the railroad and for supplies and ammunition. Shortly after departure, the train returned and the crew reported that little remained of the railroad they had built on the way up and every village along the way was filled with Boxers and Imperial Army troops. Seymour's column line of supply and communications had been cut.

Short of supplies and ammunition, growing casualties and being harried by both Boxers and Imperial Army troops, Seymour had no choice but to retreat. On June 16, he decided to fall back on Yang-Tsun, where the railroad crossed the Pei-Ho River. Later in a report, Seymour wrote, "I decided on June 6, [*sic*] to return to Yang-Tsun, where it was proposed to organize and advance by river to Peking."[3] Lord Elgin and Baron Gros' expeditionary force had followed this route when they advanced on Peking in 1860.

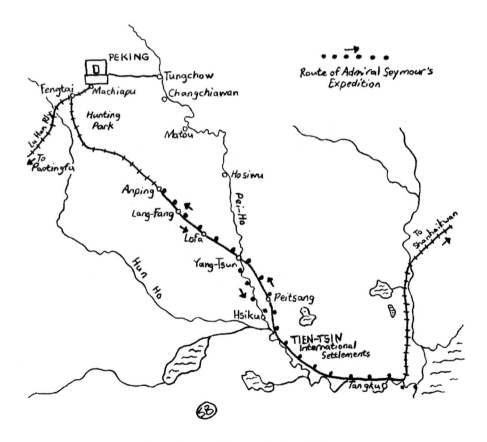

Map 3. Route of Seymour's Expedition.

The column left Lang-Fang in two sections. The first day the column traveled about 30 miles and only three miles on the second day. The second section of two trains, which followed, was attacked by Boxers and Imperial troops from Peking on 18 June. The casualties were six killed and 48 wounded. The section finally joined the first at Yang-Tsun on the evening of 18 June.

Because of the fall of the Taku forts, the Empress Dowager had ordered the Imperial Army to join the Boxers. The Imperial troops who had offered little resistance during the advance now strongly resisted the retreating column. In the face of stiff resistance, the badly mauled column finally reached Yang-Tsun only to find the railroad bridge crossing the Pei-Ho River destroyed.

Short on supplies and ammunition, hampered by wounded, and with communications with Tien-Tsin completely cut, Seymour again changed his plans.

At Yang-Tsun he commandeered junks to take the column back to Tien-Tsin. Unfortunately, there had been a prolonged drought in North China and the river was so low that junks had to be towed most of the way down river. Further, the junks could not be heavily loaded. Therefore, the column had to abandon its heavy guns and much of its equipment. This further weakened the column.

For the column, to advance, the banks on both sides of the river had to be cleared of the enemy. Instead of a compact column on the river, the towing created a long column of straggling junks. Consequently, it was difficult to protect them from the Boxers as well as Chinese cavalry and artillery. The Boxers, when defeated in one village, moved down river to the next village. While occupying the village, they selected positions from which they had to be forced either by heavy fire or bayonet point. In every case the advancing column was faced with heavy fire that was sometimes difficult to locate. Since the troops were equipped with only light arms, it was almost an impossible situation.

While the Boxers were untrained peasants, the Imperial Army was organized and trained by European officers and made a formidable foe.

From June 18 to June 20, Seymour's column slowly made its way back to Tien-Tsin, which by now was in the hands of the Boxers and the foreign concessions were again under siege.

On June 22, the column was eight miles from Tien-Tsin and near the Imperial Hsiku Arsenal. Here, the column stalled. Hampered by growing casualties, low on food, medical supplies and ammunition, and harassed on all sides, Seymour made the decision to capture the arsenal. In this last effort, the Royal Marines supported by the American Marines and Germans carried the heavily fortified arsenal after some two hours of fighting. In a dispatch, Seymour reported: "On June 23 we made a night march, arrived at daybreak opposite the imperial armory, above Tien-Tsin, where, after friendly advances, a treacherous heavy fire was opened, while our men were exposed on the opposite river bank. The enemy were kept in check by rifle fire in front, while their position was turned by a party of Marines and seamen under Major Johnson, who rushed and occupied one of the salient points, seizing the guns. The Germans, lower down, silenced two guns and then crossed the river and captured them. The armory was next occupied by the combined forces. Determined attempts to retake the armory were made on the following day, but unsuccessfully."[4]

The arsenal was stocked with ample food, badly needed medical supplies, ammunition and modern weapons. Seymour dug in to await a relief column. In one last futile attempt to establish a line of communication, a squad of British Marines tried to reach Tien-Tsin but were captured by the Boxers and decapitated.

The column had over 200 casualties. Of McCalla's 112, thirty-two were killed or wounded. According to one report, "By percentage, the small American contingent sustained almost twice as many casualties as any other in the force."[5]

Another historian has noted, "Capture of the arsenal virtually saved the force from certain annihilation (there were only a few rounds of ammunition left per man), for in it they found abundance of three things of which they were most in need — ammunition, food, and medical stores."[6]

The expedition failed because of the unexpected resistance of the Chinese, which no one thought likely or possible.

Tien-Tsin was now in the hands of the Boxers and Imperial Army troops. From the walled city of Tien-Tsin, they lay siege to the foreign concessions strung out along the Pei-Ho River.

The concessions were defended by some 2,400 allied troops, mostly Russian. Daily the concessions were raked by artillery fire. Barely able to defend it, allied forces could not send a relief column to Seymour's aid. More allied troops were needed.

6

Major Waller's Column

As the situation in North China became more serious, the Western Foreign Powers scoured their forces in the Far East for more troops. The Navy Department offered the War Department a force of 2,000 Marines. Upon closer study, however, it found that it could actually provide no more than 800 men. In fact, initially, the Corps provided only eight officers and 130 enlisted men. The Navy Department ordered Rear Admiral George C. Remey, commander in chief of the Asiatic Naval Station, to render all possible assistance to the legation in Peking. The first contingent of Marines to be ordered to North China from the Philippines was Major Littleton W. T. Waller's detachment of eight officers and 104 enlisted men that were preparing for transfer to Guam. Because of the Navy's commitment, emergency orders diverted the detachment to North China. These Marines were part of the eight officers and 130 enlisted men promised to reinforce the Marines already in North China. The officers of the detachment were First Lieutenants Smedley D. Butler, Henry Leonard, George C. Reid, R. F. Wynne, W. G. Powell, A.E. Harding, and Second Lieutenant Wade J. Jolly.

Embarking on the USS *Solace* at Cavite, the detachment sailed for Taku on June 14, 1900. Several hours after the detachment was at sea, Minister Conger in Peking got a message through to Washington stating, in part, that the foreigners in Peking "have been completely besieged within our compounds, with the entire city in the possession of a rioting, murdering mob, with no visible effort being made by the Government in any way to restrain it.... In no intelligent sense can there be said to be in existence any Chinese government whatsoever."[1]

When the *Solace* was well out in the Yellow Sea, Major Waller discovered two Marines had sneaked aboard during the night of embarkation. Rather than turn back, the Major added the two stowaways to his detachment, to bring the strength of the relief force up to eight officers and 106 enlisted.

On 19 June, Waller's detachment arrived at Taku and at 0330 hours debarked at Tangku. Thirty Marines from the USS *Nashville* reinforced the detachment. This reinforcement brought with them a Colt machine gun and an antique 3-inch landing gun. The Colt machine gun was an early machine gun that fired 6mm ammunition.

Commandeering a Chinese train, and with the help of machinist's mates and water tenders from the gunboat USS *Monocacy*, Waller coaxed the engine to life. Loading the train with spare ties, spare rails and the Marine detachment, Waller departed Tangku for Tien-Tsin.

Repairing the tracks they advanced, the detachment was halted by a blown-up bridge twelve miles short of Tien-Tsin. Abandoning the train, the Marines joined a battalion of 440 Russian infantry whose headway had been blocked by the Boxers.

A conference was held between the two commanders and it was decided to remain where they were until reinforced by British and Russian troops that were landing at Taku. With that decision, both commands went into bivouac.

At about 0200 hours on June 21, the colonel commanding the Russian troops notified Major Waller that he was resuming his advance and requested that the Marines join him.

Waller recognized the strength of the Chinese resistance and was reluctant to continue the attack with such a small force, especially when reinforcements were expected the next day. After some discussion, he reluctantly gave in to the demands of the Russian colonel that the combined forces continue the attack.

Waller's strength now totaled eight officers and 123 enlisted and the Russians' strength was about 400. At this point, they were relieved of at least one burden: "The 3-inch naval gun, having proved defective, was thrown into the river."[2] Later, Lieutenant Powell said after "dragging and pulling the wretched cannon across the first creek, it was such damned nuisance that we dumped it into the next creek. It was useless to try to advance with this encumbrance."[3]

At 0200 hours on June 20, the Marines and Russian infantry, fighting from village to village, resumed their advance. Lieutenant Powell with the Colt machine gun was in advance, followed by the Russians. The Marines were in the rear. There was little opposition until the advance force reached the Imperial Arsenal, where they received light flanking fire. Marine sharpshooters quickly silenced it.

As the advance continued, the force received heavy fire from a wall about 300 yards to its front, and flanking fire from a point some 900 yards away. The estimated strength was some 2,000 Boxers and Imperial troops.

The Colt gun, with assisting rifle fire, kept the frontal fire down. Marines, supported by some Russians, charged the right front and rear to meet the flanking fire.

Shortly thereafter, the Russian colonel notified Major Waller he was withdrawing from the front. The withdrawal was anything but orderly. Lieutenant Butler described it as "the Russians, who had borne the brunt of the fire, now had enough. They filtered through us, running back as fast as their boots would carry them."[4] The Russians formed up some one half mile to the right of the Marines and then withdrew to a position about four miles below the previous night's bivouac.

The Russian withdrawal exposed the left flank of the Marines to severe fire. The Marines then had to withdraw.

The Colt, having jammed several times, was discarded and abandoned by Lieutenant Powell. This left the Marines in a precarious position. The advancing enemy was stubbornly resisted by the Marines' rear guard, where their skill with rifles proved effective.

A four-hour running battle was kept up until the Marines reached their camp. "The retreat was conducted so well that all the wounded were brought back by hand, the dead, however, had to be left behind."[5]

During the withdrawal, it was discovered that Private Carter, who had been wounded earlier, was unaccounted for. Lieutenants Smedley D. Butler and A. E. Harding and four enlisted from the rear guard turned back to look for Carter. They found him in a mud puddle near the railroad track. He had a compound fracture of the left leg. The bone stuck out through the flesh. Carter was in such agony from the pain that he begged to be left behind to die. Butler and Harding made a chair out of their hands to support Carter, two of the enlisted men took his feet and the rescue party moved out. The remaining two enlisted men provided covering fire. Under continual attack and fire from Chinese cavalry and artillery, the six Marines carried the wounded man seven miles without the aid of a stretcher.

Upon learning that the rescue party had turned back, Lieutenant Leonard and 25 men from the rear guard returned to support the returning Marines. With these reinforcements, the Marines were able to hold back the enemy with a steady fire and prevent the Chinese from cutting them off from the main body. On a stretcher improvised out of a poncho and two rifles with bayonets fixed, four men now carried Carter.

The four enlisted men, two of which were themselves wounded, were awarded the Medal of Honor. Since officers were not eligible for the Medal of Honor in those days, Butler and Harding were both brevetted captains for gallantry.

Having been in the field since 0200 hours, the Marines were near the point of exhaustion. Their spirits were badly in need of revival. As Butler told it, the courage of two old enlisted men revived their sagging spirits. "An old corporal who marched with us was shot on the inside of the leg. He limped along for fifteen miles without complaining or mentioning his wound. The old Marine gave the rest of us an invaluable object lesson. Another old Marine, a sergeant, was walking beside me. Crack! A stream of blood trickled down his face. The sergeant pulled his hat down over the wound and walked right on."[6] By nightfall, Waller's detachment, having hiked 30 miles, fought all day on nothing but hardtack, and having sustained 10 killed and wounded, were back where they had started — on the railroad 12 miles from Tien-Tsin.

For the next two days, Waller marked time awaiting the arrival of a force of some 2,000 British, Russians, Germans, Italians, and Japanese. During this interval, Admiral Kempff sent the following dispatches to the Secretary of the Navy concerning Waller's engagements:

Chefoo, China
June 23, 1900

Latest. Marines under Waller and four hundred Russians have engaged with the Chinese army near Tientsin. Could not break through lines.

Kempff[7]

Chefoo, China
June 24, 1900.

An ambush near Tientsin on twenty-first, four of Waller's command killed, seven wounded. Three inch and Colt's automatic abandoned.

Kempff.[8]

With the arrival of reinforcements, Waller made common cause with the 600-man British naval force under the command of Commander Christopher Cradock, RN. In two columns at about 0400 hours on 23 June, the combined force resumed its advance on Tien-Tsin. The Marines led the British column and occupied the right of the firing line.

After marching through a sandstorm and engaging in heavy fighting, the column reached Tien-Tsin at about 1330 hours. When the British Marine column reached Tien-Tsin, they were forced to cross the Pei-Ho River on a crude pontoon bridge made of logs.

Butler said, "The first person to greet us when we jumped ashore at Tien-Tsin was Mr. Charles Denby. Mr. Denby knew how to welcome throat-parched Marines. He handed each of us a bottle of beer. We broke the tops off with our bayonets. The taste of that beer after eating dust for two days! That was something to remember."[9]

The Marine detachment led the way up Victoria Road while the Europeans, saved for the second time, plied the relieving troops with beer.

Waller lost one killed and three wounded during the day's fighting.

After they reached Tien-Tsin, the allied forces had two major operations to complete before the area was secured. First, The Seymour column besieged in the Hsiku Arsenal some eight miles beyond Tien-Tsin had to be relieved. This arsenal was later known to China Marines as the French Arsenal. Second, the Boxer stronghold within the walled city of Tien-Tsin had to be taken.

It should be noted that the area called Tien-Tsin was made of the walled city of Tien-Tsin and an area along the Pei-Ho River where all foreign nationals resided and conducted business. Under earlier treaties all foreigner nationals were forbidden to reside or conduct business within the walled Chinese City of Tien-Tsin. Consequently, they were assigned concessions along the Pei-Ho River. The concessions were named according to the nationality living there, i.e., British, Russian, French, Japanese, etc. The Americans did not have an area designated as the American Concession.

On June 26, after some 12 hours of rest, a mixed allied force of some 1,800 men under the command of Russian Lieutenant Colonel Shirinsky moved out before dawn to rescue Seymour's beleaguered column at the Hsiku Arsenal. The resistance was light. The relief column reached the arsenal before noon on June 26 and lifted the siege, fired the arsenal and escorted the battered column back to the foreign settlement. When the fire reached the magazines, they blew up with a roar and the sky for miles around was filled with smoke. The relief column encountered little resistance on their way back.

Seymour's column had 232 wounded, including 28 Marines and 62 dead, among them four Marines. Included in Seymour's column were Captain Bowman McCalla, USN, and some 112 American Marines and sailors.

Captain McCalla returned to the foreign settlement riding a donkey. He had been wounded in the instep of his left foot and his back had been peppered with buckshot. When he peeled off his shirt, several of the lead chunks were still embedded in his back. McCalla turned over his command over to Major Waller, who thereby became the American commander in chief ashore in North China.

Admiral Seymour gave credit to the generalship of McCalla that made it possible for the column's return to Tien-Tsin, saying, "That my command pulled out safely is due to Capt. McCalla. The credit is his, not mine, and I shall recommend to the Queen that he and his men be recommended by her to the President of the United States."[10]

Major Waller's Marines still had another fight before the confrontation with the Boxers in the walled city of Tien-Tsin. The East Arsenal, held by some 7,000 Boxers, had to be captured to protect the allied force's rear.

The Russians made an attack on the arsenal on June 27 that came near to being a disaster and they were forced to withdraw. They then called for reinforcements from the British and Waller's Marines. Major Waller sent First Lieutenant Harding and some 40 Marines to their assistance under the direct command of Commander Christopher Cradock of the Royal Navy. Waller had made common cause with Cradock during the advance on Tien-Tsin on June 23. Together the Marines and British charged the fortifications, the Marines being the first over the parapets. The Boxers were driven out, the arsenal captured and the Boxers retreated. The Marines lost one man.

Of the operation to date, Major Waller wrote:

> Our men have marched 97 miles in five days, fighting all the way. They have lived on one meal a day for six days, but they have been cheerful and willing always. They have gained the highest praise from all present and have earned my love and confidence. They are like Falstaff's army in appearance, but with brave hearts and bright weapons...."[11]

On the outside of the envelope of his report, which he sent through Commander Frederick M. Wise of the USS *Monocacy,* Waller wrote this note:

> Captain Wise: Please open and read and add Russian casualties, 2 killed, 9 wounded. I need whiskey.

> L.W.T.W.[12]

Rear Admiral Kempff, commanding the China Squadron, added the forwarding endorsement:

I would suggest a suitable medal for Major Waller and five percent additional pay for life for various grades he may reach.... It is with our Marines under Major Waller as with the force with Captain McCalla, foreign officers have only the highest praise for their fighting qualities.[13]

Later, Brig. Gen. Daggett, USA, wrote:

During the last five days, this little band of about 130 officers and men had marched nearly 100 miles; they had been under fire about ten hours of this time; they had lived on scant rations; as must necessarily be the case on campaigns and in proximity of the enemy; 4 men killed in battle, and nine more wounded. During this short campaign, the Marines, officers, and men, have behaved like soldiers, and reflect credit on American arms. Especially creditable was the retreat on the 22nd of June, where Major Waller's men resisted alone and unaided the hordes of pursing Chinamen, bringing off all his wounded without ambulances or stretchers. Less skillfully handled soldiers would have been overwhelmed and massacred.[14]

With the relief of Admiral Seymour's column from the Hsiku Arsenal and the East Arsenal under European control of the allied forces, preparations were started to take the walled city of Tien-Tsin.

7

The Capture of Tien-Tsin

The foreign settlement, which was called foreign concessions, lay outside the walled city of Tien-Tsin and along the Pei-Ho River. A high wall some ten miles in length surrounded these concessions. When the Boxers lay siege to the concessions on 13 June, a barricade of bales of camel wool two miles long and two bales high was built along the waterfront one night. This stopped the Chinese across the river from raking the compounds along the river with incessant rifle fire. After that, the streets were barricaded with sandbags, bales of silk, cotton, wool, camel hair and bolts of cloth against a sudden rush of Chinese. The construction of the improvised barricades was inspired and supervised by an American mining engineer, Herbert Hoover, who later became the thirty-first president of the United States.

The Chinese attacked the concession in strength and shelled it with guns mounted on the walls surrounding Tien-Tsin. On the night of June 15, the French concession was burned to the ground. Not having the military force to defend the ten-mile perimeter, the allied forces shortened their lines to some five miles.

By the night of June 20, the Tien-Tsin garrison was low on ammunition. James Watts, a young English civilian, and three Russian Cossacks volunteered to make the 12-hour ride to Taku for help. At night, Watts and the Cossacks slipped through the Chinese lines and, after swimming the Pei-Ho River twice, reached Taku with the message.[1]

A British Rear Admiral at Taku sent the following dispatch to his home government:

Che-Foo, June 23.

> Only one runner has gotten through from Tientsin [*sic*] for five days. No information could be obtained except that the foreign settlements had been almost entirely destroyed, and that our people were fighting hard.[2]

Later a second dispatch was sent:

> A French [*sic*] officer, who has succeeded in getting through from Tien-Tsin to Taku, says that the Russians alone had lost 150 killed and 300 wounded.[3]

Capture of Taku Forts

Not only were the concessions under attack, but the Chinese forces occupying the Taku forts threatened to cut off the foreign settlements at Tien-Tsin from the foreign fleet anchored off Taku Bar.

The Pei-Ho River was China's highway into the interior of North China. Starting in the interior of North China, the river flowed southeast, passing within fourteen miles of Peking. After meandering some 85 miles across the plains it reached the city of Tien-Tsin, where it made a slight bend before continuing on its way to the Yellow Sea some 40 miles away. Here, at Taku, the Pei-Ho dumped its waters into the sea.

In 1421, Emperor Yung Lo, of the Ming Dynasty, made Tien-Tsin a garrison city to protect Peking, which later became the capital of China. The area along the river between Taku and Tien-Tsin became the center of defense and chief arsenal of North China. In this area were permanent camps where there were usually some 30,000 troops, infantry, cavalry and artillery, armed with Mauser rifles and Krupp guns. The cavalry also carried Mauser carbines. The troops stationed in this area were disciplined troops, having been instructed and drilled by German and French officers.

During the ensuing years, four forts were built near the mouth of the Pei-Ho River, which was some 200 yards wide. Two larger forts were on the right bank and two smaller ones on the left. (See Map 4.) The approaches to the forts from the Gulf of Pe-chi-Li were difficult because of mud flats. These mud flats were similar to those the Marines faced during the Inchon Landings of 1950. The armament of the Taku forts consisted of heavy Krupp guns.

The Pei-Ho River was the only reliable supply line between Tien-Tsin and the foreign fleet at Taku. In addition, because there were no telegraph lines between Tien-Tsin and Taku, the river also became the means of communication between the foreign military commanders in Tien-Tsin and the fleet anchorage at the Taku Bar. Daily small dispatch boats scurried up and down the river with dispatches for the various foreign admirals or the military commanders in Tien-Tsin. Dispatches destined for foreign governments were taken by small coastal steamers across the Gulf of Pe-chi-Li to either Chefoo or Tsingtao to be transmitted by telegraph to their respective governments. If the Chinese cut the supply lines, not only would Tien-Tsin fall, but the beleaguered legations in Peking would be forced to capitulate.

During the early part of May, the Chinese government made no effort to hamper the movement of communication and supplies of the foreign powers along the Pei-Ho River. By this time some 27 foreign warships were in the Gulf of Pe-chi-Li off Taku Bar. Among this fleet of warships were the USS *Newark,* USS *Oregon,* USS *Brooklyn* and the USS *Nashville.* The USS *Wheeling,* which had been on station at Taku earlier, had been withdrawn before the arrival of the USS *Newark.* Ten miles up stream was the river port town of Tangku, where the railway started for Tien-Tsin and

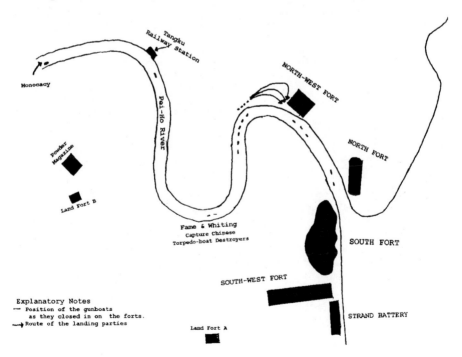

Map 4. Operations against Taku forts, June 17, 1900.

Peking. There were gunboats of several nations tied up there. Among these gunboats was the USS *Monocacy*. Commander Frederick M. Wise commanded her.[4] Commander Wise, who spoke several foreign languages, was commander of all nations at the base of Tangku, with representatives from each of the allies to assist him.[5]

During early June, the Chinese began to assemble large numbers of troops in the vicinity of the forts. The admirals were concerned but took no action. However, on 16 June, when the Chinese laid torpedoes (mines) in the river and all communications and supply lines were interrupted, "the naval commanders in council decided to send an ultimatum calling for the disbandment of the troops and announcing that if this demand was not complied with before 2 P.M. (0200 hours) on 17 June, the united squadron would destroy the forts.[6]

At Taku Bar, 12 miles out at sea, the depth of the water varied from 2 feet to 17 feet according to the tide. Only ships of shallow draft could be brought across the bar to attack the forts. The allied admirals finally mustered nine ships of shallow draft and moved them to the mouth of the Pei-Ho River in preparation for an attack on the forts.

Shortly after midnight on 17 June, in obedience to orders from Peking conveyed in a personal edict of the Empress Dowager Tzu Hsi, by the advice of Kang-Yi, President of the Ministry of War, the forts opened fire with Krupp guns on the international fleet. Thereafter, the nine allied ships launched their attack. The wire connecting the harbor torpedoes had been cut during the night before the bombardment began.

Before the bombardment began, the USS *Monocacy* moved up river from the port of Tangku. The British ships, *Whiting* and *Flame*, both torpedo-boat destroyers, moved down river to join in the attack. En route, the two ships captured four Chinese torpedo-boat destroyers in the bend of the river below Tangku. After silencing the Southwest Fort and the South Fort at the mouth of the river, the fleet continued their attack on the North Fort and the Northwest Fort. During the six or eight gun battle, the magazines of two of the forts were blown up, killing and wounding hundreds of Chinese. Shortly thereafter, a landing party of some 2,000 Russian sailors and Japanese Marines went ashore to secure the area. With the capture of the forts, the allied powers not only restored their communication and supply line to Tien-Tsin, but also held the key port of entry to all of North China.

The attack on the forts cost the British two ships. The casualties reported by the international force were 21 killed and 62 wounded. The Russians had heavy casualties, 16 killed and 50 wounded, due to the blowing up of the magazine on board the *Korietz*, a heavy cruiser.

"The U.S. Navy's *Monocacy*, a turtle-shaped wooden paddle steamer laid down in 1863 and possessing negligible fire power"[7] was two miles upstream when attack was made. Although the *Monocacy* came under rifle fire from both banks and was hit in the bow by a stray shell, it stayed out of the fight. Commander Wise later wrote: "I feel a natural regret, shared no doubt by the officers, that duty and orders prevented the old *Monocacy* from giving her ancient smooth bores a last chance."[8]

Admiral Kempff's initial orders to Wise were, "He may do anything proper in his judgment to conserve American interest of any kind in China."[9]

At that time the attitude of the Chinese government was technically friendly and the United States did not want to engage in any act that looked like war or to put the United States in a position of taking part in acts of aggression. The allied admirals were very critical of the American policy.

Kempff had sent dispatches to the Navy Department asking for instructions about acting in concert with foreign powers. The replies to his dispatches were, according to the *New York Times*, always the same: "to do whatever he thinks best for the protection of American interest, but to avoid anything that would look like an alliance."[10] The article continued, "In the early days of the Chinese trouble, 'alliance' and 'concert' were considered synonymous terms."[11]

Judging from several dispatches Kempff sent, it is doubtful if he was quite certain where "concert" ended and "alliance" began. When asked to join forces with the allied powers in taking the Taku forts, "Kempff asked a specific question — whether he can act in concert for the purpose of having the Taku forts turned over to the admirals."[12]

Again he was told "to take any action as may appear advisable to protect American interest, but to avoid alliances."[13]

In response to Commander Wise's failure to join the attack on the Taku forts, Kempff, in a dispatch dated 7 July 1900 to the Secretary of the Navy, seemed to have made up his mind on how he interpreted his orders. His dispatch read: "*Monocacy* did not return fire because Commander Wise did not interpret my written orders of 15 June as I intended. I instructed make war in return if directly attacked. Commander Wise did not consider that he was directly attacked, as firing was at night and wild. I took a different view and ordered [him to] make common cause [the] protection [of] life and property, and to fire against those opposing this purpose."[14]

After the attack on the Taku forts a headline in the *New York Times* read:

CHINA IS AT WAR WITH THE WORLD

London, June 19 — China declared War against the world when Taku Forts opened fired on the International fleet."[15]

With the fall of the forts, the Empress Dowager declared war on the allied powers and issued an edict ordering the Imperial troops to join the Boxers. The impact of the edict was immediate. On June 20, the 55-day siege of the Legations in Peking began with an assault on the Austrian mission. Seymour's column, which had advanced to Anping with little opposition from the Imperial troops, now came under heavy attack from the Chinese troops. In Tien-Tsin, Imperial troops joined the Boxers in the siege of the beleaguered foreign concessions. Now that China had declared war on the allied powers, Washington abandoned its role as uncongenial onlooker and the American commanders no longer operated under ambiguous orders.

Chinese artillery commenced heavy firing on the concessions on June 16 and 17 and continued until the native city was captured. On the June 18, a force of some 10,000 Boxer and Imperial troops stormed the defenses of the concessions. Although the allied force's lines were stretched to a breaking point defending the five-mile perimeter which enclosed the concessions, the attacking horde was repulsed.

American Reinforcements Arrive

While Waller's detachment of Marines and the allied forces were engaged in the defense of the concessions at Tien-Tsin, more American reinforcements were on the way.

The first American force to arrive was the Ninth Infantry (First and Second Battalions only) under the command of Colonel E.H. Liscum. Landing at Taku on 6 July, the Ninth Infantry was immediately sent to Tien-Tsin via the railroad that was being operated by sailors from the USS *Monocacy*. The Ninth Infantry's strength was 15 officers and 430 enlisted.

Under mustached old Colonel Robert L. Meade, the remainder of the First Marine Regiment at Cavite embarked on the cruiser USS *Brooklyn* for Taku.[16] Meade's regiment was composed of one infantry battalion, regimental headquarters, an artillery company (with three 3-inch naval landing guns and three Colt automatic guns), 18 officers and 300 enlisted.

After putting in at Nagasaki, Japan, for coal, the *Brooklyn* reached Taku Roads in early July. The roadstead was crowded with ships of all nations — British, German, French, Russian, Austrian, Italian, and Japanese, all clearly identified by their national flag. Among this fleet of warships, little tugs and steamers scurried about while Chinese junks with their bamboo sails added to the confusion.

Shortly after arrival, a small steamer came alongside the *Brooklyn.* According to Wise's account, "The Marines boarded her, each man with his rifle and knapsack, mess sergeants looking after their cooking equipment, Navy doctors and hospital corpsmen getting their stores aboard."[17] The steamer cast off and headed for the mouth of the Pei-Ho River and the port of Tangku. Passing the Taku forts, which the allied powers had captured several weeks before, the steamer reached Tangku and tied up alongside the *Monocacy.* Disembarking with its equipment, the regiment bivouacked for the night. Sentries were posted, evening chow cooked and eaten, and the men then rolled up in their blankets and went to sleep.

Early the next morning large barges were brought up and the regiment, with its equipment, embarked. The barges were lashed together and towed up river by a tug.

Although the foreign concessions were only forty miles up river, it was late afternoon before the regiment reached its destination. Long before the barges were warped into the British concession, the regiment heard the distant rumble of artillery as the Chinese shelled the foreign concessions.

Major Waller and some of his officers met the incoming regiment. Disembarking, the regiment marched to the far side of the British concession to be billeted. Lieutenant Wise later wrote: "The English were damned glad to see us. They had put out tubs of beer packed in ice. Captain S. Bayly of HMS *Aurora,* commander of the defenses of the foreign settlement was standing beside the beer. 'I say, my lads, don't hesitate to take that,' he called out. 'They offer it today. Tomorrow they'll think about it. The third day they'll be asking you war prices for it.'"[18] Taking him at his word, the Marines did not hesitate.

The regiment was quartered in large warehouses surrounded by a large courtyard. Each company was assigned a warehouse. Major Waller's outfit was also quartered there.

Of the first night ashore, Lieutenant Wise wrote: "Our quarters were a large empty room. We had not eaten since morning. As each company had its own kitchen outfit, supper was started. The men stacked their rifles and dropped their knapsacks on whatever part of the floor that took their particular fancy. From then on for many days, that bit of floor was all the luxury they were to know. It was bed, chair; anything else they wished to use it for."[19] The food "was canned but plentiful; sent up from the ships at Taku."[20]

Once quartered, the regiment settled into the regular Marine Corps routine — inspection of rifles and equipment, sentries, bugle calls from reveille to taps. Companies were assigned outpost duty, usually one day out of three.

Although the foreign concessions were shelled constantly and raked by sniper fire, the off-duty men were allowed liberty from 1200 hours until 1700 hours. It was stipulated the "the ringing of a bell at a certain hall meant an attack and each man must report at once to his company."[21]

The arrival of the regiment increased the Marines' strength in Tien-Tsin to 26 officers and about 423 enlisted men, 415 which were fit for duty. With the Ninth Infantry, the American forces in the Tien-Tsin area now totaled about 1,000 men and officers. Colonel Meade, senior officer present, commanded the American forces.

The American forces were brigaded with the 2,200-man British force under the command of Brig. Gen. A.R.F. Dorward. The British force was made up of the Second Battalion, Royal Welsh Fusiliers, Royal Navy and Marines, as well as Ghurkas, Sikhs, and Bengal Lancers, all colonial troops. The Allied Forces now mustered some 5,650 troops in the Tien-Tsin area. More than half of the force was British and American, the remainder being French, German, Japanese and Russians.

Attacking the Walled City of Tien-Tsin

In a council of war the allied commanders agreed that the walled city of Tien-Tsin had to be taken before a relief column could be sent to relieve the siege of the legations at Peking.

Neither Colonels Meade nor Liscum participated in drawing up the plans to take the city. After the British, French, and Japanese made plans, the American colonels were called in and the overall operation explained. Neither of these officers had time to reconnoiter the ground over which their force would move. If such had been permitted, faulty disposition of troops, which caused unnecessary loss of life, might have been prevented.[22]

The allied force was made up of about 900 Americans, 2,000 British, 600 French, 250 Germans, 1,600 Japanese and 2,300 Russians. The combined strength of the force was about 5,600 men. The allied artillery consisted of five 12-pounder naval guns brought from HMS *Terrible* and the Americans' three 3-inch naval guns and three Colt Automatic guns. The Japanese, French, and Russians also had some artillery.

Two walls ringed the native city of Tien-Tsin. About a 1,000 yards outside the thirty-foot stone wall surrounding Tien-Tsin was a mud wall ten feet high, thirty feet wide at the base and ten feet broad at the top. The mud wall had been built by General Son Ko Hin Sin during the Tai-ping Rebellion (1850–1865) as a defense against the British and French invasion of 1860. The wall, however, was never defended and became known as Son Ko Hin Sin's Folly.

The stone wall surrounding the city of Tien-Tsin was about twenty-four feet thick and thirty feet high. The Chinese had mounted their artillery on top of the wall and used it to shell the foreign concessions.

The terrain between the two walls was a flat plain covered with Chinese graves, large salt mounds, rice paddies, sewage canals, and large and small ponds, some that were as much as eight feet deep. To hamper an attacking force, the Chinese flooded the plain by diverting water from adjoining canals. The flooding turned the area into a quagmire of mud and muck from the sewage canals.

At 0300 hours on July 13, the men of the First Marine Regiment were awakened for the attack on Tien-Tsin. After dressing, eating and being

Marines rest before attacking the Walled City of Tien-Tsin, July 13, 1900. (Marine Corps University Archives, Quantico, Virginia.)

inspected to assure that all men had ammunition and full canteens, the regiment waited for orders.

Colonel Robert L. Meade was commander of the Marine Regiment as well as second in command of the brigade. Captain C.G. Long commanded the Second Battalion made up of Companies A, C, D, and E. Captain Ben H. Fuller commanded Company F and an artillery company of three 3-inch naval guns and three Colt automatic guns.

Herbert Hoover, a young American engineer, "was requested by Colonel [sic] Waller, in command of the American Marines, to accompany them as sort of a guide in their part of the attack on the Chinese."[23] In his memoir Hoover wrote, "I was familiar with the topographic details from horseback riding about the settlement with Mrs. Hoover."[24]

According to the plan of attack, the Marines had the extreme left flank; on their right were the Royal Welsh Fusiliers; still further to the right was the Ninth Infantry supporting a British brigade. The causeway leading to the Taku Gate, the only entry to the city on the south wall, was assigned to the Japanese, who were not under the command of Dorward. The French and the Russians attacked the north wall of the city. The

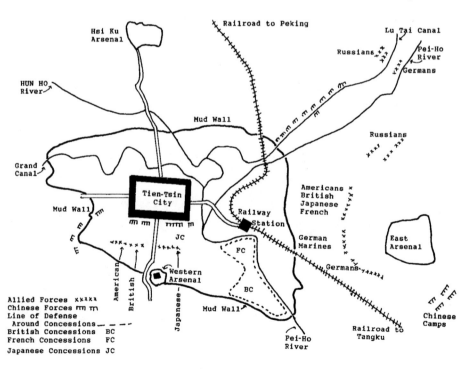

Map 5. Operations Around Tien-Tsin.

American-British forces were to attack across the plain inside the mud wall and near the West Arsenal that was also inside the mud wall.

At about 0300 hours on July 13, the American-British forces moved out in extended order to attack the south wall of the city. Although the attack had commenced around 0300 hours, it was not until around 0500 hours that orders came for the Marine Regiment to move out. It was almost dawn before the Marine Regiment reached the mud wall. Here, the Marines halted to wait for further orders from General Dorward. Daylight was just breaking around 0630 hours when Colonel Meade received orders from General Dorward to move forward and support the British Fusiliers. The regiment stretched out in a line of skirmishes and scrambled over the mud wall. The Marine Regiment, less Captain Fuller's command, advance by squads across the mud flat.

The Marines were armed with the Krag-Jorgensen rifle.[25] In addition to their ammunition belt, they carried a small haversack, blanket roll and canteen.

As the Marines struggled through the morass to reach the walled city, the Chinese artillery on the wall opened up and were joined by a steady stream of fire from modern rifles, matchlocks, and gingals.[26]

The salt mounds, graves and low dikes of the rice paddies provided their only cover as the Marines advanced in rushes of 50 to 75 yards. About 600 yards from the city wall they took cover in a long natural ditch, nearly six feet deep. Lying flat against the inner side, the Marines opened fire across the marsh that stretched to the Wall City. Targets were scarce. The Chinese, from their concealment behind the wall's parapets, were poor targets. To keep the Chinese penned down, the Marines poured rifle fire against the parapets that topped the stone wall. As usual, the Chinese rifle fire was high.[27]

By noon, the temperature had climbed to over one hundred degrees. The men were wet and covered with muck for their struggle across the plain. Water was scarce. Ammunition was running low. The Marines, having eaten around 0300 hours, were hungry. No supplies were coming up. To put it mildly, the men were miserable.

Colonel Meade and Major Waller came up and inspected the firing line. Each cautioned the men about excessive use of ammunition and water.

Toward evening, a horde of Chinese swarmed out of the west gate. It appeared that they were going to make a sortie against the Marines' left flank. Lieutenants Butler and Wise with about seventy-five men climbed out of the ditch and advanced toward the threatening Chinese. The Chinese hesitated and did not continue their advance.

Shortly after the Marines climbed over the rice paddy dikes, Private

Partridge was shot and fell backwards. He had an ugly gash in his left shoulder, but was bleeding so little that his wound was not considered serious. After Partridge received a field dressing, the party pushed on for about another fifty yards, shooting every inch of the way. The Chinese who had been threatening the left flank filtered back through the gate. The Marines were now close to the stone wall. Thousands of Chinese lined the wall. A terrific fire poured down on the Marines. At this point, a runner from Colonel Meade overtook them with orders to return to the lines of skirmish in the ditch. This party, which included some Welsh Fusiliers, was the only unit to actually reach their objective, the stone wall of the city.

On the way back, the party picked up Partridge. It was while helping to carry Partridge back that Butler was wounded in the right thigh. Partridge's wound proved to be serious and he died while still on the skirmish line in the ditch. A sergeant and Lt. Leonard helped Butler to the aid station, while a bugler carried his pack and revolver.

The Marine Regiment was on the extreme left of the line. Chinese artillery and sniper fire enfiladed their left flank.[28] With the enfilading enemy fire and fearing an assault on the left flank, Captain C.G. Long, commanding the Second Battalion, moved the battalion slightly to the left to counter any enemy assault. Once the flank was secured and to guard against any attack, he sent Lieutenants R.F. Wynne and Wade L. Jolly and fifty men still further to the left to secure that flank.

The Marines remained in the skirmish line in the ditch until around 2000 hours, when they were ordered to the rear. The withdrawal, though difficult, was accomplished by a few men at a time rushing from cover to cover. All the wounded were carried to the rear.

While the Marine rifle companies were assaulting the walls of the city, Captain Fuller's artillery took up position behind the mud wall near the West Arsenal. The three 3-inch naval guns were on the right and the three Colt automatic guns on the left of the arsenal. At a range of about 2,200 yards, the naval guns fired about 75 rounds into the walled city. The Chinese soon located the battery and brought it under fire of their 4.7-inch Krupp guns. The fire was so effective that Fuller moved his guns inside the arsenal and to the left of the gate. From this position, he fired another 30 rounds into the city. After expending his ammunition, he moved the guns outside behind the arsenal's walls.

The Colt automatic guns were put into action, but were not effective. One Colt was put into action on the left of the Marines, but soon was disabled. Under Lieutenants Parker and L.M. Little, the gun crew was sent to reinforce the left of the line at the front.

Around 0930 house General Dorward ordered the remainder of Captain Fuller's Colt gun company, along with Lieutenant W.H. Clifford, to reinforce the Ninth Infantry on the right of the allied forces. The Marines advanced by alternate rushes over a field raked with enemy fire. When they were about 200 yards in the rear of the Ninth Infantry, they were ordered to proceed no further. The Marines took shelter in ditches and behind graves and salt mounds, where they stayed for the remainder of the day. From this position, however, they protected the Ninth Infantry's right flank and rendered assistance in caring for the infantry's wounded.

Around 2000 hours the Ninth Infantry, the Marines and the British forces were ordered to withdraw. The Marines and British covered the withdrawal. Later the Commanding Officer of the Ninth Infantry commended these units. He wrote, "Our final withdrawal was handsomely covered by the British naval troops and United States Marines sent to our aid by General Dorward. These gallant men also aided us in the removal of our wounded."[29]

After a day of inconclusive action and under intensive fire, Dorward's command was back at the Western Arsenal, where they had launched their attack at dawn.

The Marine Regiment found shelter behind the mud wall, which provided cover from the Chinese small arms fire. A water cart as well as food and ammunition had been brought up from the British concession. The Marines slaked their thirst, ate, filled their canteens and stuffed their belts and haversacks with ammunition. Then, they rolled up in their blankets and turned in.

Of the 451 Marines engaged in the day's action, twenty-one were casualties, including six officers. Captain A.R. Davis was struck in the chest with a round from a gingal and killed instantly. First Lt. Henry Leonard, who had assisted Butler to the help station earlier, with the aid of Sergeant Clarence E. Sutton, also carried 1st Lt. S.D. Hiller, who was badly wounded, to the aid station. Leonard was later wounded in the left arm and was taken to the aid station by Sergeant J.M. Adams and Corporal H.C. Adriance. Much later Leonard's arm became infected and it was necessary to amputate the arm at the shoulder.[30] Captains C.G. Long and W.B. Lemly were also wounded.

The Ninth Infantry suffered more heavily, with 18 killed and 77 wounded. Their commanding officer, Colonel E.H. Liscum, was killed with the regimental colors in his hands. His last words were, "Keep up the fire!"[31]

Of the attack, Hoover later wrote, "We came under sharp fire from the Chinese located on its old walls. We were out in the open plains with little cover except Chinese graves. I was completely scared, especially when some of the Marines next to me were hit. I was unarmed and I could scarcely make my feet move forward. I ask the officer I was accompanying if I could have a rifle. He produced one from a wounded Marine and I at once experienced a curious psychological change for I was no longer scared, although I never fired a shot. I can recommend that men carry weapons when they go into battle — it is a great comfort.[32] The Chinese artillery and small arms fire continued to rake the allied lines throughout the night.

While the allied forces were attacking the Walled City of Tien-Tsin, Marines and French soldiers were stationed at the railway station. Fifty men from the Ninth Infantry reinforced them. During the morning, the Chinese shelled the station. Shrapnel bursts killed two and wounded five of the Ninth Infantry. The Marines lost one killed and four wounded. Several French soldiers were killed and wounded.

The forcing of the Taku Gate had been assigned to the Japanese, who had attacked straight up the causeway leading to the gate. After taking heavy losses, they finally succeeded in reaching the gate, were able to plant two tins of gun cotton against the gate, and attach a fuse. For some reason, they were never able to detonate the gun cotton from a safe distance. Finally, after three attempts, a Japanese engineer, with box of wooden matches, ran forward and lit the fuse. The explosion blew the gate open. The engineer perished.

Many years later Marines in their island hopping campaigns across the Pacific experienced this same type of Japanese reckless, suicidal action in their kamikaze attacks.

By daybreak on July 14, the allied troops poured through the breached gates and into the city. During the early hours of the morning the Marines were awakened and ordered to prepare to move out. After eating cold food that had been brought up the night before, they stood by for orders.

Just before daybreak, orders came down for the Marines to move out. Straight down the causeway and through the Taku Gate they marched. The Walled City had fallen. The organized resistance had ended by the time the Marines entered the city. Nothing remained but snipers who had to be wiped out house by house. The bulk of the enemy had fled.

Following the fall of the Walled City of Tien-Tsin, the city was divided into four sections, the American, the British, the French, and the Japanese. Major Waller with Marines and Captain Foote with a company from the Ninth Infantry patrolled the American sector.

Looting was rampant. "Soldiers of all nations joined in the orgy," wrote Lieutenant Wise. "Men of the allies staggered through the streets, arms and backs piled high with silks, furs and brocades, with gold and silver and jewels."[33]

The Americans were under strict orders not to loot.

The Marines guarding the yamen of the salt commissioner found a large amount of silver bullion that had been melted and formed into ingots. Some of the silver coins were fused into a mass. The silver was valued at over $376,300. The treasure was removed to the Hong Kong and Shanghai Bank and sold to Mr. C.H.C. Miller, Agent for J.P. Morgan. The amount was deposited in the U.S. Treasury. Later the money was returned to China.[34]

In reporting this find, Admiral Remey, the Asiatic Station Commander, sent the following dispatch:

> Chefoo
> Bureau of Navigation, Washington
> Received July 25, 1900

> Taku 24th. Marines have found silver specie, partly melted in ruins of mint. Amounting to one-third or half million dollars. Has been transferred to headquarters in settlement for protection. I recommend it be sold to bankers Tien-Tsin to relieve us of encumbrance, and funds held for further disposition. Colonel Meade to Mar Island Hospital rheumatism; Major Waller succeeds command First Regiment. My obtainable information clears Marines of any imputation burning houses or looting Tien-Tsin.

> Remey[35]

This dispatch not only dealt with the question of looting but reported the change of command of the First Marine Regiment from Colonel Meade to Major Waller. Later a second dispatch was sent in response to inquires of the Americans' looting.

> Chefoo, China
> July 29, 1900
> Corbin-Washington

> Tientsin July 25. Looting American troops walled City Tientsin, unfounded and denied. Silver taken from burned mint under direction of Colonel Meade, commanding, who was invalided today. No property destroyed except under military exigency. American troops have order to protect life and property noncombatants in American southeast quarter assigned to them. Will forward reports commander of American guards in city.

> Coolidge[36]

With the fall of Tien-Tsin, the Boxer and Imperial troops' opposition in the area ended. The allied powers could now concentrate on the relief of the besieged legations in Peking.

The Marines remained in the city for about ten days before being withdrawn to their warehouse quarters in the British Concession. After the Tien-Tsin operation, "Major Waller in closing his report of the operation, made a pessimistic statement: 'There seems small chance of any movement toward Peking for three weeks.'"[37]

It is interesting to note that during the operations against Tien-Tsin a bond of friendship was formed between the First Marine Regiment and the Royal Welsh Fusiliers. "Ever since the Boxer Uprising it has been an annual custom of the two corps that, on St. David's Day (March 1), the National Holiday of Wales, the Commandant of the Marine Corps and the Colonel of the Royal Welsh exchange the traditional watchword of Wales— '... and Saint David!'"[38]

Robert Moskin's book on the Marine Corps notes, "Years later, the First Marine Regiment asked John Philip Sousa to write a march to honor its British comrades in China. *The Royal Welsh Fusiliers* was first played at the Gridiron Club dinner in Washington on April 26, 1930; present was President Hoover, who had been at Tientsin."[39]

8

The Siege of the Legations at Peking

While turmoil reigned from Taku to Tien-Tsin, the eye of the storm, Peking, remained calm.

In May 1900, life at the Legation Quarter community was much the same as always. The Quarter was a compact little world completely isolated from the remainder of the city of Peking. While business was conducted primarily during the morning hours, the afternoons and evenings were devoted to visiting back and forth, strolling along Legation Street, shopping at Imbeck's, picnicking, formal calls, lawn parties, formal dinners at the various foreign compounds and horse racing, particularly in the spring and fall.

Engrossed in themselves, residents gave little attention to the Boxers as they moved north from Shantung Province toward Peking. The "Old China Hands" thought they understood. They felt the uprising was another one that usually followed floods, famine or some other disaster, which the Chinese usually blamed on foreigners, and would blow itself out after a short time.

The Boxers finally arrived in Peking and began demonstrating. As the tension mounted, the foreign ministers applied to the Tsung Li Yamen (The Chinese Imperial Foreign Office, usually referred to as the Yamen) for legation guards. When their request was approved, they immediately cabled their respective governments.

Meanwhile, life in the foreign community continued much as always. By the end of May, diplomatic families were preparing to move to their summer homes in the Western Hills. In fact, on 26 May, Mrs. Herbert

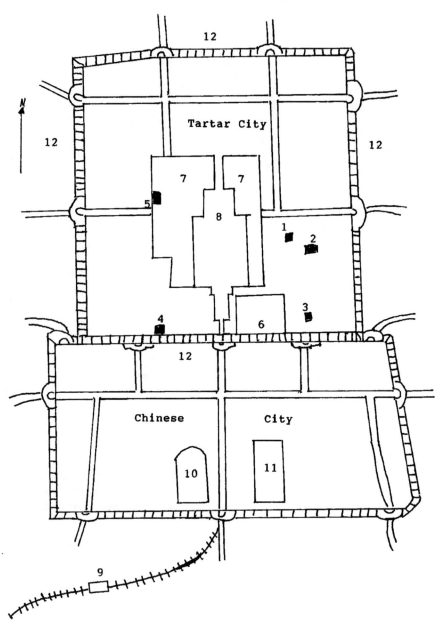

Map 6. City of Peking—1900. Places identified by number: 1. East Cathedral; 2. Tsung Li Yamen; 3. Methodist Mission; 4. South Cathedral; 5. Peitang Cathedral; 6. Legations; 7. Imperial City; 8. Forbidden City; 9. Machiapu Railroad Terminal; 10. Temple of Agriculture; 11. Temple of Heaven; 12. Tartar Wall.

Squires, wife of the American First Secretary, and her family were already settled in their summer home. For their protection the Tsung Li Yamen had provided a guard of twelve Chinese soldiers.

It was on this date the Fengtai railway sheds and station were burned by the Boxers and the Belgian engineers and their families at Chang Hsin Tien, some 16 miles away, were besieged.

Under cover, Dr. C.E. Morrison, correspondent for the *London Times,* visited the Fengtai area for a firsthand view of the destruction. While returning to Peking to file his story at the telegraph office, he remembered the Squire family. Instead of continuing on to the city, he joined the Squire family in their summer home. He found the family huddled in their residence and the area practically deserted. The twelve Chinese soldiers had abandoned their posts and fled to the safety of their barracks in the city. Seeking loot, most of the Chinese in the area had joined the Boxers.

As Morrison feared, Mr. Squires was unable to join his family that afternoon because the city gates had been closed for the night. Dr. Morrison remained on guard with the family throughout the night. The next morning, Mr. Squires arrived with a Russian Cossack guard, which he had borrowed from the Russian Minister. (Under the Treaty of Nertchinsh of 1689, the Russians were the first foreign powers to establish diplomatic relationships with China and were allowed to keep a small guard; its strength was seven Cossacks.) By mid-afternoon the Squire family along with their numerous servants were back in their residence in the Legation Quarter.

Meanwhile, M. Auguste Chamot, Swiss proprietor of the Hotel de Peking, with his American wife, formed a volunteer rescue party and, on horseback, rode to Chang Hsin Tien and brought the besieged Belgians into the Legation Quarter.

Fortunately, late in the evening of 31 May, the legation guards arrived at the Machiapu Station outside the Yung Ting Men (*Men* in Mandarian means gate) in the south wall of the Chinese City. (See Map 6). As the guards marched through the streets to the Legation Quarter, Chinese lined the streets.

A day or two after the arrival of the legation guards, life in the Quarter settled back to normal.

In his last letter from Peking dated 3 June 1900, Captain John T. Myers wrote:

"We marched here three days ago with a column of 350 English, French, Germans, Russians, Japs, and Italians. We headed the column, and I was the 'first man in.' There is a big row on, and the situation is very grave, the Boxers killing missionaries everywhere. I expect to be here for many months. I

On 31 May 1900, the Marine Detachment arrived in Peking. Sullen Chinese onlookers gazed curiously as the Marines, in heavy marching order, entered the Legation Quarter. (Marine Corps University Archives, Quantico, Virginia.)

am in command with 54 men, a colt gun, one officer and young surgeon. Our entry was not opposed, but the crowds were deadly silent. One thing is sure, if they do rise, we are inside the second wall, and in a trap, but I do not think trouble will come. Hope not, anyway."[1] Time proved Myers correct on being in a trap, but he failed when he predicted the Chinese would not rebel.

While life in the foreign community was somewhat relaxed, out in the provinces the Boxers burned, murdered and looted. When missionaries asked for military escorts to rescue outlying missions, the foreign ministers refused, explaining they could not risk the safety of the Quarter by sending out any of the legation guards.

As rioting spread throughout the city, the foreign ministers wired Tien-Tsin for addition legation guards. They were notified that Admiral Seymour would leave at once with a relief force.

On 3 June, as the heat in the city increased and in face of escalating violence, Lady MacDonald, the British Foreign Minister's wife, sent her family under the care of Miss Armstrong, her sister, to their summer home in the Western Hills. Despite the shortage of legation guards, a guard of thirty British Marines accompanied the family.

On 8 June, the ministers and military leaders met in council to formulate plans to defend the Legation Quarter as far east as Hata Men Street. Because of the shortage of legation guards, the ministers were eventually forced to amend their original plans. (See Map 7 below for these changes.) Note that the Austrian and Belgium Legations were not included within the defense perimeter. Although Captain Myers tried to hold the Belgium Legation with an outpost, his position was overrun and he was forced to withdraw his outpost. After that, the legation was ransacked, looted and burned.

The ministers further agreed that the Methodist Mission and the Peitang Cathedral, both located outside the Legation Quarter, should be held.

Before these defense lines were drawn and barricades erected to restrict the flow of traffic through the Legation Quarter, incidents had to occur which would force the hands of the foreign ministers. In the past,

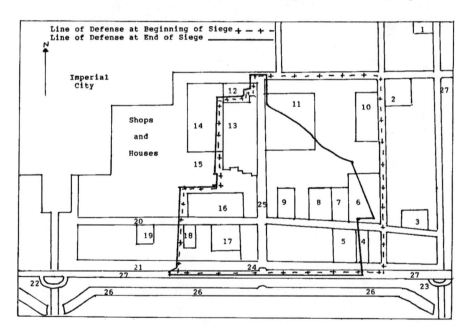

Map 7. Legation Quarter, 1900. Identified by number: 1. Belgian Legation (Burnt); 2. Austrian Legation (Burnt); 3. Italian Legation (Burnt); 4. Pekin Club; 5. German Legation; 6. French Legation; 7. Hotel de Peking; 8. Japanese Legation; 9. Spanish Legation; 10. Customs; 11. The Fu; 12. Hamlin Library; 13. British Legation; 14. Imperial Carriage Pk.; 15. Mongol Market; 16 Russian Legation; 17. American Legation; 18. Russian Bank; 19. Dutch Legation (Burnt); 20. Legation Street; 21. Wall Street; 22. Chien Men; 23. Hata Men; 24. Water Gate; 25. Canal; 26. Moat; 27. Tartar Wall

seeking a peaceful solution, the foreign ministers, wanting to appease the Yamen, had not done anything that might be considered hostile. The same sort of thinking prevented them from fortifying the Legation Quarter until they were forced to do so by the threat of annihilation. The first of these events occurred on the night of June 12. During the night the Roman Catholic Church, "Tungchou," and other missions were burned and the Chinese Christians nearby were massacred. During the morning of 13 June, another incident happened that could only happen in China.

Amid all this carnage, Baron von Ketteler, the German Minister, walking along Legation Street, encountered two Boxers on a cart armed with swords and dressed with red sashes and headbands. Ketteler, feeling the men were insolent, attacked them with his walking stick. One of the men fled, the other, however, was captured. Grasping the offender, Ketteler dragged him into the German Legation and locked him up to await punishment. Ketteler refused to give the man up to the Yamen authorities, insisting the man should be executed on the bridge on the following day. Later, however, he relented and released the man.

During the afternoon of the same day, a party of German and Italian Marines raided a temple where the Boxers were said to be drilling. The Boxers, being forewarned, fled and the raiding party only captured a few weapons and a quantity of red cord, which the Boxers used as girdles. Still later in the afternoon, rumors said that two legation servants had been killed while shopping outside Chien Men. Only after these incidents were orders given to clear and barricade the Legation Quarter.

While other legation guards cleared and barricaded designated streets throughout the Legation Quarter, Captain Myers joined forces with British Captain B.M. Strouts, and Russian Baron von Rahden, and with detachments of men made sorties along Legation and Wall Streets. Wall Street ran parallel to Tartar Wall.

They cleared these streets of Chinese and built barricades from above the Dutch Legation to below the Italian Legation. With Tartar Wall on the south and these barricades in place, the southern part of the Legation Quarter was closed to traffic. Except for the barricades above the Dutch Legation, this became the final southern line of defense. The barricade at the Dutch Legation was held until the legation was burned. Then the barricade was pulled back to the final line of defense.

Although there was no assault on the Legation Quarter before 21 June, sniper fire was troublesome. During the early morning hours, numerous volleys of rifle fire raked the Marines and Russian barricades.

On 8 June, Captain Myers sent a corporal and nine privates to the American Methodist Mission, which was located outside the Legation

The gateway to the American Legation. Also shown is the barricade built across Legation Street. The Chinese had a similar barricade across Legation Street about 20 yards away. (Marine Corps University Archives, Quantico, Virginia.)

Quarter, with orders to hold it until the relief column arrived. The Methodist Mission Compound was the largest, nearest and best fortified of all the missions in the city. Dr. Dunlap Gamewell, a missionary, had fortified the mission, and with adequate provisions of food and water, it was felt that it could withstand any reasonable assault. Therefore, it was selected as a refuge for all the missionaries and some 1,500 Chinese Christian converts.

Before the arrival of the Marines, Dr. Gamewell had already commenced reinforcing the mission's walls. Masons bricked up all unnecessary doors; windows were also bricked up and looped-holed and all drains leading from the mission were secured with iron bars. Barricades were built across the streets in front and in the rear of the mission and platforms were built along the inner walls of the mission for sentries.

To hamper the Boxers in case of a breakthrough, barbed wire was stretched across the courts and deep ditches were dug beyond the barbed wire. The chapel was designated as the last line of defense. As a final effort, large quantities of bricks were piled on the roof of the chapel to be hurled down upon any attacking Boxers who might break through.

To further strengthen the mission, on 9 June, Captain Newt Hall,

The Methodist Mission. Note the windows have been bricked up. The barbed wire in the foreground is to prevent the Chinese soldiers and Boxers from rushing the mission. (Marine Corps University Archives, Quantico, Virginia.)

Corporal Dahlgren and nine privates reinforced the other Marines at the mission. Captain Myers protested sending Marine guards to the mission, pointing out that it was not advisable to divide his small force of Marines. The ministers, however, insisted on having the Marines sent to the mission, instead of bringing the missionaries and the converts into the defense lines.

Since the British also had people at the mission, they sent two British Marines and ten extra rifles. To insure the rifles would be effectively used, a Marine sergeant put some of the missionaries through a regular rifle drill every day. The mission now had some 35 rifles for its defense.

**A Marine patrol returning from clearing the streets at the Mission Chapel.
(Marine Corps University Archives, Quantico, Virginia.)**

In addition to defending the Methodist Mission, the ministers had also
elected to defend the Peitang Cathedral, located east of P'ing Tse Men
inside the walls of the Imperial city (see Map 6, page 64). Forty-three men
from the French and Italian legation guards were detailed to help Bishop
Favier defend the cathedral.

With the split of his command, Captain Myers had no officers to share
the responsibilities of the guard or to give his men sufficient time off
duty each twenty-four hours. Being the only Marine officer present in the
Legation Quarter, Myers was especially overworked. Usually, he could

get about four hours of sleep each night and that was taken in catnaps in a folding chair. Even then, when a critical situation developed that needed his attention, the sergeant of the guard had to awaken him.

Captain Myers was not the only one feeling the effects of the under-manned guard. Dr. T.M. Lippett reported that many of the men should be on the sick list. It was hard for him to imagine how the overworked men felt when at any moment thousands of half-crazed fanatics might break into the Legation Quarter. The strain was constant. The men carried their rifles with them at all times, even when eating.

Mary Hooker wrote in her journal that one evening while eating, the Marines left their mess four times to rush to their barricades. Quite often the Marine bugler sounded "call to arms" several times throughout the day. Each time, off-duty Marines responded. Most of the time these were not serious attacks. Boxers and rioters running amok in the city after loot would decide on the spur of the moment to devil the foreigners. Never-theless, each "call to arms" had to be taken seriously.

During the early part of June foreigners still moved about the city procuring supplies and taking care of business. For their protection, armed Marine guards accompanied each party that went out into the city. These armed excursions put an additional strain on the already overextended guard detachment.

On 9 June, the Boxers burned the grandstand at the race course. Chinese troops stood by and watched.

After many failures, on 10 June, a courier sent out by Mr. Squires returned. The courier, a former gardener, managed to get through to Captain McCalla, who was with the Seymour column. He also delivered messages to the other commanders who made up the force. Captain McCalla notified Minister Conger that the Seymour column of 1,600 men of all nationalities had reached Lang-Fang, thirty miles from Peking, and was pushing on as fast as the railroad tracks could be repaired. The returning courier also delivered messages from all the commanders in the column to their respective ministers.

Not knowing the extent of the damage to the railroad, the people in the Legation Quarter felt the relief column would arrive by 1000 hours the next day and planned to meet the incoming troops.

On 11 June, many of the foreigners in Peking went to the railroad station to greet the relief column when it arrived. Along with other legation guards, Captain Myers with 10 Marines and 20 carts to transport their baggage waited until 1100 hours for the arrival of the relief column.

When the column did not show up by noon, the Europeans returned to the Quarter. That afternoon, Japanese Chancellor Sugiyama set out alone for the railway station to check on the possible arrival of Seymour's column. At Yung Ting Men he was seized by General Tung Fu Hsiang's soldiers and brought before an officer, who ordered his immediate decapitation. General Tung Fu Hsiang was commander of the Muslim soldiers, who were feared all over China for barbarity. The decapitated head was sent to General Hsiang.

The MacDonald family remained in their summer home until 11 June, when looting in the hills forced their return to the Legation Quarter. It was well the family was back in the Legation Quarter, because events took a serious turn when the Japanese Chancellor was murdered. On 12 June, the British summer residence was looted and burned.

On 13 June, the Methodist Mission's street chapel, a few minutes' walk from the mission, was set on fire and burned. When it seemed the rioters were going to move against the mission, Captain Hall and eight Marines, with bayonets fixed, charged down the street screaming. The rioters fled without the Marines making contact. When the Marines returned, one remarked, "It was the yelling the boys let out that sent the crowd flying."[2]

Once Mrs. Gamewell asked Captain Hall how she could help in case of an attack.

> The Captain heard me through and then replied: "The most helpful thing a woman can do in a fight is to keep out of the way." Then with still unsmiling countenance he said: "There is one thing you can do. When the fighting begins you can take charge of the hysterical women and keep them quiet."[3]

When the comment was repeated to the mission women, they found it amusing. These were unusual women. They had all been through riots, floods and famines before, and some, like Mrs. Gamewell, had endured the Chungking Riot of July 1886. While the women might have found the remark amusing, later it might have contributed to the civilians' dislike of Hall. The flamboyant Myers was well liked while the taciturn Hall was not.

As the heat of summer set in and temperatures climbed to over 100 degrees, it was noticed by Mrs. Gamewell that Marines still wore their heavy winter uniforms. When asked why they endured such discomfort, one told her,

> One day while at dinner on shipboard, the order was given to report on shore at once for Peking. There was no time to consider the possible heat of summer in Peking, or prepare other than the clothing we wore. They had come in haste as they were, in response to the call from Peking for legation guards.[4]

The women of the mission took up a collection, and while it was still possible to make purchases at the shops they procured enough navy-blue drilling and brass buttons to outfit twenty Marines (at the mission) with lightweight uniforms.

For a pattern a suit was ripped up. Since it was selected because it would fit the average man, adjustment had to be made to meet each Marine's physical structure. Once the uniforms were cut out, they were taken to the Marine quarters and individually fitted. When completed, each uniform was tagged with a sewn in cloth strip with the Marine's name on it.

When asked about pockets on the close fitting jackets, the Marines specified, unhesitatingly, four. Four pockets and a row of brass buttons and a little stand up collar were pronounced satisfactory. There was, however, one point on which the Marines were particular, "that was that there should be no hint of flare where the trousers met the feet," for the soldiers of the Marine Corps were anxious that no extra width of trousers should cause them to be mistaken for sailors. The Marines were not too concerned with the fit of the uniforms. The coolness of the lightweight uniforms offset the fit.[5]

Sara Pike Conger, wife of the American Minister, in her book mentioned this incident. She wrote: "Some of the missionaries are making trousers for our Marines. Their change of clothing did not reach them from Tien-Tsin. These Marines are sorely tried, for their clothing are soiled and warm and they have to wear them day and night."[6] From this statement, apparently the missionary women at least made trousers for all the Marine guards.

On 14 June, Boxers charged down every street leading into the Legation Quarter and found them blocked by flimsy barricades, yet manned by legation guards. After one volley, they withdrew, leaving behind several dead and great pikes and swords of the true old Chinese pattern. Throughout the night of 14 June, the Boxers tried to gain entrance through every possible street leading into the Legation Quarters, and each time found their way blocked.

On 15 June, the Boxers torched the Nan T'ang Catholic Mission and systematically started slaughtering Chinese Christian converts. A sortie of 10 Marines along with 20 Russian sailors and W. N. Pethick and M. Duysberg were sent to the mission to rescue the converts. Pethick and Dysberg, both proficient in the Chinese language, acted as interpreters. Amidst the ruins, the Marines and sailors surprised a group of Boxers who were looting and killing Chinese families. A short one-sided fight followed. Over 60 Boxers were killed before the group fled. The rescue party found piles of mutilated corpses of women, children and old men who had not been able to escape the fury of the Boxers. One journalist wrote, "Many were found roasted alive and massacred as not to be recognized." Several hundred women and children were found hidden in the surrounding alleys and ruins and brought to the defense perimeter. The other legation guards also joined in rescue work.

On Saturday, 16 June, a sortie of 10 Marines, 20 British, six Japanese and a few volunteers ventured forth to rescue other Chinese Christians. As they neared a Taoist Temple north of the Austrian Legation, they heard screams of Chinese Christians being murdered by Boxers. Storming the temple, they opened fire on some 50 Boxers who were in full dress armed with spears and swords. No quarter was given. Mutilated bodies of converts were found scattered about the temple. Because of the rapid response of the rescue party, a few converts were saved and brought back to the Legation Quarter.

After one of these sorties Marine Sergeant Walker told Mary Hooker "he had sent eight devils to glory; many of his shots he had seen take effect, and others he hoped soon would take effect."[7]

Finally, after three days of continuous rescue work, Captain Myers decided that with all the night watches and the long hours of daytime duty, the Marines could no longer endure it. So rescue work was discontinued. The other legation guards also stopped for the same reason.

Of the rescue work, Captain Myers later wrote: "It was realized at the time that these rescuing parties served to inflame the Boxer element more deeply against the foreigners, but it was more than flesh and blood could stand to see the terrible burned and lacerated bodies of those who escaped to our lines, and refuse to send aid to their comrades known to be still within the power of the fiendish Boxer hordes."[8]

During this period, the Chinese Imperial army took no part in fighting. They did, nevertheless, keep the Legation Quarter under observation.

On 17 June, the allied forces captured the Taku Forts at the mouth of the Pei-Ho River.

On the same day, Chinese soldiers fired on the Marine barricade on Legation Street. The Marines returned fire, killing one Chinese soldier. Despite this incident, while the Quarter was probed from time to time, it did not come under further fire from the Chinese army.

Despite the fact that the Chinese soldiers had first opened fire on the Marines' barricade, the Chinese cited the incident as the cause for the Chinese army entering the fray. Much later, when the ministers were trying to negotiate the lifting of the siege, the Yamen reminded them that their actions were the cause of the Chinese army's attack on the Legation Quarter.

The Allied Forces capturing the Taku Forts on the same day may have caused this incident. The Empress Dowager considered the capture of the forts an act of war. After 17 June, the political situation changed completely.

Dropping all pretense of neutrality, on the morning of 19 June, the Tsung Li Yamen delivered an edict to the eleven foreign ministers stating that a state of war existed and explaining that all relations were broken. Further, they demanded that all foreigners leave the city within twenty-four hours. The edict specifically stated that the evacuation must be accomplished by 1600 hours on the following day, 20 June. The edict also stated that the Chinese government would provide an army escort to guarantee their safety en route to Tien-Tsin.

The ministers and the military leaders met in council in the Spanish Legation to determine whether they should accept this ultimatum. The military officers counseled against acceptance. They pointed out there were not enough legation guards to provide adequate security for a column strung out for miles along the road to Tien-Tsin. Further, they did not trust the Chinese government to provide security for the departing foreigners. The ministers argued about what to do. Finally, it was agreed they should accept the offer, but to do so they needed more time to work out the details. In a reply to the edict, they requested an audience with the Yamen at 0900 hours the next morning to plan the evacuation.

At 0900 hours on the morning of 20 June, the ministers awaited a reply to their request for an audience, but no answer came. The consensus was to wait a little longer.

A little before 1000 hours, Baron Klemens von Ketteler, the German foreign minister, short on patience, decided to go to the Yamen and get a reply to their request. Accompanied by four guards, Ketteler in his official sedan chair, followed by his secretary, Herr Heinrich Cordes, both unarmed, set out for the Yamen. For reasons known only by Ketteler, shortly after leaving the Legation Quarter, he dismissed his guards and continued on his way. With only his two *maffus* in front as outriders, he proceeded in the same style as a Chinese mandarin would go through the street. As he passed through the Arch of Honor on Hata Men Street, just below the Yamen, a Chinese soldier, under the command of a lieutenant, stepped out from the curb. Pushing his rifle through the window of the Baron's sedan chair, he opened fire. Ketteler was killed instantly and Cordes was wounded. Cordes managed to escape and make his way to the American Methodist compound where he reported Ketteler's assassination. Later he was moved to the Quarter's hospital. The two *maffus*, being mounted, also escaped and brought word of Ketteler's murder back to the Legation Quarter.

A party of the legation guards made a sortie to recover the minister's body. When it became evident that the Chinese troops might possibly cut off the party from the Legation Quarter, they called off the search and returned to their defense lines.

Ketteler's assassination opened the ministers' eyes to their real position and the real attitude of the Imperial troops. The question of being escorted by them to the coast was never again considered for a moment. It also confirmed what the military leaders had pointed out — the Chinese government could not or would not protect the foreigners if they left the Legation Quarter. The ministers decided to dig in and await the arrival of Seymour's column.

With that decision, the ministers were faced with many problems. One of the foremost was what to do with the American Methodist Mission. Since the mission was approximately a mile from the Legation Quarter, the ministers felt it was no longer feasible to hold it.

On 20 June, orders were given to abandon the mission. A detachment of German Marines was sent to the mission to carry the stretcher bearing Mr. Cordes and help escort the European missionaries to the Legation Quarter. The main responsibility of guarding these noncombatants fell to Captain Hall and his men. Sergeant I. Fanning along with Private Oscar J. Upham was with the rear guard when the mission was evacuated. Soldiers of the Imperial Army, Boxers and rioters lined the evacuation route watching, but made no hostile moves.

The British Legation Compound covered some seven acres. Because of its size and having several wells of potable water, the compound was designated as the final line of defense.

Earlier in the day, all the Europeans, except for the guards, within the Legation Quarter were moved into the British Compound. A steady stream of men, women and children carrying bundles, trunks and grips poured through the main gate of the British compound and were assigned quarters. When the Europeans from the Methodist Mission arrived, they too were quartered there.

Crowded into the British Legation compound which measured about 300 yards long and contained about a dozen houses and a chapel, were 191 men, 147 women and 76 children, in all 414 foreign noncombatants. Madame Paula von Rosthorn, the wife of the Austrian Chargé d'Affaires, and Madame Chamot, of the Hotel de Peking, along with three children, stayed with their husbands throughout the siege. Thus, in the Quarter were some 472 foreigners besides the legation guards. In the Fu palace were some 3,000 Chinese Christians.

The Bell Tower which stood outside the chapel in the British Legation became the center of life in the Quarter. It stood near the crossroads of four lanes. Large bulletin boards were erected near the bell, which became the headquarters of the municipal government. Here the names of general committees and the heads of subcommittees were posted. Anyone who had suggestions could post their desires and anyone fitted for any kind of work knew exactly to whom to offer their services.

On the bulletin boards were posted all kinds of notices, scraps of news, rumors of the relief force, messages received from abroad, translation of Chinese edicts and other things that interested or amused the besieged people.

Partially sheltered from shot and shell by shade trees, the Bell Tower was suited to be the center of community life. Here, in the cool of the evening, people assembled to discuss affairs, to joke, to grumble or to await instructions or orders.

The Bell Tower was a memorial of the Queen's Jubilee. It was only struck once during the siege; no one was injured.

Monsieur Auguste Chamot was a Swiss in charge of the Hotel de Peking. His heroic wife was a San Francisco woman. When the other women in Peking left their homes and took refuge in the British Legation, Mrs. Chamot remained with her husband. With rifle in hand she took her regular hours of watching at the loopholes of the barricade erected across Legation Street between Hotel de Peking and the German Legation. M. Chamot started a bakery in the hotel and daily baked hundreds of loaves of bread for the besieged. Once, after a shell burst in the bakery room, Mrs. Chamot, with rifle in hand, kept the coolies working while her husband served with the guard. On one occasion while manning the barricade, M. Chamot was wounded in the hand by a Boxer spear but continued to work in the bakery as well as taking his turn at the barricade.

The abandonment of the mission created a second problem, what to do with the Chinese Christian converts who had taken refuge there. Recalling the earlier slaughter of converts, the ministers knew if the converts were left behind, the Boxers would kill them.

Due to the number of converts, there was not enough space within the Legations to house them. Dr. G.E. Morrison and Professor Heberty James soon solved that problem. The palace of Prince Su was within the defense perimeter of the legation guards. Since the prince was not using the palace, Morrison and James wangled the use of the prince's palace, or "The Fu" (in Mandarin *fu* means palace, mansion or great house, including the grounds) as it was usually called, to quarter the converts. Before it was all over, some 3,000 Chinese Christian converts were crowded into the Fu. All of these Chinese were not coolies. Many of them were scholars, merchants, teachers and other educated people. Later these Chinese became the labor force to build barricades and breastworks for the defense of the Quarter and perform other manual labor.

Another problem that required immediate attention was food for over 3,000 people now within the defense perimeter. Mr. Squires, the American First Secretary, a former army officer, was foresighted enough to lay in a store of rice, canned vegetables and meat as well as ammunition for his personal rifles and shotguns. As for the remainder of the Europeans, little had been done to collect food for the siege.

After the evacuation of the mission, working parties returned and brought back all the food and supplies that had been left behind in the haste of evacuation. Conveniently, some 125 ponies that were assembled in the Legation Quarter for the annual spring races guaranteed fresh meat. On the afternoon of 21 June, Mr. Squires, aided by his fifteen-year-old son Fargo, and many of the missionaries collected food for the besieged legation. Although not quite sure of their authority to do so, they collected anything in sight that might be used for food — a flock of sheep grazing near the British Legation, a cow, some eight thousand bushels of wheat at the Prosperity Grain Shop, and tons of rice stored near the Imperial Drainage Canal. Fortunately, the foraging parties found an abundance of fodder within the defended area for the livestock that would later be their source of meat.

Two of the foreign food shops in Peking were Inbeck's and Kierfuff's located well within the defense lines. The third was next door to the American Legation. Forging parties went to these stores and brought supplies of canned meat and vegetables, coffee, tea, cocoa, sugar, jam, tinned milk, white flour, tobacco, wines and spirits. The general public was more pleased with the tobacco, wine and spirits than the missionaries in charge.

Later, the proprietors of these stores, who had taken refuge in the Legation Quarters, authorized what was left of the supplies to be moved to the British Legation.

Because many Chinese stores which were located between the legations and near the Quarter had been abandoned, the foraging parties took anything they felt they needed — thousands of yards of cloth for sandbags and hospital use, clothing, kitchen utensils, buckets in which to carry water in case of fire, stores of coal and a Chinese gristmill. The gristmill was later set up and provided the defenders with flour.

Mr. Fenn, designated as miller to operate the ten-mule-powered gristmill, produced flour from the supply of wheat taken earlier. At first, he operated the mill where he found it. When rifle fire made the location untenable, he moved the mill to the British Legation and continued milling until the relief column arrived.

Throughout the day, a constant stream of Peking carts moving these supplies rumbled into the British compound.

Although the Hotel de Peking remained in the hands of M. Auguste Chamot, its ample cellars provided the besieged with more than 1,000 cases of Dry Monople champagne and a vast store of anchovy paste.

Precisely at 1600 hours on 20 June, as stated in the edict, the Chinese opened fire on the French Legation. A French sentry fell with a shot through the head. The siege had started.

Throughout the day there were several short assaults by a mixture of Chinese soldiers and Boxers on various defenses around the Legation Quarter. Sniping, however, continued all day. While the legation guards had to conserve ammunition, as the supply was limited, the Chinese had no such restrictions. They fired tremendous amounts, almost without aiming. They crouched behind a wall or barricade, loaded, pointed their guns over the wall and without exposing themselves or aiming, pulled the trigger.

As can be seen on Map 7, a large part of the Legation Quarter was abandoned on 20 June. It should further be noted that the defense lines were shortened on 22 June and again on 14 August. The final line of defense is marked with heavy black lines.

When the lines of defense were shortened on 20 June, the Marines' sector in the extemporized defense plan was the southwest quadrant around the American Legation and on the Tartar Wall some 400 yards east of Chien Men. This included the barricade at the west end of Wall Street and the American Legation. The Marines shared the barricade at the west end of Legation Street with the Russian sailors. The Marines were primarily responsible for Tartar Wall and the American Legation while the Russian sailors held the Russian Legation.

The southeast quadrant, to the Marines' rear, was the German-Austrian position. The Japanese and civilian volunteers manned the northeast quadrant usually referred to as Prince Su's Palace or simply "The Fu."

The French and the Italians defended the sector between the southeast quadrant and the northeast quadrant.

The Royal British Marines and British volunteers defended the northwest quadrant. Backing the British Legation was the Hanlin Academy (Library). Because the library contained centuries of Chinese culture, the British felt the Chinese would never attack from that corner of their sector.

The whole perimeter measured about a mile and a half in circumference. It included most of the legations, various foreign banks, the club, and Hotel de Peking. M. Chamot and his wife stayed at the hotel throughout the siege, grinding flour and baking bread for the besieged foreigners.

First Lieutenant Graf Alfred von Soden commanded 50 German Marines of the Third Sea Battalion, which held the Wall during the first days of the siege. However, on 24 June, Chinese soldiers charged down the wide top of the Wall and poured heavy fire into the entire Legation Quarter. The Germans cleared the Wall of snipers down to Chien Men. The lack of cover on top of the Wall made holding the Wall difficult and they fell back.

Captain Myers attempted several times to take position on the Wall, but blinding smoke and Chinese rifle fire forced the Marines back each time. On his third attempt, Myers led his men back up the stone ramp and this time established a permanent position. The Chinese soldiers charged Myers' position with war bugles blaring and flags flying, trying to drive the Marines from the wall. Their assault failed and they retreated with heavy losses. Building a stone barricade that faced west toward Chien Men, the Marines now had a firm foothold on the Wall.

The German Marines succeeded in securing a foothold on the Wall some 500 yards to the Marines' rear. Their barricade faced east toward Hata Men. Both of these stone barricades were flimsy affairs. The Germans manned this barricade with some 15 men. In towers over both Chien Men and Hata Men the Chinese had observation posts and artillery that shelled the American and German positions.

The key point in the defense of the Legation Quarter was the 60-foot-high and 40-foot-wide Tartar Wall. The wall had loopholed parapets three feet high at the sides, and square bastions 100 yards apart on the outside face. At wide intervals along the inside face was a pair of inclined ramps eight feet wide for mounting the wall.

Anyone controlling the 60-foot wall that overlooked the Legation Quarter would dominate it. For the Marines, the siege became an endurance contest for control of the Wall. The Marines kept a guard of 15 men atop the Wall, relieving them at night. A half-dozen Marines manned a barricade at the foot of the ramp and another seven or eight held a barricade on Legation Street. Moving to and from the Wall was especially dangerous during the day for Marines and their own Chinese barricade builders, as they had to use the ramp exposed to Chinese sniper fire. Consequently, the relief of guards on the Wall was made at night. This made a twelve-hour tour of duty on the wall necessary. The first four Marines to die were all shot through the head by snipers while moving along this ramp.

The Marines had an outpost defending the Russian Bank just outside the American Legation. While on duty at this outpost, Private Charles B. King was killed by a sniper's bullet through the head. Later Private Herman Helm was struck in the head by a piece of shrapnel while on the stone

View of Tartar Wall that surrounded the Legation Quarter, Tartar City, Imperial City and Forbidden City. The left ramp leading to the top of Tartar Wall
was controlled by the Marines. The ramp to the right was controlled by the Chinese. Note the series of barricades on the left ramp. To the extreme right is the
Chien Men Watch Tower which was controlled by the Chinese. (Marine Corps
University Archives, Quantico, Virginia.)

ramp leading to the top of Tartar Wall. He was taken to the hospital in
the British Legation where he was kept for the remainder of the siege.

The Chinese mounted several pieces of artillery near Chien Men and
built a series of barricades that put them even closer to the Marines' barricades. From these positions, the Chinese kept the Marine sector of the Wall
under continuous artillery and rifle fire as they burned and burrowed their
way closer to the legations. Sir Claude MacDonald would later write, "Captain Myers' post on the wall is the peg which holds the whole thing together."[9]

With continued pressure of the Chinese and Boxers on the defense
lines and the shortage of legation guards, many of the outlying legations
were abandoned. One of the first to be abandoned was the Belgium Legation, which was some distance from the Quarter. A party of Austrian
Marines went to the legation and escorted the minister and his staff back
to the defense lines. Shortly after the evacuation, the Chinese looted and
burned the compound.

Finally, on 22 June, the Austrian Marines vacated their legation. The Austrian Marines joined the French and strengthened their defense lines. This legation compound was also looted and burned.

The next concentrated attack was against the Dutch Legation west of the American Legation. The first barricades had been set up to include the Dutch Legation. Captain Myers tried to hold the barricade and protect the Dutch Legation. He ordered his Marines to turn the Colt machine gun on the crowd. It was of no avail. Finally, he had to pull his men back and abandon the compound. The Boxers promptly looted and burned it.

After the initial attack on 20 June, the defense perimeter was again shortened on 22 June. (See Map 7.)

It is surprising that no attention had been given to building defenses to enable the Legation Quarter to withstand a siege. Before 20 June, the defenses were jerry-built by military men trained to fight in the open, not to build barricades and fortifications. The ministers and military leaders recognized the weakness of the existing barricades and knew something had to be done. Dr. Frank Dunlap Gamewell, the missionary who had planned the defenses of the abandoned Methodist Mission, was selected to plan and build the fortifications. Dr. Gamewell was not an ordinary missionary. Before becoming a missionary, he had gone to both Rensselaer Polytechnic and Cornell engineering schools and studied engineering. He knew about construction — a Mauser bullet would penetrate one-quarter inch of brick, a Krupp shell 54 inches. There was no longer any haphazard planning. One of his first tasks was to demolish buildings adjoining the Legation Quarter that might serve as cover to the enemy. The timbers and brickwork from the destruction of these buildings were used to build barricades and breastworks. Bombproofs, blockhouses and barricades were built to withstand artillery fire. The blockhouses and barricades were constructed with gun ports that gave protection to the men using them and trenches 12 to 14 feet deep were dug to counter Chinese mines. Gamewell left nothing to chance.

The "bombproofs" were cellars where people might take shelter during shellings. These were trenches about six feet deep, covered with a roof of timbers, boards, and several feet of earth or sandbags. Until the rains came in July, these shelters were often used by the noncombatants. After the rains came they filled with water and were no longer used.

His recommendations for barricades and counter-mining to protect against Chinese undermining were carried out as nearly as possible. Undermining was one of the Chineses' principal means of destroying barricades and breastworks.

Gamewell left nothing to chance. Everything that could be done was by an engineer of experience. Given carte blanche authority, day and night he pedaled about the Quarter on his bicycle supervising the building of new defenses and strengthening old ones.

The coolies helped in building barricades and bombproofs, filling sandbags and doing necessary sanitary work. In building and reinforcing the barricades and breastworks, they worked shoulder to shoulder with the legation guards and were exposed to harassing fire from the Chinese. Many were killed or wounded.

Thousands of sandbags were needed to build barricades and breastworks. One diarist estimated that over one hundred thousand sandbags were made and used in the construction of defense lines. The women working with sewing machines and by hand made the sandbags according to Dr. Gamewell's specifications.

Materials of all kinds were used — satin curtains, monogrammed linen sheets, brocades and tapestries seized from Prince Su's Fu and anything else that could be turned into sandbags. Mary Hooker wrote, "There was no doubt that the sky-blue, blood red, yellow and many other colored sandbags made the most colorful barricades and breastworks in the history of warfare."[10]

Credit must be given to the missionaries that took refuge in the Legation Quarter. Once there, they did not become passive drones. While the military was involved with the defense of the Legation Quarter, it was the missionaries who organized a sort of municipal council for the management of the civil affairs of the Legation Quarter. Committees were appointed to organize, supervise and handle the distribution of food, building of barricades, breastworks and other fortifications, the work of coolie labor, the fire brigade, sanitation and all the other things necessary for people to live together in harmony.

All Chinese coolies, servants, cooks, and retainers of the Europeans, which numbered over 1,000, were enrolled as laborers, given badges to sew on their sleeves, and were given fixed hours for their employment on public works for general defense. Later, this labor pool was increased with other Chinese converts from the Fu.

A hospital was equipped under Doctors Velde and Poole. Dr. Velde was a surgeon in the German army who had been decorated by the German Emperor. His forte was surgery but he lacked the general practitioner's knowledge for the general care of patients. Both Drs. Velde and Poole were skilled in battlefield surgery. Miss Lambert, a trained nurse from the Anglican Mission, was the head nurse and supplied the skills the two doctors lacked. She was assisted by a number of ladies, most of them missionaries. All medical supplies from the various legations were pooled at the hospital, and by some means made to last until the end of the siege.

Latrines and garbage tanks were built and the Quarter put under proper sanitation regulations, all supervised by Doctors Robert Coltman, Lowry and Ingles.

At the beginning of the siege, the foreign community had laid in enough supplies to last at least a fortnight or perhaps a little longer. Until July 28, every household lived on what they had gathered for itself at the beginning of the siege; only the staples of life — flour, rice and meat — were supplied from the general stores. Consequently, many of the families formed messes and shared their supplies. There was the Mission Mess, the Customs Mess, the Soldiers' Mess, and Lady MacDonald Mess, to name a few.

If the siege had continued for any length of time, it was evident that all stores would have to be pooled and rationed out per head. Therefore, an order went out on July 28 that every household would send in a list of its stores in tea, sugar, canned meat and vegetables, and other foods. While it did not become necessary to carry out the order to pool these supplies, it did become necessary to reduce the general stores and pony meat to half ration.

No one really knew how many trained Chinese troops were in the area. Admiral Kempff, while in Peking, estimated there were some 20,000 Chinese troops, not counting the thousands of Boxers and rioters that joined in the attack.

Not only did the Boxers attack, but also trained soldiers with European guns. During the siege at one time or another such Chinese units as "General Tung Fu-hsiang's fierce Khansu — ten thousand Mohammedan cutthroats feared by even the Chinese, The Imperial Bannerman, Prince Tuan's Glorified Tigers, and Jung Lu's huge Peking Field Force" attacked the Legation Quarter.[11]

The Boxer hordes attacked with screaming curses, armed with old flintlocks, muzzle-loaders, spears, tridents, gingals, swords, flaming arrows, sky rockets, hot bricks that showered down from out of nowhere and anything else that could be considered a weapon.

In an attempt to start fires within the Quarter, fanatic Boxers carrying bamboo poles with kerosene-soaked rags tied to the end often dashed up to a barricade or a wall and attempted to hurl the poles over the wall. Occasionally they succeeded, but most of the time they were stopped short of the wall. They attacked in crowds and little groups, all still believing they were invulnerable to the foreigners' bullets. It did not seem to matter. As soon as some fell, others took their place. The Chinese troops, armed with modern weapons, were more cautious. Single snipers accounted for most of the Legation's causalities.

The Imperial troops were poor artillery men, but with the huge ten-foot-long, three-man gingals, which they used like rifles, they were deadly. The shouting, screaming, blare of trumpets, and gunfire never seemed to cease.

On the morning of 22 June, the legation guards began to fall back. Austrians, Germans, Italians, Japanese, Americans, and Russians all converged on the British Legation Compound, which had been designed as the final line of defense. At the time, the defenses were not under a major assault. For a short time, confusion reigned as the military commanders tried to determine what had caused the sudden withdrawal. Finally, it appeared Captain Thomann, skipper of the Austrian cruiser *Zenta*, had given the order to withdraw. Captain Thomann, present at the time but not a member of the legation guards, had assumed command by virtue of seniority. The result of his idiotic order was almost disastrous. Once order was restored, the legation guards returned to their defense sectors. Fortunately, the Chinese had not realized the legation guards were falling back and had not occupied the vacated positions. With the exception of the barricade at the Customs Lane, all sectors were reoccupied.

The foregoing account is the way most writers who were present during the siege described the withdrawal. Mary Hooker's account of the withdrawal differs greatly from most accounts. In her book, *Behind the Scenes in Peking*, she wrote:

> On June 22, an unaccountable terror swept over the entire length and breadth of the legation lines. The wave of terror started when the French Marines left their Legation to the Boxers and ran all the way to the British Legation where they reported their Legation as lost. Because of this, the German Marines also became frightened. After fleeing halfway up Legation Street, they stopped and returned to their breastworks. They not only returned to their lines of defense, but sent men to the French Legation to resist if the Boxers should attack.
>
> The Russians' compound was the only passage-way by which the American Marines could escape and retire to the British Legation. It was understood that in the case of withdrawal, the Russian Marines [actually sailors] would not close their big gate that opened on Legation Street until the American Marines had entered the Russian Compound. Together the American Marines and the Russian Marines [*sic*] would hold that position as long as possible and then retreat to the British Legation.
>
> Thinking a general withdrawal had been ordered, the American Marines retreated to the Russian gate only to find it locked and barred. No one was in the vicinity to open the gate. Left with no other alternative, they returned to the wall and manned their positions. Later it

was learned that the Russians had left a smaller gate further down the street open, but neglected to tell the Marines.

By chance, when the Marines returned to their breastworks, they found two Russian Marines [sailors] still manning their sector of the Wall [*sic*]. Somehow, in the confusion of withdrawal, their comrades had left them behind.

Later, the French Marines returned to their sector and relieved the German Marines who had temporarily manned it.

The French and German Legation occupied two important positions in the Legation district defense. They were constantly under attack by the Boxers. If the Boxers had attacked during the hours' panic, the Legation district might have been overrun.[12]

This variation of the withdrawal is given to show that accounts kept by people who were present during the siege varied greatly.

Following this incident, Captain Thomann was relieved of his self-appointed post. Sir Claude MacDonald, the British Foreign Minister, was selected to coordinate the military operations. He was not the supreme commander, because the legation guards remained under the command of their respective ministers. If a minister did not feel an order was justified, he did not carry it out. Further, Sir Claude did not have a reserve force that could be used in critical situations. Captain Thomann was later killed during an assault on the French-Austrian breastworks.

On 23 June, General Chang Foo Shiang's soldiers attacked the west barricades. Gunfire pounded the defenses until about 1130 hours. Then the Chinese did the unexpected; they fired the Hanlin (Academy) Library just north of the British Legation. Until this moment, the British assumed the Chinese would not endanger their great library of Chinese culture. The Chinese fired the library with the intent that the flames would spread to the adjoining British Legation.

There were five wells in the British Legation. Three of the wells contained potable water while the other two were brackish. Using these wells, a bucket brigade was formed to fight the flames. Anything that would hold water was used to keep the flames from spreading; "buckets, kettles, pans, and finally dozens of chamber pots with which the legation was amazingly well supplied." Women, children, coolies and all others that were not needed in the defense lines joined the bucket brigade.

To hamper the efforts of the bucket brigade, Chinese snipers opened fire. Marines and the Royal British Marines were kept busy eliminating the snipers. Late evening found the Hanlin Library destroyed, but the British Legation was intact.

The burning of the library was coordinated with an attack on all fronts. On top of Tartar Wall hordes of Chinese tried to sweep the German and American Marines off the wall. If the attack had been successful, enemy guns would have commanded the entire Legation Quarter. Somehow, both the German and American Marines managed to keep the Chinese off their sector of the Wall. To further keep the Marines busy, the Russo-Chinese Bank that joined the American Legation on the west was blown up and burned. The fire also destroyed the Marines' quarters. After the Marine quarters were burned, Minister Conger's residence became the Marines' quarters. The kitchen became their galley and the long butler's pantry their mess hall. Other rooms became their sleeping quarters. Earlier, Minister Conger and family had moved to the British Legation.

The Japanese barely managed to hang on to the Fu. It was one of the worst days yet for the defenders of the legations.

During the evening of 24 June, the Boxers again attacked and set fire to the buildings in the Empress Dowager's Carriage Park. Had there been a wind blowing the fire in the direction of the British Legation, all might have been lost. The British Legation was the final bastion of defense. All the women and children were quartered there and the food supplies were stored there. Providence was in favor of the Legation Quarter that day. The fires were extinguished by the bucket brigade.

Captain Halliday, the Royal Marines' commanding officer, led the counterattack that broke up the attack. Although shot through the shoulder and lung while covering the withdrawal, he managed to drop three of the attacking Chinese with his revolver and then stagger to the hospital under his own power. The feat won him the Victorian Cross.

During the burning of the Hanlin Library, the defenders only had rifle fire to contend with but during this fire Chinese brought up a 3-inch field piece and opened fire on the Legation Quarter. Some 70 rounds fell on the Quarter.

Other than some people being scorched and burned by the fire, no casualties resulted from the sniper fire. The burning of the Carriage Park and the Hanlin Library benefited the defenders. Not only did the British Marines have a clear field of fire, but also there was less cover for snipers.

During this attack Captain Myers, who had gotten up barricades facing west toward Chien Men, led a party of 20 Marines along the wall against some 2,000 Chinese entrenched behind successive barricades, several with big guns.

During the attack a piece of shell struck the shoulder-piece of the Colt machine gun while another struck the wall near the gun to bring down bricks on the gun. For a while, J. Mitchell, the gunner, thought he might have to abandon the gun. Somehow, he managed to free the gun from the rubble and get it down the ramp to the safety of the barricade. Later he repaired the Colt and returned it to service.

Although Myers never gained any ground with this attack, neither did he lose any. During this assault, the Italian one-pounder supported Myers.

After weeks of hard work, however, the Marines on Tartar Wall were now entrenched in a place of great strength; walls of the barricades were 10 feet or more thick, trenches 150 yards long connected the east and west barricades. The bastion that overlooked the ramps were fortified to make passage up and down safe. Before the fortification was in place, Marines, creeping from point to point behind insufficient barricades, passed up and down the ramp under fire.

Many Chinese who attacked the barricades were killed. Mr. F.D. Cheshire, of the American Legation, was the Marines' interpreter. He also supervised the coolies who helped the Marines strengthen the barricades on Tartar Wall. For the sake of community health, he also spent much of his time supervising the gang in collecting and throwing dead bodies over the wall. "Since he came in touch with so many corpses, he told the Marines that he should be dubbed Major General of the Corpses. This was one of the gruesome tales to emerge from the siege."[13]

Throughout the siege the people were able to maintain their sense of humor, which helped them through some trying times. One diarist wrote, "Although the Legations have waited some two weeks for the appearance of the Seymour Column, the people have not entirely lost their sense of humor. Sir Robert Hart, Chief of Customs, suggested that when he (Seymour) got there they call him Admiral See-no-more, or if the Queen wished to promote him for his rapid advance on Peking, she could call him Lord Slow-come."

On 25 June, the Chinese attacked down the top of the Wall and along Wall Street at the base of the Wall, but were driven back with heavy casualties. Private Harry Gold was wounded during the morning attack. While on the ramp returning to his post at the barricade atop the wall, Private Martin M.L. Mueller was also wounded. A sniper's bullet first hit Mueller's rifle at the magazine and then glanced off and hit him in the leg above the knee. Shortly after midnight, while moving along the barricade, Sergeant John Fanning, an old time Marine, was struck in the head by a random bullet. He was killed instantly. A journalist later wrote, "A good sergeant or corporal is missed as much when wounded or killed as an officer; it is especially true for our own Marines, for in many instances they do the work of an officer, and take as much responsibility."[14]

Giving up their assault, the Chinese continued to rake the Marines' breastworks with rifle fire.

On 25 June, the supply of beef was exhausted. There remained, however, a small flock of sheep. The mutton was reserved for women, children and the sick. A quarter of a pound of mutton was issued to each woman every third day. For the remainder of the European community, two horses or mules were slaughtered daily and distributed to the various messes. With some 1,293 Europeans to feed daily, the ration of horse meat was small. Many of the Europeans felt that mule meat was better than horse. And, some Europeans came to prefer horse meat over tinned meat. Dr. Robert Coltman later wrote that horse meat was good eating, and he doubted not that he had some of that kind of beef before in substitution for the genuine article. "A number of people who were using it assured me it was very good. First we tried the liver, fried with a small scrap of bacon, and were please to find it tasted just like beef-liver. Then we tried some of the meat curried, and now we are having excellent sausages of the meat, which helps the rice to be more palatable. We are allowed one pound of horse meat per adult individual each day."

Mrs. Gamewell wrote that "horse meat cut into steaks, covered with hot water, simmered for three hours; then browned in fat with added spices was quite tasty."[15]

"Usually the meat was cooked in a big cauldron in one of the courts in which nearly half a carcass was boiled at once. The long-continued boiling that was necessary to cook so large pieces, seemed to take away the wild taste that the flesh other wise had, and when our mess had orders which gave us a part of such boiled meat, it found more flavor than other forms of cooked horse flesh."[16]

Peter Fleming later wrote, "Pony meat and rice were [the] staple diet, washed down by champagne of which there was a copious amount from Inbeck's and Kierulff's."[17]

The coolies who built the defenses and did other manual labor had a mess. They were issued a ration of horse meat and rice daily. The Chinese converts in the Fu subsisted on a diet of millet. As the siege dragged on, the Chinese converts' rations were reduced. In desperation, all the trees and shrubbery in the Fu were stripped of foliage, bark, leaves and small branches that were consumed as food.

Shortly after 20 June, the Marines were in a bad way about food. On arrival in Peking they contracted with a Chinese merchant to feed them at so much per man. When the Chinese cut off the merchant's source of supply, the Marines had no food stores to fall back on.

Fortunately, Mr. Squires was able to feed the Marines from his storeroom. Large caldrons of rice seasoned with corned beef were prepared in the Squires' compound for delivery to the Marines. It was difficult to get food to them because constant sniper fire made it dangerous to move about the Legation Quarter.

Mrs. Squires sustained the Marine guard with hot biscuits and coffee sent out at midnight and at various times throughout the day. She also worked as a nurse in the hospital.

M. Chamot undertook to feed a number of refugees that had fled to the Legation Quarter. His supplies were basic — horse meat, rice, some tinned vegetables and a kind of coarse brown bread baked at his hotel. He not only personally supervised the cooking for two messes in the British Legation, but also delivered food to the location. Twice a day he made the trip, once at twelve o'clock and again at six. Since anyone moving about the Quarter was fair game for Chinese snipers, Chamot risked his life during each of the trips. Mary Hooker commented, "Chamot's Hotel de Peking is known in the siege vernacular as the Swiss legation."[18]

On 26 June, an assaulting Chinese force hard pressed the Marines on the Wall. Not only were they attacking on the Wall, but were also firing on the Marines' position from the street below. The Marines turned the Colt machine gun on them and killed about 50; the rest fled. In need of reinforcements, Sir Claude MacDonald told the French commanding officer to send 10 men to reinforce the Marines. The officer refused point blank, so 10 Royal British Marines were sent instead. With reinforcements, the assault was fought off.

There always seemed to be elements of dissension among the commanding officers of the various nations. As the siege continued, the racial friendships and animosities became obvious, as Hooker noted. "The British and Americans are almost one people; although the expression 'Damn Yankee!' and 'Damn lime-juicer!' are interchangeable, they are used in a spirit of affection."[19]

Although the British disliked the Russians, the Marines and Russian sailors were the best of friends. Fortunately, their duties did not often bring the British and Russians into contact with one another.

The Russian guards were sailors from the battleships *Navarine* and *Veliku*. They mustered 72 men under naval Lieutenant Baron von Rahden and Sub-Lieutenant Carl von Dehn. Before the siege, seven trans–Baikalen Cossack guards were in Peking before the arrival of other allied legation guards.

Baron von Rahden ordered his men to work and fight side by side with the Marines. In doing so, he hoped to improve the efficiency of his untrained men. Coltman recounted, "Baron von Rahden, their commander, stated that on arrival in Peking his men were mostly green farmers, recently enlisted as sailors. Very few of them had any experience or even knew how to properly handle their rifles. After a few weeks association with the well trained American Marines under constant fire, they had developed wonderfully fast, and he felt, at the end of the siege, that he had a body of men who were well trained, steady, and cool."[20]

One journalist wrote that during the heavy attacks by Tung Fu Hsiang's soldiers at the west end of Legation Street, these Russian sailors behaved with great courage, and with their American Marine companions never failed to drive the Khansu ruffians back. Finally, the Chinese became discouraged at the lack of success in rushes, and settled down to a policy of sniping from behind their heavy barricades.

Dr. Coltman noted in his journal that when all troops left their posts and returned to the British Legation, owing to a mistaken order, four Russian sailors remained at the barricade commanding the Mongol Market. (The Mongol Market was a large open square bordered by houses, in which the Mongols pitched their tents when they came to Peking during the winter to sell their fur and frozen game.) This kept the Chinese from being aware of the general retreat. It then made it possible for the French, German, Austrians and American forces to return to their positions without a cost of life.

While the other allied forces were satisfied to have Chinese Christians build their barricades, trenches and other fortifications, the Russian sailors did more manual labor than any others of the besieged. The Russian sailors pitched in and built, as well as manned, all their own barricades.

Hooker observed, "The Germans are somewhat by themselves and fraternize with no one."[21] The dislike of the French for the Germans was quite obvious. The Japanese were pro–English and anti–Russian. As for the Italians, Hooker wrote, "One can only hope for Italy's sake that the soldiers in Peking are the worst she has."[22] Despite these likes, dislikes and animosities, the international force was valiant in its defense of the Legation Quarter during the siege.

On 27 June, the Chinese breached their barricade on Tartar Wall and a mass of soldiers scrambled through. Forming up, they charged down the Wall toward the Marines' barricade. Contrary to the usual charge, which was made with screaming and blaring bugles, this charge was made in an uncanny silence. Myers ordered his men to withhold fire until the Chinese were in close range. When the Chinese were within about 200 yards of the Marines' barricade, he ordered the Marines to fire. The deadly fire from the rifles and Colt machine gun drove the Chinese back with heavy losses. Throughout the night, during a severe thunderstorm that drenched the Marines to the bone, the Chinese continued to pour continuous fire into the Marines' barricade.

It was long believed by some that the Chinese would never fight in a storm. Some believed that the Chinese people's dread of getting wet could be compared to that of cats. A rainstorm was sufficient excuse for any Chinese to break any engagement. If rains fell, he did not think it necessary to make any excuse; he knew he would not be expected. This attack dispelled that belief. Many times during the siege, the Chinese attacked during thunderstorms.

Nigel Oliphant had this to say about the attack: "We heard last night a party of 30 Boxers, including a few soldiers, actually came over their barricade and tried to rush the Americans' position. This is the first time they have tried that game, and I expect it will be the last time as the Americans turned their Colt quick-fire on them and killed at least half, besides no doubt, wounding some, whom their friends dragged back to their barricade."[23] One journalist later wrote: "So long as the Americans can hold the Wall, I think our Legation will be in no danger."

During this attack the Boxers also launched an attack against the Germans' position to the east of the Marines' barricade. The Germans repulsed the attack.

After the assault on 27 June, the Chinese did not try another frontal attack. During the night, however, they settled down to pushing their barricade down the Wall stone by stone. The Marines also continued to strengthen their barricade.

During the afternoon of 28 June, the Chinese mounted a gun on their barricade in the Mongol Market. Firing four shells in succession brought down the upper story of a house in which the legation guards had a post. Several more shells exploded over the hospital, a pony was killed, but no was injured. Although the shelling was doing damage, abruptly it ceased. Later in the evening they again shelled the same area, doing little damage.

Because of the gun's location, it was decided to send a raiding party out to capture it. Accordingly, at about 0300 hours on the morning of 29 June, a party of Marines from all nations assembled at the Bell Tower. The raid was a failure. The raiding party became lost in a maze of blind alleys and burned out houses. The Chinese took advantage of this confusion and opened fire from the walls of surrounding compounds. The raiding party retreated without casualties. Strangely enough, for some reason, the Chinese removed the gun and afterwards made no attempt to renew the struggle at this point. Indirectly, however, the raid was successful, the gun was gone.

Later in the day on 28 June, the Chinese brought up a 3-inch Krupp and shelled the Fu. They also attacked the Marine barricade on the Wall

Section of burned houses outside the Legation Quarter, as viewed from the Marine position on the east ramp. (Marine Corps University Archives, Quantico, Virginia.)

and were repulsed with heavy losses. After the attack Private Upham wrote in his diary, "dead Chinks are getting very numerous up here."[24]

On the night of 30 June, while the Chinese were probing Myers' barricade, Private John W. Tutcher, while looking through a loophole in the barricade, was killed by a sniper's bullet through the eye. Tutcher was the second man killed at this loophole. On 30 June, a Russian was killed with a head shot. Private John H. Schroeder was also wounded in the elbow. Schroeder later died of his wound. Private Upham noted in his diary, "They [Chinese snipers] can put 5 shots out of 6 through a loophole 3 inches square and don't need a field glass to do it."[25]

The Chinese also launched an attack against the German Marines at the east end of the Wall defense perimeter. Shortly after dawn on 1 July, Lieutenant von Soden's Marines came under fire from three cannons in the Hata Men Tower. Shortly thereafter, the German detachment, commanded at the time by a corporal, retreated. While retreating, he signaled to the Marines that they were overrun. The Marines, seeing their rear threatened, withdrew to the lower barricade.

After anxious council of war with Ministers Conger and MacDonald,

Captain Myers with 14 Marines, reinforced with 10 Royal Marines and 10 Russian sailors, returned to the Wall. By 1100 hours, the barricade was retaken. The Germans, however, were unable to regain their former position on the Wall.

With no defense to the east, Myers was forced to build a barricade across the Wall to protect his rear. A working party of coolies and some 400 sandbags were sent to build the barricade as well as reinforce the existing barricade.

This maneuver cost Myers three casualties. While building the barricade, a chance shot came through a loophole and struck Private John Kennedy in the head. Private Thomas F. Hall, a shipmate, was hit in the knee. Private Joseph Silva was also wounded.

Captain Myers had been on the Wall continuously since 25 June. With little sleep, he was approaching exhaustion. He had taken full responsibility for directing the defense of the Wall, leaving Captain Hall responsible for the American compound below. On 1 July, Minister Conger ordered Myers to turn over his command of the Wall to Hall and go below for rest.

When Hall assumed command of the barricade on the Wall, he received an unusual order from Minister Conger. In writing, Conger threatened to prefer charges against Hall "if you leave until you are absolutely driven out."[26] This unusual order would become a part of the dossier used against Hall when charged with cowardice.

On 2 July, the Marines still required British Marine reinforcements to hold the Wall. Despite these reinforcements, the Chinese, under cover of heavy rifle fire, continued to push their barricade closer to the Marines' barricade. Stone by stone they raised barricades that protected them from the Marines' rifle fire. In defiance of heavy losses, the Chinese advanced their barricade until it was some 35 feet from the Marines' barricade with a flanking wall and a 15-foot tower across the bastion to the Marines' left. (See Map 8.) With the tower overlooking their barricade, their position became untenable. The Marines were forced to withdraw to the barricade at the foot of the ramp leading to the top of the Wall. Rain fell throughout the night of 2 July.

During this rain, the French Legation compound wall was breached by the Chinese. The French did not completely abandon their Legation. They fell back to a previously prepared secondary entrenchment in the western part of the legation compound. This new line of defense was very weak but was rapidly strengthened with sandbags and bricks by a working party of coolies. Even then, it was considered a very precarious defense. The French and Austrian Marines stubbornly resisted all attacks and held

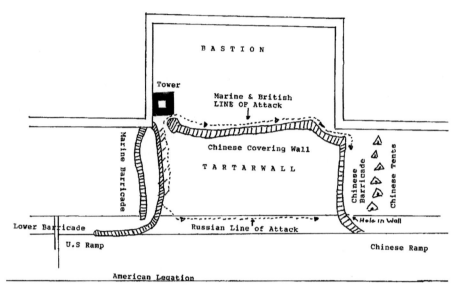

Map 8. Captain Myers' Line of Attack on 2 July 1900.

the lines. After viewing the lines, one Marine remarked, "Our place is bad enough, but this is worse."[27]

Since the Wall commanded the entire Legation Quarter, it was necessary to retake the Wall barricade immediately.

By now, Captain Myers had returned to command the Wall barricades. At 0130 hours on 3 July in a heavy rainstorm, Myers assembled an assault force of 30 Marines, 26 British Marines and 15 Russian sailors in the American Legation. Myers' instructions were simple. The Russian sailors under the command of Baron von Rahden would attack on the inside of the Wall, taking the Chinese left flank and gaining a position to command the inside ramp. The American and British Marines would charge the Chinese right flank, coming around behind the Chinese 15-foot tower and flanking wall. (See Map 8.) According to Coltman's account:

> Before starting, Captain Myers had briefly addressed his men, telling them the vital necessity of capturing the barricade. "Men," he said, "we must take that place at all costs or be driven off the wall! Once off the wall, the legations will lie at the mercy of the Chinese, and we, with all the women and children, will be butchered. This is our opportunity. I expect every man to do his duty. We cannot stop to pick up any who may be wounded, but must press on and accomplish the work, leaving the wounded until we return. If I fall, Sergeant

Murphy of the British Marines succeeds to command; if he falls, Corporal Hunt of the American Marines succeeds him. Now, when I give command, spring over the barricade, and follow me.[28]

Nigel Oliphant, one of the British volunteers who had once served with the British Grays, thought Myers' speech was a bit theatrical. Whether it was or not really did not matter. After the short speech, Myers gave the command "GO!" and led his men up the ramp and onto the Wall. The Chinese poured heavy rifle fire onto the Marines' barricade which delayed the storming party from climbing over the barricade. During a lull in the

Private Albert G. Turner stands guard at a post in the Methodist Mission. On the night of July 3, he died in Myers' attack on the Chinese barricade on Tartar Wall. He was one of the best shots of the Marine garrison. (Marine Corps University Archives, Quantico, Virginia.)

fire, Myers led his party around the end of the barricade and onto the bastion. Privates Robert E. Thomas and Albert Turner led the attack as the party moved out onto the bastion. During the attack, Myers ran into a spear implanted in the wall, which tore into his thigh. He fell, disabled. Mixed with the Royal Marines, Thomas and Turner along with Corporal Martin Hunt continued the attack. As the storming party approached the Chinese barricade, Turner was shot through the head. The storming party swarmed over the barricade, surprising the defenders, who only got off one quick volley. In the struggle that followed 15 Chinese were shot or bayoneted. Private Thomas was hit in the stomach and died soon thereafter. The attack caused the Chinese to flee down the Wall to another barricade. Corporal Gregory and one other British Marine were wounded in the fight.

On the Marines' right flank, von Rahden's Russian sailors were fiercely opposed and finally driven back to their barricade. Two Russian sailors were wounded in the struggle. Von Rahden was injured when a brick from the barricade fell and hit him on the head.

Within a half hour, the Boxers' barricade became the new front line for the Marines that they held until the siege was lifted. The charge cost the Chinese 65 known dead. Two Chinese regimental flags were taken as trophies.

Captain Myers later wrote that Privates Albert Turner and Robert E. Thomas, who were killed during the assault, were "two of the best men in the guard." Both men were interned in the Russian cemetery.

During the remainder of the siege, the Marines' barricade on the Wall came under heavy rifle and cannon fire, but it was never again seriously threatened. Thereafter, the Chinese main thrusts were on the Japanese sector at the Fu and the French breastworks in the southeast sector of the Legation Quarter. The retention of the captured barricade on the Wall made it possible for the Marines to ascend the ramp without being exposed to Chinese fire.

Many rifles and bandoleers of ammunition were collected after the assault. Because of the scarcity of ammunition, these were essential in the defense of the Legation Quarter.

Although the assault may seem small, it was considered one of the major assaults of the siege. One diarist later wrote, "It eventually proved to be one of the most important factors in the successful conduct of the siege and turned our precarious foothold on the Wall into a sound defense position."

When a monument to the British Marines was erected outside the Admiralty in London, one bas-relief depicted the American Marine Captain leading his men on the Peking Wall.[29]

Captain Myers' wound became badly infected and on 29 June, he came down with typhoid. For the remainder of the siege, Myers was on the sick list. This left the Marine legation guard under the command of Captain Hall.

Earlier, Surgeon Lippett, while seated in front of the Marines' quarters smoking a cigarette, was wounded when a bullet ricocheted off a nearby tree and struck him in the thigh, fracturing the bone. It was feared at the time that his leg would have to be amputated. Fortunately, Dr. Velde, a German surgeon, managed to save his leg. Dr. Lowery, a missionary doctor, replaced Lippett as the Marines' doctor.

Myers' victory was celebrated on July 4, the following day. Alban Millett commented, "Although the American civilians praised the Marines, many Europeans deemed the detachment too skittish, undisciplined, and given to drunkenness. It was said that only Captain Myers' presence kept them on the Wall. Nonetheless, most of the defenders admitted that the Marines were expert marksmen in the anti-sniper war around the legation."[30]

With their victory on the Wall, the Marines' questioned honor was restored and they were toasted throughout the Legation Quarter. This charge was one of the two major victories of the siege.

In celebration, Minister Conger brought out the framed copy of the Declaration of Independence that hung in his office — a bullet had pierced the lines that criticized George III — and read it to the Americans. It was a day of rejoicing. Meanwhile, "Mrs. Conger slipped quietly to the little plot where six Marines now lay buried. Gently she covered the graves with a silk American flag."[31] Another historian added, "On the Wall, a sniper spoiled Private Fred D. Moody's celebration by wounding him in the leg."[32]

To protect the children from flying bullets and exploding shells, they were not permitted to play outside in the compound. One of their favorite games was called "Boxers," in which they copied what the adults were doing outside. The younger children were always forced to be the attacking Chinese. Sometimes the older children got carried away in the defense of their positions and gave the younger children some real lumps on their heads. As Mary Hooker wrote, "The construction of barricades and their whoops of *Sha! Sha!* (kill! kill!) was creditable to the real thing and it is a good thing that they don't realize what this many mean, and we hope that relief will come before they lose their spirit and before they know."[33] Although several children died from disease, none were killed by enemy gunfire.

The American Legation compound was under continuous fire from both rifles and artillery. The American flag that flew at the entrance of the compound was a target for both snipers and shellfire. On 6 July, a shell struck the roof of the gateway building and the pole and flag fell through the roof together. A Marine snatched the flag up and hoisted it to the top of a nearby tree. The flag flew from this tree until the Legation Quarter was relieved.

On the same day the Japanese Marines, supported by Gunner's Mate Mitchell and the Colt machine gun, made a sortie to capture the cannon that was battering the Fu. Too many houses, however, concealed the whereabouts of the Krupp and after having three men wounded, they were obliged to return unsuccessfully. The cannon continued to be troublesome during the remainder of the siege.

Men with former military experience formed volunteer companies and armed themselves with anything they could find. One group of volunteers was composed of 32 Japanese ex-soldiers and sailors and 43 Europeans. Because they lashed knives to the barrels of their rifles, they were known as the "Carving Knife Brigade." This group served with the Japanese and French in the eastern line of defense. The second group of some 50 Europeans was known as the "Thornhills' Roughs." Made up mainly of British who had previously served in the British army, it did garrison duty in the British barricades.

There were times when hundreds of rifles were let loose at one time on the defense lines. Portions of solid brick walls were pulverized by continuous rifle fire against them. Most of the time, however, the firing was limited to snipers. The Mannlicher and Mauser rifles used by the Chinese troops fired ammunition filled with smokeless powder. The Chinese snipes concealed themselves in trees and other high places that overlooked the Legation Quarter. It was difficult to locate snipers because the smokeless powder did not betray their positions.

Mrs. Gamewell wrote in her diary of one sniper incident. "One day one of our American soldiers [Marines], who is a fine marksman, strolled by where I worked. They told me that he and two others were detailed to watch for a Chinese sharpshooter who had the range of a certain walk of the British Legation, which was frequented by women and children of the Legation. For many hours they kept the grim watch, and then the crack of a rifle was followed by the falling of a human body, and the laconic report was passed in: 'We got him.'"[34]

Mary Hooker also wrote of the Marines' marksmanship. "The Marines have the reputation of being crack shots. It was noticed that when the American Marines aim they bring down their game — whether the game is a Chinese soldier's head or a Boxer."[35]

The residences in the city of Peking were enclosed in a series of interlocking compounds opening onto the street. The compound walls were solid and anywhere from 10 to 15 feet high. Until the Chinese found positions that overlooked the Legation Quarter, these high walls provided some protection from sniper fire. Keeping under cover of the high walls, people could move about the Quarter unseen and with some degree of security. Once the Chinese snipers found positions that overlooked the Quarter, people moved about at their own risk.

After Myers' attack on the Wall, the defense settled into a snipers' war between the barricades. As the Chinese made more and better use of their artillery, the need for a counter-battery was acute.

The legation guards had three machine guns—the American Colt machine gun, an Austrian Maxim and the British five barrel Nordenfelt, 13 years old and incapable of firing more than four rounds without jamming. Except for the Colt machine gun, which had some 8,000 rounds, the ammunition for the other machine guns was limited. These guns were moved about the legation perimeter to beat off assaults that could not be stopped by rifle fire. While valuable, the machine guns could not serve as artillery.

By 1 July, the need for artillery was critical. Except for the Italian one-pounder with 120 shells, the legation guard had no artillery. By July only 14 shells remained for the little gun. When the shells were expended, Gunner's Mate Joseph Mitchell, USN, found that the empty shell cases of the Italian one-pounder could be reloaded. Not only were spent bullets that the Chinese had fired into the various legation compounds picked up, but pewter vessels from the Chinese houses around the Legation Quarter as well as candlesticks, vases, images and anything else that could be melted down were turned in to ammunition. A forge was set up, the objects melted down, and turned into grapeshot in improvised molds. Once, three quarts of spent bullets were picked up in the American Legation compound.

"We are manufacturing lead bullets for the use in the Italian one-pounder, as the proper shells for the latter [are] almost exhausted. We can still use the old shell cases, which are being diligently hunted for. The lead bullets we make measure about one inch at the base, and are about four inches long, being cone-shaped."[36]

When the shell cases were reloaded, and there being no primers for them, revolver cartridges were readily used instead. When the grapeshot was tried in the gun it worked very well, though it was feared that the harder metal of which they were made would be ruinous to the rifling of the gun.

Still feeling a need for heavier artillery, Mitchell set about fashioning a gun with the hopes of firing the Russian nine-pounder shells. During the afternoon of 7, July the Americans began making a gun out of some

Marines service "The Old International," Legation Quarter, Peking, China, 1900. (Marine Corps University Archives, Quantico, Virginia.)

brass tubing taken their fire engine. They wired the tubes to strengthen them.[37] While so engaged they were faced with the problem of a breech for their gun. Before this makeshift gun was completed, Chinese coolies found an old 1860 bronze British cannon in the back of a blacksmith shop. Mitchell felt that this muzzle-loading relic might be adapted to fire the ammunition made for the Russian nine-pounder that had been left behind at Tien-Tsin. With the help of a Welshman named Thomas, Mitchell built a new cannon from the old relic. The cannon was adapted to fire the nine-inch Russian ammunition. The cannon turned out to be a remarkable mongrel — a British barrel found by a Chinese coolie, mounted on a spare Italian gun carriage, firing Russian ammunition by an American-British gun crew. The cannon was christened "The Old International." The Marines called the cannon "Old Betsy" or sometime just "Old Crock." Others in the Quarter often referred to the cannon as "Boxer Bill" or "Dowager Express."

On 8 July, "Old Betsy" was fired for the first time. Because no one knew what would happen when "Old Betsy" was fired, it was placed in front of a barricade and a fuse laid. After Mitchell had hastily retreated behind the barricade, it was fired. The gun went off with a roar, recoiled several feet, but did not burst. The Legation Quarter now had artillery.

Some 60 rounds of ammunition for the Russian nine-pounder that had been left behind by oversight in Tien-Tsin had been dropped in a well during the panic of 2 July. It was fished up, and the shells, after having their damp charges renewed, were found more or less to fit the breech of "Old Betsy."

The first round that was fired went through three walls. Although the gun was not very accurate, the recoil was terrific, it always looked as if it might explode and it made a devastating roar, the defenders now had another way to fire back.

The cannon had no sights and was not accurate for long range work. However, on barricades and breastworks 30 yards or so away, it inflicted heavy damage. Mitchell also learned that grapeshot could be fired from "Old Betsy." Many times, after firing a concussion shell, he followed up with a charge of grapeshot in the form of old nails, or bits of scrap iron. One Englishman noted, "it has killed more men than all the rest put together."

In pretense of having more artillery than they had, the defending forces continuously shifted their two guns, the Italian one-pounder and "Old Betsy," around the Legation Quarter. Tartar Wall, the Fu, the Han-lin earthworks, the British stables, and the main gate at one time or another all used these guns in their defense.[38]

From prisoners taken, it was learned that the Chinese believed the legations had several thousand troops under arms. One reason the Chinese thought this was because of the number of Chinese that were killed. They attributed this to the legation guards. However, it reality, they were killed by their own bullets and shells which were aimed high, passed over the Legation Quarter and dropped among their own people.

Although the Chinese cannons boomed from morning until night, the shortness of the range prevented many of the shells from dropping into the Legation Quarter. When the muzzles of the cannons were elevated to pass over the buildings surrounding the Quarter, the projectiles flew harmlessly overhead and usually fell beyond, killing many Chinese.

With rifles, the untrained Chinese were remarkably bad marksmen. They usually fired by holding their rifles up so that the muzzles barely projected above the barricade, then pressed the trigger and quickly withdrew the rifle. They seldom exposed themselves firing their rifles. The firing usually did no damage. Thousands of rounds passed over the Legation Quarter and killed hundreds of Chinese a long way from the Quarter.

Because of the number of Chinese killed or wounded outside the Legation Quarter, it was the gossip of the teashops and restaurants around the city that several thousand troops defended the Legation Quarter.

Upham wrote that on 9 July, "The Chinks got past the Japs and started building a barricade across the street along the north wall of the Fu. The Japs got ladders and when the Chinks leaned their rifles against the wall to carry bricks, the Japs reached over and gathered in all the guns, as they were getting the last one the Chinks saw them and made a break but the Japs got five before they could get to cover."[39]

On July 12, the Chinese troops moved up so close to the Hanlin earthworks that they leaned their banner against the British Legation wall. At this time, Gunner's Mate Mitchell and "Old Betsy" were temporarily defending the earthworks. This impudence was too much for Mitchell. He leaned over the wall and grabbed the flag. A Chinese soldier grabbed the other end of the flag. All firing ceased while both sides watched the

Marines from the USS *Oregon* were a part of the legation guard at Peking. Private Upham, third from the right in the front rank, kept a detailed diary of the 55 day siege. (Marine Corps University Archives, Quantico, Virginia.)

tug-of-war for the flag. Finally, in desperation, Mitchell scooped up a hand full of dirt and flung it in the face of the Chinese soldier who then let go of the flag. Clutching the torn red and black banner, Mitchell dropped back to safety behind the legation wall. As the defenders cheered Mitchell's victory, the Chinese answered with a hail of rifle fire.

Inside the Legation Quarter conditions worsened. Sanitation was abominable. Chinese corpses and dead horses and dogs were scattered beyond the defense lines. Because of the constant sniper fire, these bodies could not be removed and buried. With temperatures reaching 110 degrees in the shade, the stench of decaying bodies was awful. To add to the stench of sewage and decaying bodies was the body odor of the defenders crowded together in the Legation Quarter. Many refugees possessed only they clothing they arrived in. The legation guards seldom took their clothes off. During the drought that preceded the rains, no one took a bath. The stench was appalling.

Although there were several wells in the Legation Quarter, there was concern lest the water supply fail. Therefore, at the beginning of the siege, water was rationed. Because of rationing, no bathing was permitted. The rains that started in July assured the water committee there would be an adequate supply of water. While the general order for rationing was not rescinded, it was less carefully observed. People who could find a bit of privacy indulged in the luxury of an occasional bath. With the accumulation of dirty clothes came the need of a means of washing them.

About this time a laundry was started which added to the general comfort of the community. Mr. Brazier, the Commissioner of Customs, managed the laundry. Securing the services of coolies from The Fu, he set the laundry up in a building in the British Compound. In the cool of the evening, Mr. Brazier sat at a table near the wash house receiving and checking in bundles of soiled laundry and dispensing stacks of clean laundry. Since the clothes could not be starched or ironed, they were wrinkled, but they were clean. Baths and clean clothing enhanced the morale of the community, especially during the hot, humid weather of July and August.

Since there was a plentiful supply of tobacco, "men who smoked have a cigar in their mouth from morning until night as a protection from the unseen horror, and even some women, principally Italian and Russian, found relief in the constant smoking of cigarettes."[40] Those that smoked did so to overcome the smell rather than for the sake of their nerves.

The rainy season began around July. The previous dry heat was nothing compared to the humidity that came with the rains. With the rains came mosquitoes and fleas. The flies were always with the besieged. Because of the bodies that were beyond the fortifications, little could be done to eradicate them. The torrential rains filled the canals and left puddles of water standing everywhere; all became havens for mosquitoes. These were beyond the control of the defenders.

As for fleas, they multiplied and thrived in the moist conditions that prevailed. At night, the defenders had not only to endure the bites of mosquitoes but also the fleas. The few mosquito nets that were available were reserved for the wounded and children. Throughout the summer these insects plagued the Legation Quarter defenders.

Throughout the siege the Chinese used mines against the walls of the Legation Quarter. They brought in coal miners from the Western Hills and set them to tunneling under the Legation defenses. To countermine, Dr. Gamewell successfully dug deep trenches along the defense lines where it was evident the Chinese were mining. In most cases, the mines were not effective. Around 1800 hours on July 13, however, the Chinese detonated their most effective mine beneath the French breastworks. The explosion destroyed the breastworks. The first explosion buried four men. The second blast killed another man. The French Marines dug into the ruins and managed to hold the position. The French now held about one-third of the original French Legation. The attack and explosion cost the lives of three French Marines and another three were wounded.

The Chinese fire on the Wall was continuous. Captain Hall, who now commanded them, ordered the Marines to refrain from firing unless they had a sure shot. "The Marines proved to be deadly snipers. Every shot fired," wrote Pvt. Oscar I. Upham, "there is a Chinese funeral on hand."[41]

On 12 July, Captain Hall was ordered to advance the Marine barricade atop Tartar Wall 100 yards to cover the east side of the Legation Quarter and the Water Gate. With the help of Chinese converts, the stone barricade was moved forward 50 yards during the night of the 12th.

In an attempt to bypass the barricade, the Chinese came down off the wall from Hata Men and charged up Wall Street, which paralleled the Tartar Wall inside the Legation Quarter. After the Chinese passed the German Legation, the Marines on the Wall opened fire. The Chinese became confused as soldiers fell from the overhead fire. "They didn't seem to know where to go," wrote Pvt. Upham. "We had a regular picnic with them."[42] When the remaining Chinese attempted to charge up the wall ramp, German Marines broke the charge with rifle fire and the survivors retreated.

During the night of the 14th, working parties of coolies advanced the barricade to the first bastion overlooking Water Gate. One of the reasons for advancing the east barricade to Water Gate was to provide a place of entry for the relief column. Chinese rifle fire was intense but no Marines were wounded. The barricade was now only 250 yards from the Chinese barricade.

For several days, a den of some 60 snipers in a house west of the Russian Legation harassed the defenders along the western perimeter. Finally, Captain Hall gave the order to clean out the snipers. At about 1500 hours on 15 July, a sortie of four Marines and 20 Russian sailors made an attack on the compound where the snipers were holed up. When they arrived at the wall of the compound surrounding the house, they found there was no way to get into the compound. So each man picked up several bricks from the rubble that littered the street, and at a given signal, with shouts and abusive language, started heaving the bricks over the wall into the compound. This continued until the alarmed Chinese fled. The men took the compound without a shot being fired.[43]

At this time, Chinese troops at other locations commenced a brisk fire that lasted some ten minutes or so. There were no casualties to the detail.

On 15 July, Capt. Hall, accompanied by Pvt. Dan Daly, moved forward across another 200 yards of open ground and entered the next bastion to locate the Chinese skirmish line and to build a new barricade. Before coming atop the wall, Captain Hall had left orders that if he and Daly were not fired upon within 10 minutes, Privates William L. Carr and Upham would bring up a working party of coolies. Each of the coolies was to bring sandbags so that the new barricade across the Wall could be completed by morning.

When the working party did not arrive in the specified time, Hall reluctantly left Pvt. Daly to hold the position while he returned to the Marine barricade in search of the working party. Here, under heavy fire, Private Dan Daly alone with his bayoneted rifle held the position until Hall and the working party returned. After the siege, Daly was awarded the Medal of Honor — the first of two he would be awarded during his career as a Marine.

At the barricade, Hall found Carr and Upham had not been able to bring up the working party because they had no one to interpret for them. Due to constant sniper fire, Chinese coolies disliked working on the Wall. Hall ordered Carr and Upham to join Daly on the Wall. Finally, he located a member of the Belgian Legation to serve as an interpreter who persuaded the coolies to accompany Hall. After much delay, 25 coolies with sandbags moved up the wall and out across the no-man's land to the Marine privates' position. The construction of the barricade progressed with little difficulty. While the coolies worked on the barricade, the German commander asked Hall to fire several volleys down the wall to prevent the Chinese from mounting a cannon that would command the Germans' position. When Hall complied with the request, the return fire was so great that he had to stop construction on the barricade until it died down. By morning, the barricade was firmly in place. When dawn broke, the Chinese snipers opened fire on the new barricade. Once the barricade was complete, Privates Butts, Davis and Fischer relieved Daly. Later, Fischer was standing watch at the barricade when a bullet shattered a brick near his head. "That was damn close," he remarked, and moved toward cover when another bullet hit him in the chest. He was dead within 10 minutes.

On 14 July, the ministers received a letter signed "Prince Ching and Others." In essence, the letter pointed out the futility of their situation and requested that the ministers and their families move to the Yamen where they would be protected until they could be sent home. One condition made it impossible for the ministers to even consider the request. In concluding the letter, Prince Ching wrote, "But at the time of leaving the Legation there must on no account whatever be taken any single armed foreign soldier, in order to prevent doubt and fear on the part of the troops and people, leading to untoward incidents."[44] (See Appendix D for complete text of letter.)

No one in the Legation Quarter intended to leave the fortified legations. The ministers, however, felt that the Chinese government might want to negotiate some kind of peace. In a letter of reply, the ministers suggested that if the Chinese were in earnest, a cease-fire would be the best way to show it.

"Now that that there is mutual agreement that there is to be no more fighting," replied Prince Ching and Others, "there may be peace and quiet."[45] With that, an uneasy truce began on July 17.

Over the next several days, letters continued to be exchanged. On July 16, a message was brought in cipher to Mr. Conger from the State Department, Washington. It simply stated, "Give tidings to bearer."[46] To say the least, it was unclear to the ministers as to the intent of the message. An enclosed letter told the American Minister he could answer the telegram. Knowing the reply would be an open telegram and subject to change, Mr. Conger declined.

The next day Mr. Conger received another telegram from Chinese Minister Wu in Washington. This telegram read, "China sent greetings and aid by the United States, and desires to know the health of Mr. Conger."[47] This time Mr. Conger was permitted to reply in cipher. Wanting to send a clear and strong message, Conger cabled: "We are holding our last positions under shot and shell in the British Legation, and will be massacred shortly if help does not come."[48]

Taking advantage of this, the other ministers all sent cipher messages to their governments, hoping they also might be sent. The next day, however, these cipher messages were returned with no apology.

During this uneasy truce letters continued to be exchanged. The Yamen stated the ministers could send open telegrams to their governments that all was well. The ministers declined, saying they would never send a telegram unless in cipher.

Keeping the lines of communications open and negotiating bought the ministers time. One day more brought the relief columns one day nearer.

On 18 July, during the truce, Chinese continued to build their barricade on Legation Street. Upham wrote: "We brought the 'Old International' from the British Legation and set it up and trained it on them, we stuck up a large sign with Chinese characters on it telling them to knock it off, which they refused to do, so we turned her loose and knocked their barricade down, they took the hint."[49]

During the truce Upham wrote in his diary, "A Chinese colonel on the wall was holding a conversation with one of our officers, he eagerly asked who those men were who wore the big hats, and being told that they were American Marines he shook his head and said, 'I don't understand at all, they don't shoot very often, but when they do I lose a man, my men are afraid of them.'"

On 20 July, in reply to a request for ice, eggs and fresh fruit for the women and children, three carts loaded with melons, six bags of flour, eggplants and other Chinese vegetables arrived. These were sent "to the ministers by the Yamen as a sign of good feelings."[50]

Later, "Several cart loads of melons arrived from Prince Ching and Others. Another shipment came with the Empress Dowager's compliments.... Chinese soldiers conducted a lively black market first in eggs, then in ammunition."[51]

During periods of ceasefire Chinese soldiers often exposed themselves without fear. Standing on top of their barricades, they called out to the legation guards professing friendship. On these occasions they often sold eggs to the besieged guards. On one occasion Japanese Marines bought rifles and ammunition from Chinese soldiers for fifteen dollars apiece. Only in China is this not only credible but also probable. In the afternoon of 27 July, "The Yamen sent 15 carts full of melons, brinjals and ice, and 1000 catties (about 1500 pounds) of fine flour."[52]

From time to time the ministers sent out numerous couriers in hopes that some would get through and inform the world of their plight. Most of the paid couriers lowered over Tartar Wall just disappeared. It was not until 18 July that they received the first word from the outside. A messenger sent out by the Japanese minister at the end of June returned to report that a mixed relief force of some 13,000 troops would leave Tien-Tsin on

20 July. The days dragged by; no relief force was sighted. Then on 28 July, another messenger arrived. This messenger was a Chinese student the American missionaries had lowered from the Tartar Wall on 4 July. Disguised as a beggar, he had made his way to Tien-Tsin. Now he was back with a letter for Sir Claude from the British consul, and it could not have been more discouraging. As of 22 July, the relief force had not even been organized. "There are plenty of troops on the way," the message vaguely concluded, "if you can keep yourselves in food."[53]

On 1 August, Japanese Colonel Shiba received a message from Tien-Tsin which stated: "Your letter of 22d received. Departure of troops from Tien-Tsin delayed by difficulties of transportation, but advance will be made in two or three days. Will write again as soon as estimated date of arrival in Peking is fixed."[54]

About the same time, Minister MacDonald received a somewhat mangled but authentic telegram from London. Among other things, the telegram stated that the Chinese troops, after severe fighting, had been routed from Tien-Tsin on 15 July and arrangements for the relief of the Legation were being hastened.

The message and the telegram proved that reports brought in earlier by some of the paid messengers were unreliable. As so often happened in the past, the paid couriers often gave the ministers the information they wanted to hear and were not completely trustworthy.

"It was a great disappointment, after being told that the relief columns were within two days, to hear that they have not yet started and have not fixed a date for starting,"[55] wrote Coltman.

After 1 August, many authentic letters managed to reach the Legations. Each letter brought encouraging news. Extracts from various letters from Tien-Tsin read:

> Mr. E.K. Lowery to Ms. Lowery, July 30, Bearer arrived last Friday evening, with news from Peking.... The 9th and 14th Regiments, United States, already in Tien-Tsin, 6th Cavalry at Taku on its way up.[56]
> Consul Ragsdale to Mr. Conger, July 28 ... Advance of troops tomorrow probable.[57]

From J.S. Mallory, Lieutenant Colonel, 41st Infantry:

> A relief column of 10,000 is on the point of starting for Peking; more to follow. God grant they may be in time.[58]

One of the most informative was a letter from Colonel Warren to Captain Myers:

Have been trying to reach you ever since June 21. Relieved the foreign settlement (Tien-Tsin) June 21. Seymour, June 24. Captured east arsenal June 26, captured west arsenal July 10; captured Tien-Tsin city July 14. Will advance in two days. Column 10,000 strong — English, American and Japanese; 40,000 more following in a few days. Hold on by all means. First column will support you and divert enemy from you. There will be eight regiments of United States Infantry; three cavalry and two batteries of artillery; also 500 Marines. Infantry will be in the first column. Enemy strongly entrenched seventeen miles north of here (Yangtsun), and at two points farther on.[59]

Of all the letters and messages received by the various legation officials, from a military standpoint, this was the most comprehensive summary of all the military action in the Taku and Tien-Tsin theater.

Food had now become a problem — it was running out. There was no fresh meat; the last of the ponies had been slaughtered. The Food Committee took stock of the food supply on 1 August. They figured that there was enough food to give each person one pound of wheat and one-third pound of rice a day for nine days.

On 7 August, the besieged legations all went on half rations. The rations of the Chinese refugees in the Fu, whose food had primarily been millet, were also reduced, now resorted to stripped leaves and bark from trees and eating dogs and cats. Many of their children died from malnutrition.

On 2 August, volunteers from the Custom Service took up a new position on the Mongol Market southeast of the British Legation. By 9 August, sniper fire became troublesome in this sector. Finally, it became necessary to move the Nordenfelt machine gun to this sector. On a parapet built against the west wall of the British Legation, the gun soon silenced the snipers.

The uneasy truce was often broken by sniper fire. Finally, it collapsed altogether on 9 August. A new Shansi regiment took over the attack on the Legation Quarter. They had the latest repeating rifles and swore to finish the foreigners off, "leaving neither fowl or dog."[60] They swept through the Mongol Market on the west, where they were met with a devastating fire from the legation guards. At last, they fell back among the ruins of the Mongol Market.

On 10 August, another messenger arrived with word that the relief force was at last underway. It had left Tien-Tsin on 4 August, and would approach Peking from the east. Most important were the words, "Probable date of arrival at Peking August 13 or 14."[61] In the message, General Gaselee, commander of the relieving force, wrote, "Keep up your spirits."[62]

As the relief force approached, the Chinese in Peking tried to over-whelm the legation defenders. Fighting on 11 and 12 August was constant and general attacks fierce. The Chinese continued to build higher and stronger barricades, which were matched by the defenders. These attacks were accompanied by constant blowing of trumpets and the shrill cries of "Sha!" "Sha!" Sha!" (Kill! Kill! Kill!). The legation guards for the first time during the siege could not conserve ammunition. They answered back vol-ley for volley.

On the evening of Monday, 13 August, the Chinese attacked the Mon-gol Market position in force. The Shansi regiments again stormed the west wall of the British Legation while the Japanese and the Italians in the Fu reeled under a furious attack but managed to hold their positions. The defenders brought to bear all the artillery they had to hold their positions. "Old Betsy" along with Gunner's Mate Mitchell was brought to the British lines to defend the Mongol Market lines. On the same day, the Yamen sent

British Marine manning "The Old International" at a barricade in the Mongol Market sector. (Marine Corps University Archives, Quantico, Virginia.)

word that if the Legation defenders ceased fire, the Chinese would also hold their fire. Although this was agreed to, heavy fire from the Chinese continued.

In the evening the observers in the British Legation noticed activity in an emplacement high up in a wall of the Imperial City that overlooked the Legation Quarter. It was not long until it was learned the Chinese had brought up and mounted a new 2-inch quick firing Krupp gun. While in operation, the Krupp did more damage to the Legation Quarter than the smoothbores had in five weeks of bombardment.

As a countermeasure, the Colt machine gun and the Austrian Maxin were brought up at dusk and trained on the embrasure at 200 and 300 yards. Firing through the darkness over fixed sights, the machine guns soon put the Krupp out of action. Because of the heavy fusillade, the machine guns were kept busy throughout the night beating off assaults and preventing the Chinese from overrunning various breastworks.

Fours hours later the Chinese made the most terrific attack of the siege. Violent attacks at two-hour intervals continued throughout the night. Amidst the din, the defenders could hear Chinese officers urging on their men, "Don't be afraid, don't be afraid — we can get through!"[63]

Gunner's Mate Mitchell was a badly wounded while sitting behind "Old Betsy." A bullet passed through a rifle porthole and shattered his arm. It was thought for a time the arm would have to be amputated but with the later arrival of the relief column with medical supplies, his arm was saved. When the gun fire of the relief column was later heard outside the city, he remarked: "Oh, you can keep up your devilish racket now, but in a little while longer you will be silent enough!"[64]

The legation guards held their sectors. The Chinese charge broke and the regiments withdrew.

About 0215 hours on the morning of August 15, all firing stopped. It was relatively quiet. Then, in the distance, the rumble of artillery fire could be heard from the east. A little later and much closer, machine gun fire was also heard. The long awaited relief force had arrived.

During the morning hours of the 15th, Captain Hall watched shells fall on Tung Pien Men, where the Russians and Americans were trying to smash their way through. To the north shells battered the Chih Hua Men, as the Japanese fought to gain entrance to Tartar City. The British found light resistance when they took Hsia Kuo Men. Once inside the Chinese City they knew just where to go, for the Legation sector of Tartar Wall was marked with flags. Further, an earlier message from Sir Claude told the British commander, General Gaselee, that easy access to the Legation Quarter could be made through Water Gate in the Marine sector. The British

Indian troops advanced quickly without opposition and were signaled by semaphore to enter the Water Gate, a giant seven-foot sewer tunnel. Inside the Legation Quarter, Myers' Marines cleared the obstruction for them.

General Gaselle and the Seventh Rajputs emerged from the Water Gate on to Canal Street at about 1430 hours and were greeted with bottles of champagne. Just as the relief force was pouring into the British Legation, the first woman to be wounded during the siege, Mme. Cuillier, a French woman, was struck by a Mauser rifle bullet in the thigh and seriously, but not dangerously, wounded.[65]

The arrival of the Americans was somewhat later. They had spent the morning pinned down at Tung Pien Men. Finally, after scaling the wall adjacent to the gate, the American forces fought their way along a moat beside Tartar Wall. When they reached Chien Men their advance was halted for the night. General Adna R. Chaffee, commanding the American force, arrived at about 1630 hours. An account by Walter Lord described the arrival:

> From the top of the Tartar Wall an American Marine called down
> to the general: "You're just in time. We need you in our business."
> Letting this one pass, Chaffee asked, "Where can we get in?"

A view of the 60-foot Tartar Wall that greeted the Allied Relief Column when they reached Peking. (Marine Corps University Archives, Quantico, Virginia.)

"Through the canal," the Marine shouted back. "The British did it two hours ago."[66]

Later, American Marines and Russian sailors on the Wall joined a sortie of Waller's Marines that charged the Chinese on Tartar Wall, routing them and securing Chien Men. Later, they helped the incoming troops mount their guns in the Chien Men tower. On the 15th, the Marine legation guards joined Waller's Marines in Chien Men tower and along Tartar Wall to support the Ninth Infantry in their attack on the Imperial City.

The siege was lifted. "For 55 days some 480 men had held off some 20,000. The casualty figures alone showed their peril and bravery: 234 men — 49 percent of the defense force — were kill or wounded."[67]

Of the small Marine detachment in Peking, seven Marines had been killed (six of them on the Wall) and ten wounded. The seven were buried near the chapel of the Russian Legation; later, their bodies were sent home. The next day allied forces began mopping up. They relieved the isolated Peitang Cathedral, where Bishop Favier had successfully held out. S.M. Russell reported:

> As the Americans held the city wall (Tartar) adjoining their legation, very little damage was done to it. Their position on the Wall was most perilous; only a few yards off was a Chinese barricade, where a cannon had been mounted. At these close quarters they were shot at and shelled day and night.
>
> The occupation of that part of the city wall [was] essential to us, as, if the Chinese had possession of it, they could have fired straight down and shelled the Legation, making our position untenable.
>
> It was not an enviable position to be sent to; in fact it was designated by the name "hell."[68]

The day after the lifting of the siege, a journalist wrote, "Next morning we discovered two mines already laid, with powder and fuses all complete. If the troops had come one day or one night later, God only knows what the results would have been."[69]

Another of these mines was beneath the French breastworks. The longest, however, was a mine that extended about 200 feet under the British Minister's quarters. It curved to miss the British countermine. It was high and wide enough for a man to walk through without stooping. If this mine had been detonated, it would have killed or injured hundreds of the women and children quartered in the British Legation.

Sir Claude MacDonald, the British Minister, and M. Giers, Russian Minister, had high compliments for the American Marines during the siege: "Our Marines led in their intelligent work as soldiers. The accuracy of their shooting is extra-ordinary, and their ability to step forward, one after the other, on the death or retirement of [an] officer or non-commissioned officer and take his place is remarkable. They show the greatest aptitude to command, and are in no way disconcerted by the sudden increase in responsibility. In many instances which could be cited this was proved."[70]

No account of the defense of the besieged Peking Legations would be complete without comments on the charge of cowardice that was leveled against Captain Newt Hall for abandoning the defenses of the barricade on the Wall on 2 July. Was Captain Hall guilty of cowardice at Peking, or as some put it, "over-cautious?"

Many civilians in Peking who liked Captain Myers and believed he was an excellent officer, and disliked the taciturn Hall, pointed out after the siege that Hall served below while Myers commanded the defense of the Wall. It was on Hall's watch that the Chinese advanced their barricade across the open front of no-man's land between the two forces and erected a 15-foot tower, all in one day.

Typical of the talk by the civilians within the Legation Quarter was an entry in the diary of Dr. C.E. Morrison, the *London Times* correspondent, who took a leading part in the defense. "10 July — Today on the Wall there were 13 men under Captain Hall. He is never put on the Wall, his men having no confidence in his judgment. He has no control over his men...."[71]

Further charges circulated among the civilians in the Legation Quarter that Hall had hesitated to lead his men over the barricade on the final day when relief was in sight. There was also Minister Conger's written orders admonishing Hall against leaving the Wall until "absolutely driven out."

Soon after the relief force reached Peking, all this ugly talk soon came to the attention of General Chaffee, commanding the United States forces in North China. Chaffee immediately ordered his inspector-general, Captain William Crozier, who had distinguished himself during the relief column's march to Peking, to investigate the charges against Hall.

After 12 days of investigation, Crozier accumulated a dossier of nasty statements, most of which were made by civilians. Captain Myers, who was Hall's immediate superior and still ill at the time, did not testify. Later, however, in his report he made little mention of Captain Hall. Captain Crozier recommended against further action. General Chaffee approved Crozier's report and forwarded it to Major General Charles Heywood, Commandant of the Marine Corps. According to Col. Robert Heinl, General Heywood, uncle by marriage to Hall, commented that "Hall should have been court-martialed on the spot if only for his own protection."[72]

To further complicate the case, Captain Bowman H. McCalla, who commanded the Marine and naval forces on the Seymour Expedition and who commanded the USS *Newark,* recommended Hall for brevet and to be advanced 10 numbers in grade for his conduct at Peking. At about the same time, W.N. Pethick, an American civilian who had been in Peking during the siege, published an article in the widely read *Century Magazine* criticizing Hall's conduct during the siege.

Hall, meanwhile, seeking redress, asked General Chaffee for a court-martial. When Chaffee refused, Hall requested Admiral Remey, Commander in Chief, Asiatic Station, to convene a court of inquiry on his conduct. Remey approved the request. On 1 March 1901, a court of inquiry was convened at Cavite in the Philippines. After an investigation, which disclosed "great caution" on Hall's part, the court cleared the unhappy captain but in terms of which no officer could be proud — "for the reasons that he has already suffered sufficiently for the world-wide publications and criticism of his conduct in Peking."[73]

To add to the enigma, the Secretary of the Navy approved brevets to major for both Myers and Hall. Myers, however, was advanced four numbers in grade for "eminent and conspicuous conduct." Hall was not given such distinction. Finally, on 28 August 1901, Minister Conger, in a public letter, denied that he had ever preferred charges against Hall (which was true). Conger said he had personally defended Hall's conduct to Chaffee and Crozier, and referred with emotion to a "great injustice."[74]

Heinl concluded, "Hall, officially cleared and stoutly defended by many friends in the Marine Corps, got his brevet, stayed on, and ultimately retired a colonel."

9

The Relief of Peking

As predicted by Major Waller after the fall of Tien-Tsin, the International Relief Force was plagued with imperialistic rivalries that delayed their setting out for the besieged Peking. They wrangled about rank, the order of march and the need for more troops. Some felt that to succeed, the allied force would need at least 60,000 troops.

While they fiddled with plans to continue the march, more troops poured into the Tien-Tsin area: "French Zouaves in red and blue, blond Germans in pointed helmets; Italian Bersaglieri with tossing plumes, Bengal cavalry on stallions, turbaned Sikhs, Japanese, Russians.... Royal Welsh Fusiliers with three folds of ribbon down their backs."[1]

After some five weeks on the way from the United States, Major General Adna R. Chaffee, U.S. Army, a veteran of Indian fighting on the western frontier, arrived in Tien-Tsin on 30 July. Accompanying Chaffee were substantial reinforcements: two battalions of the Fourteenth Infantry; the Sixth Cavalry; and Reilly's Battery, Fifth Artillery. General Chaffee assumed command of all United States forces in North China. The army forces in North China now totaled some 2,000 men and officers.

By order of President Theodore Roosevelt, all Marines in North China were placed under the command of General Chaffee.

On August 3, Major William P. Biddle arrived from San Francisco with a battalion of Marines.[2] Joining Wallers' battalion, Biddle formed the First Marine Regiment, and, being senior, assumed command of the regiment. The First Marine Regiment now had some 35 officers and 630 enlisted men. Major Waller, second in command, also commanded the First Battalion of Marines; Captain Frank J. Moses, the Second Battalion, and Captain Ben H. Fuller, "F" Company of Artillery. Captain Dave Porter was Major Biddle's adjutant. Each company was composed of 75 to 80 men. Second Lieutenant Wise, in Captain Dunlap's company, was advanced to the grade of First Lieutenant.

First Lieutenant Butler reported that, while confined to a hospital recovering from a wound in his thigh, he "was examined for promotion to the grade of Captain. The medical board hemmed and hawed and decided I was unfit to perform the duties of captain, because of weakness through the loss of blood. Colonel Meade and Major Waller both pronounced the decision absurd. Upon their recommendations, Admiral Remey, the Commander in Chief of our naval forces in the Orient, overrode the doctors and gave me my promotion."[3]

Thus, Butler, brevetted a first lieutenant for gallantry in action during Waller's advance on Tien-Tsin was promoted to the rank of captain before his nineteenth birthday. Once promoted to Captain, Butler argued his way out of the hospital and rejoined his company as they prepared to move out.

The next ten days were spent in preparing for the march on Peking. While en route the Marines were allowed their blankets, haversacks, canteens, rifles and ammunition belts. The field galleys, rations, extra ammunition and water were all piled into springless, two-wheeled Chinese carts with a lattice house built over the body. Mules, driven by Marines, were used to pull the carts.

To protect Tien-Tsin, still far from peaceful, the International Force left some 2,000 troops there. Chaffee left six Marine officers, two navy surgeons, and 177 enlisted Marines for this duty. "The regimental surgeon, a veteran of the fighting in Samoa in 1899, had the suggestive name of Lung."[4]

With the detachment of these Marines, the First Marine Regiment's total strength consisted of about 482 men. Within the ranks of the First Marine Regiments were three future Commandants of the Marine Corps: Major William P. Biddle, Captain Wendell C. Neville, and Captain Ben H. Fuller.

The overall strength of the American force was approximately 2,500 men and officers. Because the Sixth Cavalry horses were unfit after the long sea voyage, Chaffee was forced to leave the regiment behind.

As is normal in any Marine outfit, scuttlebutt began to circulate about the indecision of the International Army moving out: Some allied commanders wanted to wait for more troops.[5] The rain season was soon to commence. Some commanders wanted to wait until the rains ended, as the country across which the allied forces must march to reach Peking would be one huge bog. Others wanted to start before the rains began.

Scuttlebutt also told the American troops about their new commander, General Chaffee. According to one account, "He was getting fed up with the delay in starting for the relief of Pekin [*sic*]. He had announced to the allied chiefs that if they didn't decide to move on Pekin [*sic*] at once, he would take all the American troops and go alone. Washington had ordered him to relieve the legation at Pekin [*sic*]. He was going to carry out his orders without delay."[6]

This scuttlebutt sounded very much like Captain McCalla's declaration at the outset of the Seymour Expedition.

Although General Lineivitch, commanding the Russian army, was the senior officer present, he was not in overall command of the International Army. Each of the contingents, more or less, operated independently. The commanders met in council daily and agreed upon vaguely made plans. Once agreed upon, each commander carried out his part with very little overall coordination with the other units.

Since the Tien-Tsin–Peking railroad was almost destroyed, the allied commanders elected to advance along the Pei-Ho River. (See Map 9.) This route was the same as the one used by the British-French expedition in 1860.

Second Lieutenant Wirt McCreary, USMC, was put in command of a fleet of 30 junks that would carry the supplies for the American column up the Pei-Ho River. Theoretically, the troops would keep in daily contact with the fleet all the way. The junks, about 60 feet long, each had a stumpy mast and lateen sails of woven reeds. Coolies walking on the riverbank towed the junks by ropes harnessed across their chests. Lowell Thomas tells this story:

> When two military junks met, the senior officer had the right of way and the junior was obliged to tie up. McCreary, being a second lieutenant, had to tie up so frequently that he was perpetually behind in his schedule. But he was a man of resourcefulness. The rank of passengers on the junks was indicated by the number of stars on the flags flying from the bamboo masts. McCreary made himself a flag out of an old blue flannel shirt. He pinned four white stars on his flag to indicate he was an admiral. Then he put on a pair of green glasses so he would not be recognized and sat like a potentate in an armed chair in the stern of his junk. He had the right of way for a month. His deception was not discovered until he collided with a junk carrying a genuine Japanese Admiral.[7]

The original date of departure was set for August 14. The Americans, British and Japanese were ready to march by August 4. The Russians could not make up their minds whether to go or not. Finally, the Russians were

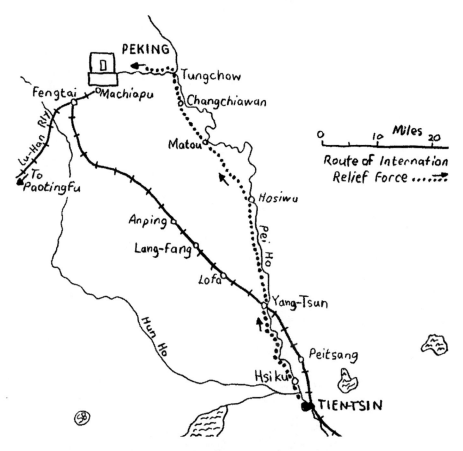

Map 9. Route of International Relief Force.

given an ultimatum "of going with us or alone at their own pleasure."[8] After a prolonged discussion, the Russians joined the force on the condition "that the British do not lead the column and carry off all the honors."[9]

Apparently, it was very important to the Russians that they get to Peking first. This may account for the fact that the Russians launched their early attack on Peking without notifying the other allied commanders.

On the night of August 3, orders were received that the march to Peking would begin on the following day. Early on the morning of August 4, the International Army prepared to move out. One thing after another delayed the march. Lt. Frederick Wise reported, "The Japanese must go first because they had the biggest army. The Russians next; they've got the next to the biggest. Then the British must get well under way before our

[American] turn came."[10] Then there were the French, who could not make up their minds whether to join the march. Finally, they mustered a small force and took their place in line ahead of the British. The Germans, Italians and Austrians also had small units that had to be fitted into the order of march.

Late in the afternoon under a scorching sun, the column started for Peking with a force of some 18,600 men and officers.

The allied forces crossed the Pei-Ho River on a military bridge built of boats and planks. Once across, it followed a high railway embankment along the river. Throughout the remainder of the afternoon, the firing was heavy as the allied forces advanced, pushing the Chinese back.

Late in the afternoon, just eight miles from Tien-Tsin, the Marines reached the Hsiku Arsenal. Here, the Marine regiment broke ranks and bivouacked for the night. Wells in the courtyard supplied the Marines with ample potable water. At about 0700 the next morning they were on the march again.

The Marines marching in the rear of the advancing column, missing most of the action and excitement, trudged along hour after hour in the

Marines en route to Peking with the Allied Relief Column. (Marine Corps University Archives, Quantico, Virginia.)

heat and dust. It was not long until their clothing was soaked with sweat and caked with dust stirred up by the advancing column. Ahead, throughout the day, heavy bursts of firing rose and subsided as the Japanese and Russians advanced against the determined Chinese. As the regiment passed through deserted villages, they encountered allied soldiers looking after aid stations. It was evident that the allied forces were taking casualties.

In the blistering heat, the water supply was soon exhausted. The rank and file had been ordered not to drink any water from wells in villages unless it was boiled. However, on the march it was impossible to stop and boil water. Therefore, out of necessity, they selected the best looking wells they could find, drew the water, and drank it to quench their thirst. Later, as was expected, dysentery made its presence known.

The column halted for ten minutes on every hour for health and comfort reasons. At 1200 hours a scanty meal of bacon or canned salmon and hardtack was eaten. This was the usual order of the march throughout the advance on Peking. They cursed and swore vengeance on the Chinese, General Chaffee, and on down the line to include the mess sergeants when the chow was bad, and it usually was.

The weather was hot and dry, and most of the allied troops were unused to field conditions. The column suffered from heat and the lack of water. Heat exhaustion caused more casualties than acts by the Chinese. Marching at the tail end of the allied column with not a chance of action eroded the morale of the regiment. As the day lengthened, the grumbling and swearing ceased and the men slogged along silently with downcast eyes.

Near the small town of Pei-tsang a cavalry troop appeared off to the right of the Marines' line of march. The cavalry troop was driven off with several volleys of rifle fire. Brief though the encounter was, the action animated the Marine ranks.

The first decisive battle was fought at Pei-tsang, a few miles north of the Hsiku Arsenal on the morning of August 5. The Japanese bore the brunt of the attack, supported by British artillery. The American forces did not participate in the battle.

All day the Marines marched along the railroad embankment and in sight of the river. At sunset, they halted just outside Pei-tsang. McCreary's fleet of junks was tied up along the riverbank. The Marines were able to get clean water for drinking. The river water was so filthy, they were unable to wash away the sweat and grime accumulated throughout the day's march. A little water splashed on their faces and hands had to suffice for a much-needed bath.

At daybreak on August 6, they were again on the march. The carts were stacked with ammunition, food and water from the junks and each man's canteen was full. One officer noted that from the looks of their blanket rolls, the men had stripped down to barest of necessities. The third day of the march was much like the previous days, a blazing sun, thirst, dust and heat.

As the Marine column approached Yang-Tsun, artillery and rifle fire grew heavier. Yang-Tsun sat in the bend of the river and just beyond the town an iron railroad bridge spanned the river. A high railway embankment led up to the bridge. There was persistent enemy resistance and allied troops were heavily engaged. Heavy artillery and rifle fire was heard off to the right of the Marine column.

The Marines, the Ninth and Fourteenth Infantry Regiments, Reilly's Battery of the Fifth Artillery and the British led the attack against an elaborate system of trenches and earthworks, strongly held and well supported by artillery. The Russians and French were in support and the Japanese were in reserve. The Marine regiment was assigned to support Reilly's Battery. The battle started early in the afternoon and by evening of August 6, Yang-Tsun had fallen.

Of the engagement, Lieutenant Wise in Dunlap's company wrote years later:

> We were halted. Word came back that we were to drive a heavy force of Chinese out of some earthworks far over to our right.
>
> We stood there with mouths and throats gritty with dust; without a drop of water in our canteens and no chance to get any. Then when it seemed we had stood there for hours that afternoon, the orders came to deploy to our right and attack.
>
> The plain in front of us was a furnace. Dust rose in thick clouds. There was no air to breathe. That heavy heat and dust left us choking.
>
> As we started forward there was a crash of sound at out rear. Our own artillery, firing over our heads, was covering our advance.
>
> We advanced a thousand yards. Down on us, every step of the way, beat that blazing sun, heavier every second.
>
> Another thousand yards. My men began to stagger again. They were taut and game, but all in. Here one turned ghastly white. There one dropped dead from heat. More and more men were staggering....
>
> Another man dropped dead from heat. Chinese bullets were whizzing over our heads. They were shooting high, as usual. We couldn't even see them yet, dust and smoke were so thick. We advanced deeper into it.
>
> My sergeants' faces were grim. Their lips drew tighter and tighter. They rapped out orders, cursing.
>
> Everybody from General Chaffee down they cursed.

A Marine staggered and lurched along.

"Come on, you gutless son-of-a-bitch!" he heard from a sergeant.

They called those men everything they could put their tongues to. Anything to madden them beyond all thought of their exhausted condition were roared by those magnificent old sergeants.

They knew their business. We kept on.

The firing ahead of us was slackening. The Chinese artillery alone was blazing away as fast as they could work the guns. But they, too, were firing high.

Through the dust and smoke those earthworks came into sight. We stopped, fired, advanced, again and again.

Now we were close to it. Behind the earthworks, the Chinese were milling. We went on. We could see them begin to break.

Off to our right I got a glimpse of a Chinese battery limbering up and rolling off as if it were on parade.

Then we were on the earthworks. Over them. Behind them.

They were empty. The Chinese, each man for himself, were vanishing rapidly amid the tombs in the dust of that endless plain....

Men and officers collapsed in the shadow of those earthworks. We couldn't have made another hundred yards to save our lives. Men sprawled on their backs, on their sides, on their stomachs, hiding their faces from the sun in their arms.[11]

During the engagement two villages were captured. The battle and intense heat cost the Marines two wounded in action and two dead from heat prostration. Compared to other allied troops, the Marines had fewer casualties from the heat. Despite the trying conditions, the allied column averaged about twelve miles a day.

Following the Yang-Tsun action, the Marines once again made contact with Lieutenant McCreary's junk fleet and to replenish their supplies and ammunition.

The next morning while the Marines were still cleaning their rifles for inspection, orders came down that the allied column would spend the day at Yang-Tsun to rest and clean up. The resting was simple, but as for cleaning up, that was almost impossible. Potable water was limited and as for the river, it was again out of the question. A hand dipped into the river came out coated with slime that dried and caked. In describing the Marines' efforts to clean up, Lieutenant Wise later wrote: "We found wells in which my men washed hands, faces and necks; then handkerchiefs and extra socks. As a pair dried on they went and the ones they replaced were washed. Clothes and shoes were brushed with anything that came to hand; haversacks turned wrong side out and hung up to air. Dust was shaken out of blankets and they were sunned and aired. Every bush was covered with Marine Corps paraphernalia and washing."[12]

Peter Fleming later recounted, "At Yang-tsun, the German, Italian and Austrian detachments were forced to turn back and return to Tien-Tsin because of their transportation and commissariat problems."[13]

General Frey, commanding the French troops, also elected to return to Tien-Tsin. His troops, mainly Tonkenese, were in poor physical condition because of extended duty in Indo-China. Further, his transport, which consisted of rickshaws and wheelbarrows, was inadequate. With the departure of these detachments, the International Army now consisted of the Japanese, Russian, British and American troops.

After resting in Yang-Tsun for a day, the International Force set out again at dawn on August 8. The line of march that had previously followed the railroad embankment that paralleled the river now followed a road that led almost due north, while the Pei-Ho River flowed on an east-west course. "The roads— normally there was only one — were narrow gullies eaten into the loess by hoofs and wheels worn down by the centuries,"[14] Fleming continued.

Each hour of march would take the allied forces further away from the river and its junk supply fleet. Consequently, the Marines piled all the supplies possible on their carts.

Although at times the officers and NCOs (noncommissioned officers) drove the men, the relationship between the enlisted men and offices was easy and friendly. In his memoirs, Captain Butler recalled a private in his company named Pete. Pete was a Greek who had served nearly thirty years in the Marine Corps. He was a little fellow, all bone and muscle, weighing around 150 pounds and wearing brass earrings. But he was all Marine. "Pete had his knapsack stuffed with bread and cheese. Some evenings, when rations were short, Pete shared his bread and cheese with me. Mold and stale as they were they went to the right spot."[15]

For the next four days the allied forces marched along the narrow roads two and sometimes three abreast through fields of ten-foot-high grain, a sort of millet the Chinese farmers called "sorghos." The heat was intense and the ten-foot grain cut off what little breeze there was. Again the shortage of water was felt and it was not long until the Marines resorted to water drawn from the village wells. Within hours dysentery appeared in the ranks. Many times, however, when the rear echelon reached a village the well had been emptied by the forward elements and they went thirsty.

Captain Smedley Butler later wrote of the march: "The blasted discomfort bothered us more than the fighting. The temperature rose as high as 140 degrees in the sun. There was no shade, not a drop of rain, nor a breath of air.

"The cavalry and artillery kicked up clouds of dust which beat back in our faces. The blistering heat burned our lungs. Nearly fifty per cent of our men fell behind during the day, overcome by the sun. In the cool of the night they would catch and start on again the next morning.... Our throats were parched, our tongues thick. We were cautioned not to drink the water along the road, but no order could keep us from anything that was in liquid form."[16]

Through all this the American forces plodded along a road broken by the advancing allied army. Heavy fighting was going on ahead, but the Americans were not involved. What hurt the Marines' morale most was the fact they were at the very end of the advancing army. The only news they could garner was from soldiers at the aid stations in the villages they passed through, or perhaps from a courier headed for the rear would stop and tell them of pitched battles of which they had heard the firing.

Evidence of looting and the Asiatic ferocity of Japanese, Cossacks, and the British native Indian Cavalry were evident in every village — bodies of all ages and both male and female were strewn everywhere.

When night came, the men slept where they halted, tormented by mosquitoes, flies and midges. Rations consisting of hardtack and bacon or perhaps canned salmon grew monotonous. After these scanty rations, the mess sergeant's life became hell. In the eyes of the rank and file, he alone was responsible for such food.

After four days of marching, eight days since leaving Tien-Tsin, the river and the junk supply fleet again came into sight. There was food, clean water, camphor-opium pills for the dysentery cases and freedom from the tall fields of grain. Here the cooks prepared a supper of corned beef, tomatoes, and potatoes. The mess sergeants had redeemed themselves.

The next morning, with carts loaded with supplies, the allied forces again left the river and trudged through unending fields of millet, corn and reeds. There was the previous heat, thirst and dust.

Early on August 9, with little opposition, Hosiwu was captured, Matou was taken at dawn on August 10, and Changchiawan on August 11. Fleming has noted, "This was the place where in 1860 the allied envoys and their escort were made prisoners while negotiating under a flag of truce. Of the thirty-nine — English, French and Indian — nineteen survived. It was in reprisal for this treatment that the British burnt down the Summer Palace, which had already been looted by the French."[17]

On August 12, ten days after leaving Tien-Tsin, the allied forces arrived at the city of Tungchow, a rich walled city fourteen miles from Peking. The city had been captured and looted by the Japanese, Cossacks, and the native Indian cavalry of the British who made war in the old barbaric way. By the time the American forces arrived, it was all over. The American forces bivouacked on the riverbank where the junk fleet had tied up. The following day the Relief Force spent a day resting and replenishing their supplies.

Throughout the campaign, each contingent had scrutinized the equipment of the others with professional curiosity. Of particular interest to the Marines were the two types of rifles with which they were armed: the Krag-Jorgensen was much admired by allied soldiers; the other, the Lee, was not.

While there was criticism among the various allied armies, the bond of friendship formed between the Marines and the Royal Welsh Fusiliers during the storming of the Walled City of Tien-Tsin was now strengthened and continues to this day.[18]

With the fall of Tungchow, rumor circulated among the allied forces that the legations had fallen and all the foreigners had been murdered. The American and British commanders, however, were reasonably sure that this was not so. On August 8, "Generals Chaffee and Gaselee received identical cipher messages, dated August 6, from Sir Claude [MacDonald]; these were accompanied by a sketch-map and gave directions about the best way of reaching the Legation. Various other messages had come since then. Though they expressed guarded confidence, all made it clear that the Legations were in acute peril."[19] Apparently this information was not shared with the Japanese and Russian commanders.

General Frey, the French commander, with a few hundred exhausted troops caught up with the allied forces at Tungchow and expected to take part in the assault. The German, Italian and Austrian detachments did not arrive until seven days later.

In council, on August 12, the allied commanders formulated vague plans for attacking the walled city of Peking. It was agreed that the allied command would advance in four parallel columns against the eastern wall of the city. The columns would advance along the Imperial Canal. The Russians on the right flank were to attack the Tung Chih Men. The Japanese, moving along the paved road that ran north of the canal, would attack the Chih Hua Men. South of the canal, the Americans would attack the Tung Pien Men, while the British objective would be the Hsia Kuo Men. The French force, north of the canal, was sandwiched between the Japanese and American columns. No troops were held in reserve. The allied commanders agreed that the allied forces would halt and bivouac three miles from the walls so that a coordinated attack could be mounted during the early morning hours of August 15. Further, the troops would be given a short rest before the assault.

Reconnaissance found no resistance between Tungchow and Peking.

Before dawn on August 14, the allied army, following the Imperial Canal, moved away from the river and out across the level plain toward Peking. Then the long delayed rains set in. Throughout most of the day, the army marched through the rain, sometimes following a road and sometimes marching through tall, dripping grass. The rains turned the roads to a quagmire of mud and made it difficult to move the artillery and supply trains. Finally, late in the afternoon, they reached the city of Peking. Under an overcast, dripping sky the allied forces bivouacked for the night as planned.

Much to the surprise of all the other allied commanders, during the early morning hours of August 15, heavy firing was heard in the direction of Peking. It was soon learned that the Russians had violated their agreement of the previous day and had moved out alone in the early morning hours in the rain to attack the Tung Pien Men, the Americans' designated objective. In doing so, they had cut diagonally across the proposed allied front. This move forced the remaining allied forces to launch their attack earlier than planned. As could be expected, confusion reigned. (See Map 10.)

To reach their objective, the Chih Hua Men, the Japanese had to pass through the attacking lines of the Russians. Further, by abandoning their assigned objective, the Russians left the Japanese right flank exposed.

Upon receiving the news, the American force, that included the First Battalion, First Marines, resumed their advance. Upon reaching the Tung

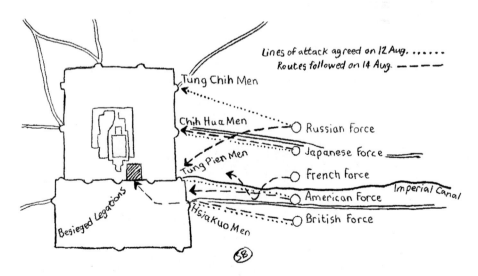

Map 10. Planned and Actual Lines of Attack.

Pien Men, the Americans found the gate jammed with Russians troops. The Russian attack had stalled and could not advance beyond the gate. With the Fourteenth Infantry in the fore, the Americans launched their attack against the Manchu Wall south of the Tung Pien Men. Scaling the wall, they opened fire on the rear of the defending Chinese. The Marines' heavy rifle fire relieved the pressure on the pinned down Russians, which enabled them to hold until reinforcements came up.

During the struggle for the Tung Pien Men, Trumpeter Calvin P. Titus of the Fourteenth Infantry, USA, placed the American flag, the first foreign colors, atop the Walled City of Peking.

The American force entered the Chinese City and by 1500 hours had fought their way along Tartar Wall to the vicinity of Chien Men. On the opposite side of Tartar Wall was the Legation Quarter. While moving along the moat at the base of Tartar Wall, the Marines discovered a small American flag flying above Tartar Wall. The Marine legation guard was holding this section of the wall. A legation guard Marine waved the flag and called out that the relieving force could enter by passing through Water Gate. Some two hours later, General Chaffee with the Fourteenth Infantry and a light battery entered the Legation Quarter through the Water Gate. The American Forces went into bivouac for the night at this location.

In a wild charge, Marines and Russian sailors from the Legation Guard cleared the Chien Men and their sector of Tartar Wall of Chinese defenders. This prevented enemy rifle fire from the wall on the bivouacked troops. Later, these same men opened Chien Men for the Fourteenth Infantry and Reilly's artillery.

Captain Butler received his second wound during the campaign while his company was breaching the Tung Pien. During this attack Butler was knocked down by a bullet that hit him in the chest and knocked the wind out of him. Butler later described the incident: "Captain Bannon and the bugler William Carr, who had helped me when I was wounded in Tien-Tsin, tore open my blouse. The bullet had struck the second button on my blouse. The ring of the flattened-out button dug a hole in my chest and carried off a part of 'South America' from the Marine Corps emblem tattooed on my chest.[20] I carried that flattened-out button in my pocket for years. Medical aid in battle was not elaborate thirty years ago. A little pad of dressing was bandaged on the wound. That was all. For weeks my chest was black as ink and every time I coughed I spit blood."[21]

Two privates were also hit during the struggle for the gate.

Meanwhile, the French force, disoriented in the rain and early morning darkness, lost their way. They blundered across the Imperial Canal and the Americans' line of attack twice. Their part in the attack was negligible.

The British Indian troops met little resistance when they attacked Hsia Kuo Men, their objective. With little opposition, they took the gate and proceeded to the Tartar Wall. "Unlike the other contingents, the British did not fight their way into Peking (their only fatal casualty died from heat-stroke); they walked; they almost sauntered in. Their cheap success was not the reward of cunning or superior intelligence; it was due to luck...."[22] Arriving near the Water Gate in Tartar Wall, a signaler appeared on the wall and with semaphore flags wagged out a message: "Come in by here." In addition, he pointed to the Water Gate, a giant seven-foot sewer tunnel directly below him. Inside the Legation Quarter, Major Myers' Marines cleared the barricades from the gate and at about 1420 hours General Gaselee with the British and Indian troops was the first to enter the Legation Quarter. Residents with bottles of champagne greeted the thirsty soldiers.

The Japanese and Russians entered the Legation Quarter late in the evening. The French did not arrive until the morning of August 16; they had done no fighting. The siege of the Legation Quarter had been lifted. The following day mopping up would commence and the remainder of the city cleared of Chinese.

In the meantime, the Japanese had captured Chih Hua Men in the face of stubborn resistance. The Tung Chih Men that had been the Russians' assigned objective and the southern part of the city remained in the hands of the Chinese. To gain control of that part of the city took considerable effort the following day.

The Russians were severely criticized by the allied commanders. It was assumed that since the Tung Pien Men was nearer the legations, General Lineivitch had deliberately moved out early, hoping, that if all went well, the Russians would be the first to enter the Legation Quarter.

At 0700 on August 16, Chaffee ordered an assault on the Imperial City in the center of Tartar City. Marines led one of the attacking columns in the initial stage. Other Marines took position in the tower over Chien Men and cleared the way for Reilly's battery to come into action.

Between Chien Men and the Imperial City were a series of courtyards. Massive gates of heavy timbers that were thickly studded with huge nails and metal braces blocked access to each courtyard. The gates were barred and heavily bolted. Reilly's Battery was to breach these gates so that the Fourteenth Infantry, led by Colonel Aaron S. Daggett, could penetrate the Imperial City and take the Forbidden City.

Captain Reilly, directing the battery fire, was in the tower with one of his guns. The main battery, however, was on the ground just inside Tartar City near Chien Men.

Captain Reilly kept a steady fire with thorite shells against the first gate. The gate took a heavy beating before it was breached. Once that was accomplished, the Fourteenth Infantry swarmed through and slowly pushed the Chinese back.

Major Waller ordered two companies of Marines to take up firing positions on Tartar Wall and in Chien Men tower to provide overhead fire against the Chinese. "We fired so rapidly that many of the rifles got hot and jammed,"[23] reported Lowell Thomas.

Once a gate was breached, Reilly shifted his fire to the gate of the next courtyard. Under artillery bombardment and the Marines' rifle fire, the Chinese troops, although continuously being reinforced, were slowly pushed back to the last wall before the Sacred City. The Chinese resisted stubbornly, but when the last gate was breached and the American troops poured through, their fire slackened. Suddenly the stubborn resistance vanished and the Chinese troops fled in all directions. Only one more massive gate stood between the Americans and the entrance to the Forbidden City. Once taken, the Americans would be the first allied troops to enter the Sacred City. The Fourteenth Infantry rushed forwarded to achieve victory. That victory, however, was denied. Suddenly they were ordered to halt, cease-fire and withdraw. No one in the attacking force could understand the reason for the withdrawal.

There were many different stories as to why the withdrawal was ordered. Wise has offered, "The most probable seems that the ministers at the legations had asked General Chaffee not to penetrate the Sacred City, because Pekin [sic] had been taken, and further destruction was unnecessary."[24]

Although it was reported that no allied troops entered the Forbidden City at this time, an article in the New York Times reported otherwise:

FIRST IN THE FORBIDDEN CITY

Capt. Lang [sic] Reports that the Honor Belongs to the American Marines.

WASHINGTON, Dec.26 — Brig. Gen. Heywood, Commandant of the Marine Corps, has forwarded to the Navy Department a letter from Capt. Charles D. Long, serving with the Marines in China, stating that the American Marines were the first to enter the Forbidden City at Peking. There has been much controversy as to whether the Russians, British, Germans, or Americans were first inside the sacred precincts, and this letter is regarded as establishing the claims of the Americans. Capt. Long gives the following account of the duties performed by Company D at Peking on Aug. 16:

"Up to that time (Aug. 16) the Forbidden City had not been

entered by any of the allied forces. Three of the four gates between the Chien-Men and the Forbidden City had been forced the previous day by the Americans, but then halted and finally withdrew to the first gate held. Receiving an order from the commanding officer of Marines to enter the Forbidden City and seize such buildings and quarters as might be most advantageous for us to hold and occupy, I moved immediately with my company, forced the fourth gate, and entered the city. Japanese sentries objected to our entering, but I did not consider their claim to any control at this point. On entering there was no opposition, the Chinese having departed, leaving their tents and banners standing. I put guards on the best of the buildings, and the regimental colors where hoisted on one of the administration buildings.

"To the best of my belief this was the first and only occupation of the Forbidden City by any of the allied forces, and the only time that any force hoisted its colors there. We remained there from about 3:30 P.M. to 5:30 P.M., when I received an order to withdraw and to leave a guard at the fourth gate. Capt. Matthews and Lieut. Little, United States Marines, were the officers in Company D with me."[25]

During this action Captain Reilly was struck in the mouth with a bullet and killed instantly. His loss, no doubt, caused the men of the Fourteenth Infantry to fight more savagely as they approached the walls of the Imperial City that stood between them and the Sacred City.

General Chaffee had assigned the Second Battalion, First Marines, the inglorious role of guarding the American pack trains, and only the First Battalion was in the forefront of the battle that covered Reilly's Battery in breaching the Chien Men. Fifteen Americans died in this engagement.

Since organized resistance was over, it remained only for the relief force to go into billets. The First Marine Regiment was assigned the southwest quarter of the Tartar City, with Major Waller as Provost Marshal. Regimental headquarters occupied the Palace of the Eighth Prince.

Lieutenant Wise later wrote: "We stopped at the Palace of the Eighth Prince, which was to be our 'barracks' for the next two months.

"It was the usual Chinese succession of quadrangular courtyards with buildings on four sides.... The men were allotted sleeping quarters in some of the buildings. Officers took others. Yet another was converted into a galley where the men's food was cooked and ate. The courtyard, paved with flagstones, was drill ground and recreation hall.... We were in a prince's palace.... By noon we were established, sentries posted, Officer of the Day appointed, the Marine Corps routine in full swing."[26]

On August 28, the allied powers decided that a representative column of foreign troops should march into Forbidden City to erase its legendary inviolability by foreigners. The Marine Corps contingent was one company from each battalion, First Marines. Captain Butler and Captain Neville commanded the companies. As the last troops cleared the north gate, a 21-gun salute proclaimed the fall of Forbidden City.

Shortly after the siege was lifted, Colonel Henry Clay Cochrane arrived in Peking and took command of the First Marine Regiment. Wise recalled Cochrane in this account:

> Colonel Cochrane was a remarkable man. But he was "ornery" and meaner than hell on duty. Keen, rigidly courteous, but cold and sarcastic.... He could not abide waste of any kind. He never permitted it by any in his command. Once the Marine baker turned out a batch of poor bread. The Colonel promptly made him pay for a sack of flour.... He was a Tartar for discipline. A Marine [who] had been drinking but wasn't exactly drunk came into the [Navy] Yard once. The Colonel smelled his breath and ordered him on bread and water for five days, for smuggling liquor into the Marine Barracks—inside himself! A man of no sympathy and no affection, but efficient to an unusual degree.... I learned a lot about soldering from him.[27]

Later Captain Butler wrote of his encounter with Colonel Cochrane: "Almost at once he had an inspection of the regiment. I know my company looked like tramps. No new clothes had been given out since we left the Philippines the first of June. Not a man was completely dressed in an American uniform. As they lined up for inspection, some wore blue or rose Chinese trousers, others mandarin coats and almost all of them were shod in Chinese silk boots.

"Cochrane looked us over and snorting in disgust [said,] 'Captain, your men don't even look like soldiers....'

"We all had rifles and ammunition and our good nature and health, which are, after all, the prime requisites for soldiering. I was furious at Cochrane, but since he was my commander, I had to control my feelings."[28]

With some persuasion by Captain Dave Porter, Major Biddle's adjutant, General Chaffee soon came to the aid of the battle-weary Marines in Cochrane's command. When Cochrane had arrived in Tien-Tsin he had brought a third battalion of Marines. The third battalion of Marines in Tien-Tsin made a full strength Marine regiment in North China. General Chaffee decided that it was necessary to establish a Marine Headquarters at Tien-Tsin and that the senior Marine officer in North China, Colonel Cochrane, should command it. Colonel Cochrane turned the command of the two battalions of Marines in Peking over to Major Biddle and departed for his new command in Tien-Tsin. Major Biddle's command once again settled down to a more relaxed state of affairs.[29]

A big rumpus was kicked up over looting in Peking. "It is true," Butler once said, "but allowances should be made for the fact that during the excitement of a campaign you do things that you yourself would be the first to criticize in the tranquil security of home."[30]

Was there looting by the Americans? Perhaps a few did. However, the American forces were under strict orders from the president of the United States to refrain from looting. American commanders carried out this order. If any looting occurred, it was kept to a minimum. Some foreign forces, however, apparently looted without limits.

After a month, affairs in North China were quiet enough to allow the Marines to return to the Philippines, where troops were badly needed. On October 3, the First Marine Regiment marched south from Peking toward Tien-Tsin. It had taken eight days to march from Yang-Tsun to Peking. It took four days on the return march to reach Yang-Tsun. At Yang-Tsun the regiment traveled by the recently rebuilt railway to Tangku, where they boarded a steamer that took them out to the Taku Bar and the waiting naval transports. On October 10, the Marine regiment sailed for Cavite in the *Brooklyn* and two transports, the *Zafiro* and *Indiana*. Two weeks later the regiment was back in Cavite. Except for one company of the Ninth Infantry, all army units were also withdrawn.

The Allied Forces celebrate their lifting of the siege of the Legation Quarter in Peking with a ceremony within the Forbidden City. (Marine Corps University Archives, Quantico, Virginia.)

Although the State Departmentz preferred Marines as legation guards in foreign countries, and over protest of General Charles Heywood, the Commandant of the Marine Corps, Secretary of War Elihu Root established a company of the Ninth Infantry as the legation guards in Peking.

The Marines had to wait until 12 September 1905, almost five years later, and at the request of the American Minister W. W. Rockhill, before returning to Peking as legation guards.

Alban Millett has observed, "The officers of the International Relief Force thought the Americans were conspicuous for their careless dress, causal discipline and lack of skill in small unit tactics. As one Japanese office observed, the Americans individually were probably the best fighters in the entire force, but the worst when not on the firing line."[31]

An unusually large number of enlisted Marines— 33 — were awarded the Medal of Honor for bravery during the Boxer Rebellion. Five Marine officers were given brevet commissions for distinguished service.

10

Marines Return to Peking

Following the Boxer Rebellion, the moribund Ch'ing Empire tried to reform itself into a modern nation. Because of its weakness and corruption, it failed and insurrection, civil war and banditry swept over China.

Many rebel groups tried to overthrow the government. One of these groups was led by General T'set Sun. Despite the political strife, as well as the normal floods, famines and disease, the Ch'ing Empire managed to keep control of the government.

It all changed on 10 October 1911, when a revolutionary army near Hankow turned against the government. By the end of the year, the rebel army controlled most of south China. In December, the leaders of the revolt met in Nanking and set up the Republic of China. Sun Yat-sen, a leader in the revolt, was named president of the new republic. Sun Yat-sen began ruling southern China in 1912.

The government of the new Republic then tried to gain control of northern China by making a secret agreement with a disloyal official of the Manchu government. Under this secret agreement Sun Yat-sen would step down as president and give the office to a Manchu military leader, Yuan Shih-k'ai. In exchange, Yuan would force the Manchu 6-year-old emperor to abdicate. Yuan would rule the republic as president. Yuan, however, betrayed the agreement and declared himself dictator.

To gain control of the government again, Sun Yat-sen and his followers formed the Kuomintang (Nationalist Party) and again revolted. The revolt failed and the leaders of the Nationalist Party fled to Japan in 1913.

Yuan tried to establish himself as emperor but failed. He died in 1916, leaving China without an effective chief of state. During this time, warlords fought each other for power. In the meantime, Sun Yat-sen continued to work for a unified China.

In 1923, Communist Russia entered the picture and supported the Nationalist Party with money, arms and advisors. In return, Russia asked the Nationalists to accept the help of the Chinese Communists.

When Sun Yat-sen died, Generalissimo Chiang Kai-shek took command of the combined Nationalist and Communist rebel armies.

In March 1927, the rebel armies captured Shanghai and the lower Yangtze valley. In April, Chiang Kai-shek turned against the Communists. Consequently, the Communists fled to the hills of Kiangsi Province. There, under the leadership of Mao Tse-tung, the Communists started building an army of their own.

After consolidating his control of southern China, in 1928, Chiang Kai-shek moved his armies north and captured Peking, bringing northern and southern China under one rule.

Because of the insurrections, civil wars and banditry, the United States, from time to time, was forced to send military troops into China to protect its citizens and their property.

When the Marines marched out of Peking in the fall of 1900, General Chaffee, on orders from Secretary of War Elihu Root, established a company of the Ninth Infantry Regiment as legation guards in Peking. This order was bitterly protested by General Charles Heywood, Commandant of the Marine Corps. In a letter to the Secretary of the Navy, Heywood wrote:

> It has always been the custom to furnish guards for the legations in a foreign country from the Marines, and this custom has not been departed from until the present guard at the legation in China was established, which was furnished by the Army. Army troops are never supposed to be sent to a foreign country except in the time of war, and, for this reason, legations guards and other guards required in foreign countries have always been furnished by the Marine Corps. It is respectfully submitted that it is eminently proper that the guard to be kept at the legation in Pekin [sic] should be furnished by the Marine Corps."[1]

Despite the protest, Secretary of War Root's order stood and an Army legation guard remained in Peking. Between 1900 and 1905, company-size detachments from the Ninth Infantry in the Philippines were rotated as the legation guards in Peking. While the United States maintained a legation guard at Peking, it depended on other nations that had armed forces stationed in Tien-Tsin to keep the railroads open and to maintain lines of communication between Peking and the sea.

On 12 September 1905, at the request of Minister W. W. Rockhill, a Marine detachment returned as guards for the American Legation in Peking.

The original assignment of the Ninth Infantry as the legation guards in Peking may have reflected the growing concern in Washington, D.C., over the role of the Marine Corps. In 1900, the Navy Department, during reorganization, designated the Marine Corps as the best possible force to defend temporary advance naval bases for the battle fleet. The Navy was moving toward organizing the Marine Corps into permanent expeditionary battalions. There were political factions, however, that sought not only to remove Marines from aboard ships, but also to dissolve the Marine Corps as a distinct branch of service and absorb the Corps into the Army. The Marine Corps fought to maintain their identity as well to keep Marines aboard ships and to develop and defend advance naval bases. It was not until 1909 that the matter was resolved in favor of the Navy Department and the Marine Corps.

In the meantime, early in 1905, the issue of substituting the Marines for the Ninth Infantry was discussed among the Departments of the Army, Navy and the Executive Office of President Theodore Roosevelt. Roosevelt felt the Marine Corps had too much political influence and supported dissolving the Corps and absorbing it into the Army. Nevertheless, on 31 July 1905, President Roosevelt signed an order directing the Marine Corps to relieve the Ninth Infantry as legation guards at Peking.

The reasons that Roosevelt signed the order for the changing of the guard are ambiguous. The opinions of Minister W. W. Rockhill may have influenced the decision. Rockhill thought the Marines provided a more prestigious guard, as they were noted for their smartness. Further, without conflicts of authority, they could also be reinforced in time of need from the Marine guards on ships of the Asiatic Fleet or from the Marine guards at navy shipyards in the Philippines.

General George F. Elliott, Major General Commandant of the Marine Corps, directed the commanding officer of the First Brigade of Marines stationed in the Philippines to transfer two officers and 100 handpicked men to Peking as legation guards.

The one hundred Marines, commanded by Captain Harry Lee, USMC, with First Lieutenant Thomas Holcomb (later to become Commandant of the Marine Corps) as junior officer, sailed from Cavite, Philippine Islands, aboard the Army transport *Logan*. On 12 September 1905, they relieved the Ninth Infantry and the legation guard in Peking became a permanent Marine duty station.

During the troubled years that followed, neither the reformed nationalists nor the regional warlords would accept either foreign exploitation or the Manchu rule. Consequently, all of China was disturbed by civil unrest. During these years, the United States government continued its vigilance.

The year 1911 marked the beginning of a revolutionary upheaval that would continue for decades. On the morning of 14 November 1911, Chinese General T'set Sun's revolutionary forces took control of the government in south China. Around the same time when revolutionary violence grew near Peking, the American Foreign Minister requested additional legation guards.

In the fall of 1911, complying with the request, a battalion of 375 Marines under the command of Major Phillip M. Bannon was sent to Peking to reinforce the existing legation guards.

Devastated by the revolution of 1911, the Manchu dynasty stepped down on 12 February 1911, and the Nationalist government assumed power under political general Yuan Shih-k'ai. Civil unrest continued as the regional warlords fought among themselves.

The Marine guard at the legation in Peking was kept at more than 500 men until May 1912, when it was reduced. The legation guard varied in size over the next ten years or so in response to the major incidents of local unrest.

As the revolutionary violence grew in North China, late in 1911, under the terms of the Protocol of 1901, the War Department was ordered to furnish a force to protect American interests and citizens in North China.

In January 1912, the Fifteenth Infantry Regiment, stationed in the Philippines, was deployed in Tien-Tsin. The force was known as the China Expedition. Later it was called the American Forces in China and finally, in 1924, named the U.S. Army Forces in China.

The Fifteenth Infantry consisted of two infantry battalions with supporting companies. Its average strength was approximately 1,000 men and officers.

From 1912 until 1917, the Fifteenth Infantry, known as the "Can Do" Regiment, was billeted in substandard buildings in Tien-Tsin. In 1917, however, after the Germans were banished from their concessions in Tien-Tsin, the Fifteenth Infantry moved into the German barracks in the old German concession.

Throughout this period the Army, in conjunction with the British, Italian, French, (Russians and Germans until 1917) and Japanese forces, protected the concessions in Tien-Tsin and guarded the lines of communications to Peking. In addition to the garrison in Tien-Tsin, company-size detachments were maintained at Chinwangtao and Tongsham.

Chinwangtao was not only a port of entry for North China, but the army also had Camp Barrows, a large rifle range and recreation area located there. The Fifteenth Infantry arrived in Tien-Tsin during January 1912 and served there until March 1938, when relieved by the Marines.

In 1912, due to revolutionary incidents, the Marine legation guard was increased to battalion strength, consisting of a Headquarters Company, the 38th, 39th and 62nd Companies and the Mounted Detachment. All these companies were rifle companies. The 39th Company, however, was also an artillery company equipped with 3-inch naval landing guns (hand drawn). The other two companies were equipped with machine guns. Sometime, around 1926, the battalion was reorganized into letter companies—Companies Able, Baker and Charlie. About that time, the companies were equipped with machine guns, 37mm howitzers and 60mm

39th Company (Artillery), Marine Legation Guard, 1924–1926. Officers: Captain W.A. Worton, commanding, Second Lieutenant J. McHugh. Staff Noncommissioned Officers: First Sergeant Burns, Gunnery Sergeant Matson, Senior Platoon Sergeant Miller. This company was the last company in the Marine Corps to be equipped with 3-inch USN Landing Guns (hand drawn). Photograph taken in front of the Chien Men Pagoda on Tartar Wall. (Marine Corps University Archives, Quantico, Virginia.)

Marines of the 39th Company snapping in on the 3-inch USN Landing Gun. (Marine Corps University Archives, Quantico, Virginia.)

Stokes trench mortars. With the 3-inch naval landing gun being phased out, the 39th Company in Peking was the last Marine Corps unit to be equipped with this gun.

The Mounted Detachment was organized shortly after the Revolution of 1911, but it was not officially recognized as a unit in the legation guard until February 1912. First commanded by 1st Lt. David Randall, USMC, the Horse Marines distinguished themselves for snappy courier service during the revolution. The mounted Marines also made a tremendous impression on the Chinese. Since "face" counted a lot with the Oriental people, it was decided after the revolution that the "face" created by the mounted detachment was too good to lose.

Originally, the detachment consisted of sixteen men; one sergeant, three corporals and twelve privates. After the revolution, Col. Dion Williams, then commanding the Embassy Guard, received permission to increase the authorized strength of the mounted detachment to one officer, two sergeants, one corporal, five privates first class and 23 privates.

In addition to the general routine of drills, inspections, and parades, the Mounted Detachment was assigned the duties of taking a census of the

American citizens residing in and around Peking. Peking was divided into four districts. Because horsemen could navigate the narrow streets in the hutungs of Peking that motorized vehicles could not, they patrolled the city. Each squad of the detachment was assigned a district to cover. The district was patrolled weekly to observe any changes of addresses that might not have been reported to the Embassy. Once a year the men visited concentration points for inspecting and renewing of flares that were used as distress signals, as well as instructing citizens within the district in their use.

In times of trouble, Americans residing in Peking were called into the Embassy compound. By day, the American flag with a blue signal pennant beneath it was hoisted on the Marine Corps' 310 foot radio tower within the compound as the signal for the assembly. At night, the display of red and blue lights from the same tower was the signal for assembly. Four shots from the field gun in the compound warned Americans to watch the tower, the highest structure in Peking, for danger signals. Even so, it was sometimes necessary for Marines to go out and bring the Americans in. This job was turned over to the Mounted Detachment.

The mounted detachment also continued the original courier service of delivering dispatches to other legations. The night patrol of the city was also taken over by the Mounted Detachment in 1933.

During the rifle range season, the detachment kept one man at the range. According to one historical account, "He set up camp about a quarter of a mile from the main camp. I don't know why, but it seemed no one wanted a stable close to them. He would pick up dispatches at the main camp, ride across country to the Legation compound, deliver the dispatches, pick up more, and return to the range."[2]

The men of the detachment wore the usual Marine uniform of khaki for summer, forestry green for winter and blues for dress. They wore breeches, boots and spurs instead of trousers. Like other Marines of the guard, because the thermometer dropped to zero and below in Peking, they wore fur hats in the winter.

The detachment was armed with one machine gun, three Browning automatic rifles, three Sub-Thompson machine guns and twenty rifles. Every man was armed with a .45 Colt automatic and a cavalry saber. The members of the machine gun crew did not carry rifles. The detachment had its own scarlet guidon.

The McClellan saddle used by the Detachment and the U.S. Cavalry was the same type that was used in the Civil War. A blanket roll consisting of a complete change of clothes, including shoes, was secured to the cantle of the saddle. Saddle bags containing toilet articles and mess gear

Mounted Detachment, First Lieutenant Charles E. Shepherd, Jr., commanding, Sergeant Thomas, 1st Platoon, Corporal McDonald, 2nd Platoon, Lieutenant Shepherd's horse — "Eau De Cologne." (Department of Defense [Marine Corps] photograph.)

were carried on the near side, and grooming gear, feed and horseshoes on the off side. In addition to that, a saber was attached to the saddle on the off side and a rifle boot on the near side.

The detachment had three races each year; two flat races of a mile and a quarter, and either a steeplechase or a paper hunt. The first three places were awarded cups and prize money.

The Detachment was equipped with the best veterinary facilities in North China, carried out by members of the detachment who were capable veterinarians and were fit to cope with any illness of animals which might arise. The shoeing of the horses was done by a Chinese blacksmith and was inspected by the Stable Watch on duty at the time. All horses were stabled in the Quartermaster Compound.

Although the Mongolian ponies were small, they could cover a surprising amount of ground in one day and still be fit to travel the next day. "They had one cardinal virtue, they were as tough as a ten-cent steak."[3]

The Mongolian ponies' weight ran from about 650 to 725 pounds and averaged 13 hands in height. They were in their prime at about six or seven years. The jump for them was about three and a half feet. Because of the size of these ponies, men picked for the detachment weighed between 140 and 170 pounds. As could be expected, each pony had a name selected by the rider or his predecessor. Some mounts had common names like Tex,

Private Gerald C. Merchant, Jr., mounted detachment, Peiping, China, 1935, in summer uniform. (Department of Defense Photography [Marine Corps]).

Pat, Blackie or Nellie. Other names were more colorful — SubMarine, Whiskey Bill, Moonshine or Syosett.

The men who rode in the Mounted Detachment were selected not only because of their light weight but for their knowledge of horsemanship, if they had any, and their clean service record.

While the Marine Corps had, from time to time during the past, used horses and mules as mounted patrols in Nicaragua and Haiti as well as on patrols of ammunition depots, the Mounted Detachment in Peking was different. The Mounted Detachment trained as a cavalry unit. All the members ran the pistol and saber courses for record. This included the pharmacist's mate that accompanied the detachment on their cross-country rides and maneuvers. (It was probably the only time in the history of the naval service that a sailor was a trained cavalryman.)

The following were the qualifications for the Pistol and Saber Courses:

> Pistol (Once over the course)
> Expert 13 hits
> Sharpshooter 10 hits
> Marksman 8 hits.
> Time limit — 55 seconds. One less hit for every second over time.
> One less hit for every time a horse broke out of a gallop.
>
> Saber (Twice over the course)
> Expert Swordsman 90%
> Excellent Swordsman 85%
> Swordsman 75%

Three points were scored for piercing the dummy with a point of the saber. Two points were scored for vigor of attack: that is, the spirit and fighting manner in which the lunges were made. If it was very good, one and one half points, and if it was fair, only one point was scored. Nothing was scored for the vigor of attack if it was considered less than fair.

There were ten dummies in the course, and the possible score was 50, making the total possible score 100. For each second over the prescribed time limit of forty-five seconds, two points were deducted from the total. For each obstacle not jumped, five points were deducted from the score. For each instance during the run that the horse assumed a gait other than a gallop, one point was deducted. This penalty was not construed as applicable in the case of run-outs, or where a horse in changing leads hit two or more beats of a trot, or in refusals.[4]

Over the years, many Marine officers commanded the Mounted Detachment. Among them was the renowned Chesty Puller, who later became a legend in the Corps. As commander, Capt. Puller "put his Horse Marines through their paces daily, excluding Saturdays and Sundays, leading them on long cross-country rides with small dust storms boiling in their wake. He rode into areas where the Japanese were training, in an effort to observe details of their tactical work."[5]

Of these rides, Pvt. Wayne Burnside was to recall, "We rode across farmland, plowed fields, and jumped mud fences. We quite often ended up at the brewery outside town. The brewmaster would bring out a wash tub full of ice and bottles of beer."[6]

From another account: "There was also a weekly sunset parade for the American colony of the ancient city—about 3,000 strong—followed by the Colonel's reception. A battalion of infantry and the cavalry detachment put on this show, the Horse Marines finished it by passing at a walk, trot, and finally a gallop, with sabers flashing."[7]

Puller was also a member of the Embassy Polo team. He played two years, being chosen as No. 1 "Griffin" of the season in 1933, and the best beginning player. His detachment team won the Hotel de Peking Cup in 1933 and the next year the Major McCallum Trophy. Like everything Puller did, he trained hard and played the same way.

Leatherneck magazine told this story in 1938:

> Captain Jinks, of the Horse Marines, who fed his horse on corn and beans, is purely a legendary character. But there was no foolin' about the Horse Marines of Peking. They were real Leathernecks on horseback.
>
> Around the office of the Marine Corps Commandant, in the Navy Building at Washington, where they are spoken of as "the mounted detachment at Peiping," [Peiking] the derisive implications of "Horse Marines" have a slightly irritating effect. "A Horse Marine," sputtered a colonel. "Why it's ridiculous-ludicrous-absurd!" But Horse Marines they were and remained so for almost thirty years.[8]

The band of the American Legation in Peking and the band of the Fourth Marine Regiment were the only bands in the Marine Corps to serve on foreign soil. The band in Peking was started around 1910. A nucleus of volunteers under the leadership of a man named Niccoli (first name and rank not known) formed a band. With instruments scrounged from who knows where and music borrowed from the British Band, which was stationed there at the time, they were well received by the foreign community.

There were only two companies stationed at the Legation at the time and the men performed their regular duties and in their spare time played with the band. Because of their success, more and better instruments were requested from Marine Corps Headquarters. The instruments arrived the following year and the band took hold.

The Post Exchange was a big help in getting the struggling band off on the right foot by purchasing some instruments and lots of sheet music. In addition, they gave each man playing in the band a dollar a month for his troubles. At the time, a private drew something like $21.00 a month, out of which he paid the navy twenty cents a month for medical care and his insurance, if he had any. Therefore, the dollar a month was bonus worth working for. Eventually, a regular band was authorized and replaced the volunteers.

In 1919, the Marine band introduced the first saxophone to North China. The band is also credited with playing a big part in making western music popular in North China. The band not only played at all Marine parades, but also held weekly concerts during the summer in the bandstand in the center of the Marine Compound.

Much of their work, however, was done away from the Marine Compound. They played at Catholic University, Yen Ching and the Yu Ying Academy, various churches and missions, several foreign embassies and some funerals.

When the guard detachment was restricted to the Marine compound during periods of civil unrest, the band played a big part in keeping the morale of the command at a high level. During these times the orchestra played for dances at the Marine clubs, YMCA, and in the gymnasium in Johnson Hall in the compound.

During the downsizing of the legation guard in 1941, the band was under the leadership of Master Sergeant August Olaguez when it was disbanded and the men returned to the States.[9]

Throughout the 1920s civil wars swept over China. Political parties, warlords and the army all struggled to gain control of the Chinese government. The struggle gave birth to anti-foreign mobs and floods of refugees that threatened Western Powers' citizens and trade. Usually starting in the south of China, the civil wars swept north until all of China was engulfed in a political upheaval that was reminiscent of the Boxer Rebellion of 1900.

The United States' foreign policy at the time was not only to protect American citizens and their property, but to also enable the Chinese to establish a stable government that could strengthen and protect its sovereignty.

To complicate matters, the Western Powers and Japan were afraid that the communist-dominated Kuomintang would encroach upon their extraterritorial treaty rights and trade. Further, both the Russians and Japanese were threatening to usurp Chinese land and power.

Left: Marine visiting the Great Wall near Chinwangtao, China. Circa 1920s. *Above:* Mounted Marine in winter uniform, circa 1920s. (Photographs from the author's collection.)

The United States hoped that the presence of its military forces, small though they were, would prevent China from being overrun by foreign powers.

The role of protecting both the American interests and China put the Marines in a precarious position because they had to accomplish both without actually engaging in combat. Consequently, the Asiatic Fleet was kept busy moving Marines about China. First, Marines were landed in South China to protect American interests. As the civil war moved north, they were moved north to Chinwangtao and Tien-Tsin to provide security for the Americans there as well as to reinforce the legation guards at Peking.

In 1922, as clashes intensified, the legation in Peking requested reinforcements. Captain Charles H. Martin and a detachment of Marines from the USS *Albany* were ordered to Peking. Arriving on 28 April, they remained until 25 May, when they were relieved and returned to the *Albany*.

The USS *Henderson*, one of the two naval transports that carried Marines and naval personnel from the States to the Far East, 1941. (Photograph from the author's collection.)

Later, a battalion of Marines under the command of Captain Roy C. Swank landed at Taku on 5 May. The battalion remained only a short time, then they were ordered to Shanghai where they remained until 11 May. Later in the year, a small battalion of Marines from the Asiatic Fleet occupied Tien-Tsin for a short time to guard American business installations and missions.

When anti-foreign mobs threatened the International Settlement in Shanghai in 1924, Captain Francis S. Kierer, commanding the First Expeditionary Force of 101 men from the Philippines, was ordered to reinforce First Lieutenant John T. Thornton's detachment of 31 men from the USS *Asheville* who were already on station. Later Thornton's detachment returned to the *Asheville*. The First Expeditionary Force, however, remained in the International Settlement. In October when the Kuomintang Party, strengthened by aid from Russia, moved against the warlords in North China, the First Expeditionary Force was ordered north to Tien-Tsin to support the legation guard in Peking. When the unrest subsided in February 1925, the First Expeditionary Force moved out and boarded the USS *Asheville*.

Captain August Wilson, with 127 men from the Second Provisional

Force in Manila, was ordered to Peking to reinforce the legation guard. Boarding the United States collier *Abarenda*, they sailed from Manila on 16 October 1925. The detachment landed in Tien-Tsin on 9 November 1925, where they stayed through the remainder of the year.[10]

In November 1926, the Commander of the Asiatic Fleet ordered Captains Walter E. McCaughtry and Carl F. Merz with 125 enlisted men from Guam to embark on the United States collier *Gold Star* and proceed to Chinwangtao to help protect American interests there.

Throughout this period of political upheaval in China, the Asiatic Fleet kept warships off the China coast with Marine units aboard ready to respond to anti-foreign violence on the mainland.

Butler's Third Brigade 1927–1928

In February 1927, the Cantonese troops under the leadership of Chiang Kai-shek threatened the International Settlement in Shanghai. It was a time of riots, panic and disruption of trade. There was fighting between the northern warlords and the southern revolutionaries, between the Kuomintang and the Communists, and between the left and right wings of the Nationalist movement. Anti-foreign disorders spread throughout China. Warships from all nations gathered at Shanghai.

During this period, small detachments of Marines were in and out of China on numerous occasions. The major intervention, however, began early in 1927, when civil war and anti-foreign violence threatened the International Settlement at Shanghai.

To reinforce the Western Powers' troops guarding the International Settlement, the Commander in Chief of the Asiatic Fleet mobilized all available Marines in the Far East, including a small battalion from Guam, into a provisional battalion of 20 officers and 455 enlisted men. Under the command of Major Julian P. Willcox, the provisional battalion of four companies landed in Shanghai on 8 February 1927.

Because ill feelings continued to run high and danger appeared so threatening, it was felt that more troops were needed for protection of the International Settlement. Therefore, the Fourth Marine Regiment, consisting of 66 officers, and 1,162 enlisted men under the command of Colonel Charles S. "Jumbo" Hill, was sent from San Diego. The Regiment arrived at Shanghai on 14 February 1927.[11]

The Marines' job in Shanghai was to help the British and the six other foreign powers present to keep the Chinese out of the International Settlement. While Hill's efforts were coordinated with other foreign forces by the senior commander, Major General John Duncan of the British Army, the Marines' primary mission was the "protection of American and foreign life and property."[12]

Despite the fact that Marines were sorely needed both as guards of the mails in the United States and in Nicaragua, Major General Commandant John A. Lejeune decided that the forces in China should be brought up to brigade strength. The Sixth Marine Regiment, which had been disbanded in October, was reorganized under the command of Colonel Harold C. Snyder with Marines drawn from naval yards on the East Coast. The Sixth Marines was reinforced with the Tenth Marines armed with 75mm guns, engineers, tanks and an aviation force that was augmented by a Marine squadron that had been stationed on Guam since March 1921. The two squadrons consisting of some 30 planes were commanded by Lt. Col. Thomas C. Turner. Once formed, the Sixth Marines were rushed by rail to San Diego for transfer to China.

Dehaviland 02B-1 of Observation Squadron 10. One of the three DHs at Tien-Tsin, 1927–28. Note "Dragon" near tails of ship number A6904. (Marine Corps University Archives, Quantico, Virginia.)

Headquarters, Marine Corps, designated Brig. Gen. Smedley D. Butler to command all the Marines in China, and ordered the Marines for duty in China to be organized into a reinforced brigade.

In San Diego, Butler organized his headquarters and several units of the brigade special troop, which included artillery, tanks, engineers and service troops. With his headquarters, one battery of artillery and the Sixth Marines, Butler sailed on the USS *Henderson* on 7 April, and arrived in Shanghai on 2 May. The remainder of the troops to form the brigade, including two extra battalions—one for each of the regiments—were mobilized at San Diego and sailed on the SS *President Grant* on April 17. The *President Grant* proceeded to Olongapo, Philippine Islands, where the Marines were transferred to the USS *Chaumont* for further movement to Shanghai. After their arrival in Shanghai, the Marine troops were designated as the Third Marine Brigade, which had a total strength of some 238 officers, 18 warrant officers and 4,170 enlisted men.

Later Butler recalled, "The Marines were sent to protect American citizens and their property. If we could not have maintained friendly relations with the Chinese and have accomplished our purpose without fighting the expedition would have been a failure...."[13]

"Mr. Coolidge looked at it in the same light apparently, because he sent us enough men to do it, and the finest equipment we ever had ... and with this splendid display of force we were able to domi-

U.S. Marines guarding Legation Quarter of Peking, China, 1927. Chien Men Tower is in the background. (Department of Defense [Marine Corps] photograph.)

nate the situation and not have to make a combination with anybody else, whose interest was so very deep we couldn't even see it. We simply announced to the other nations, "If you wish to do this, you can do it, but we cannot join in any movement which may arouse the Chinese."[14]

The United States was fortunate in this matter by having Admiral Clarence S. Williams as its Naval Commander-in-Chief in Shanghai. Admiral Williams, commanding the Asiatic Fleet, and as senior officer in Shanghai, was entitled to preside at any allied conferences. After the massacre of foreigners at Nanking, the allied powers disclosed a plan to go up the Yangtze River and destroy the Nanking forts as retaliation for the outrages against foreigners. When Admiral Williams was asked if he would join the expedition, he replied, "No, but I'll be here when you get back."[15] After that, the expedition failed in the planning stages.

In Shanghai, the mission of the foreign troops was to keep the Chinese out of the International Settlement. All the Marines could do was to see that mutinous Chinese troops didn't get out of hand and shoot Americans. As Butler put it, "It was up to me to prevent a repetition of the Boxer and Nanking difficulties."[16]

Major General Smedley Darlington Butler, USMC, in winter field uniform (uncovered). (Department of Defense [Marine Corps] photograph.)

With the men confined to a heavily populated area, little training could be accomplished. Butler supplemented the lack of training with athletics and parades. Butler kept his men busy polishing their equipment and "burnishing their mess gear until it sparkled in the sun. I even let them nickel plate their bayonets and scabbards although it was against regulation...."[17] The whole brigade spruced up with the ambitious desire to rival the smart and dazzling appearance of the Coldstream Guards, Great Britain's crack regiment."[18]

Anticipating trouble in North China, Butler went to Peking in May to consult with the American Minister, John V.A. MacMurray, to see if it was advisable to increase the guard at the American Legation. Butler soon learned that the rival

Chinese armies were battling continually in the north, and many of the troops were undisciplined and ready to break loose and go on the rampage to loot and kill unarmed civilians. He found the situation so much more critical in the north than in Shanghai he decided to move the Third Brigade to Tien-Tsin.

By early June, the Nationalist movement had mustered sufficient military strength and popular support that Generalissimo Chiang Kai-shek was able to execute his long-planned offensive against the northern warlords' alliance led by General Chang Tsu-lin. Although the Nationalist policy was not to harm foreign lives and property, it could not curb the anti-foreign mobs, urban workers who were often led by communists, or completely control their own soldiers. Consequently, civil unrest spread northward as the Nationalist Army moved north and the northern warlord alliance moved toward Peking.

By this time, many foreign ministers, fearing a civil outbreak similar to the Boxer Rebellion, had already requested reinforcements of their garrison in the Concessions in Tien-Tsin. Therefore, other foreign powers also ordered troops north to Tien-Tsin.

Butler and the Third Brigade, less the Fourth Marine Regiment, moved to Tien-Tsin early in June and established themselves in camp. Before the movement of the Brigade, Butler had sent an advance detail to Tien-Tsin. This detail, working with the Fifteenth Infantry, secured enough housing to accommodate the brigade. The detail also picked out the spot on the Bund where the landings and unloading would take place, and mapped the routes through Tien-Tsin's streets to the various sites where the men would be quartered and to the godowns, yamens and compounds where their equipment and supplies would be stored. The detail did a good job. During the landing, absolute order prevailed, and their time schedule was observed down to the minute. Butler knew there wasn't any war going on, yet he made the large-scale landing as though there were. It was Butler's way of doing things.

Some of the officers and men of the Fifteenth Regiment were on hand to observe the Marines landing in Tien-Tsin. Private Charles G. Finney was one of the spectators. Later in his book, *The Old China Hands*, he described the landing.

> Tugs brought up the first three lighters of Marines and lodged them, with much banging and clattering, against the concrete rim of the Bund. Lines were thrown ashore and made fast. The lighters were aswarm with young Americans in forest-green uniforms, very dirty, very disheveled. Each man wore a steel helmet and carried a pack, a horseshoe-shaped blanket roll, a Springfield rifle with bayonet fixed,

Top: Loading Marine Corps tank, Tien-Tsin, 1927–28. *Bottom:* Off-loading troops, Tien-Tsin, 1927–28. (Marine Corps University Archives, Quantico, Virginia.)

a cartridge belt jammed with shiny .30-06 ammunition clips, and an extra bandoleer of cartridges over his shoulder.

The three lighters' loads of Marines emptied onto the Bund; there was nothing to stop them. They had only to leap ashore; the lighters were parallel to and tied to the concrete ramp. Out of the bowels of their lighters—which had previously been used to transport coal, and hence were rather sooty—landing parties hoisted machine guns, Stokes mortars, and 27mm [actually 37mm] howitzers. They did it quickly, efficiently and seemingly without effort, as do well trained teams. They brought out sandbags; and in something like ten minutes they threw up a horseshoe shaped barricade, facing the city and sealing off their portion of the Bund. This barricade bristled with weapons.

A Lieutenant Colonel was in over-all charge of the landing. He knew exactly what he was doing. The operation reminded me of a circus's arrival, by wagonload at its show ground. It seemed at first glance to be nothing but confusion compounded. But it wasn't that at all. It was a well-planned procedure, economically and beautifully executed. Even our critical officers began to be impressed....[19]

We were amazed at the amount of material the Third Brigade brought with it: tanks, field artillery, trucks, civilian type automobiles, great heaps of military stores and twenty airplanes....[20]

The tunic the Marines wore was the high-collar World War I model with black buttons. Their pants were stuffed into canvas leggings.... Their uniforms had gathered much coal-dust grime from the trip upstream in the lighters.[21]

The U.S. Army already had the Fifteenth Infantry Regiment with strength of some 1,800 men stationed in Tien-Tsin. The legation guard in Peking now totaled some 516 officers and enlisted men, including the 22-man mounted detachment. The United States military force in North China totaled almost 7,000 men. Combined with forces of the other foreign powers, there were now approximately 17,000 foreign troops in North China.

Although the political situation remained tense, the Third Brigade settled down to watchful waiting with little if any shooting. The Brigade soon established a garrison duty routine. Although somewhat scattered about Tien-Tsin, the billets were named after men and officers killed in 1900 during the Boxer Rebellion.

Butler established a routine of drills, exercises, demonstrations, and gymkhanas, all designed to bring the brigade to a fine polish and simultaneously to show the flag most conspicuously.

In Shanghai, the British Coldstream Guards had been the Third Brigade's incentive for military perfection. In Tien-Tsin, the Fifteenth Infantry became the Brigade's spur. Stationed in Tien-Tsin since 1911, the

"Can Do" Regiment had become a "spit and polish" outfit that could be envied.

Just as Butler had bent regulations a bit by allowing the Marines to nickel-plate their bayonets, in Tien-Tsin he bent regulations a bit more. Steel helmets were burnished, shellacked, and the polished globe and anchor emblem mounted on them. Rifle stocks were scraped, boned and hand rubbed with linseed oil to achieve a high luster.

The high collar blouses of the Marines could not compare with the rolled down lapels of the army tunics. To improve the appearance of the Marines' blouses, Butler ordered the Marines' high collars to be converted into rolled lapel collars like the army's. Unfortunately, the high collars did not provide enough cloth for a decent rolled down lapel. Consequently, the lapels on the Marines' blouses were rather skimpy. The black buttons on the blouse were scraped and shined with metal polish. Rather than the desired shiny brass-like appearance, the buttons looked more like a burnished penny. One old sergeant later said, "He even had us pressing out shoestrings."

Butler went all out to achieve the "spit and polish" of the Fifteenth Regiment, however, he never quite reached their standards. The fact that the "Can Do" Regiment were garrison troops and the Marines were a combat outfit living under field conditions made the difference.

Extensive athletics among the foreign troops in the area helped maintain troop morale. Apparently, when it came to athletics, the Marines excelled. Finney later wrote, "In Tien-Tsin that year no war developed, except the war between the Marines and the Fifteenth Infantry. It was only a tepid, athletic war fought on basketball courts, baseball diamonds, in boxing rings, and one on a football field. The Marines won all these contests."[22]

Many military parades were held, sometimes as a regular garrison routine, but many times as a compliment to Chinese generals and other officials, for fostering good will.

Under the State Department interpretations of the Boxer Protocol of 1901, the Third Marine Brigade, unlike the Fifteenth Infantry and the Peking Legation Guards, had no obligation to cooperate with other foreign forces. Butler told other foreign powers' commanders that the Brigade's sole purpose was "to protect American lives only," and would not guard the Tien-Tsin railroad or join any integrated defense command for the Tien-Tsin concessions. While Butler refused to join in an integrated defense of Tien-Tsin, he was prepared to defend the city if necessary.

The officers of the Fifteenth Infantry were a little unhappy with Butler. Butler outranked their commanding officer, Gen. Joseph Castner. This

Top: Inspection of a battalion of Tenth Marines (artillery) at Tien-Tsin, China, circa 1928. Left to right: Col. Harry Lay, USMC, General Castner, USA, Brig. Gen. Smedley D. Butler, USMC, and Lt. Col. E.B. Miller, USMC. *Bottom:* Tien-Tsin, China, circa 1928. The Third Marine Brigade passes in review. (Department of Defense [Marine Corps] photographs.)

meant if any shooting started, the Fifteenth Infantry would have to fight under a Marine general.

All American citizens in China were encouraged to come to either the protected areas of Shanghai in the south or Tien-Tsin in the North. A few people did stay out in the interior, but they did so at their own risk and understood that expeditions could not be sent out to bring them in. In North China, there were some two million Chinese under arms. Any military column that was sent into the interior would be chewed up.

Butler tried to persuade Minister MacMurray to move the legation and all Americans in Peking to Tien-Tsin to simplify the task of protecting them. When MacMurray refused, Butler organized a "striking force" of some 2,000 men ready to move out on a two-hour notice to Peking to evacuate all Americans if necessary. Trucks armed with machine guns and ammunition and pre-loaded with rations for a self-supporting foray of ten days were always ready to move out. To transport people, benches were built that could be mounted on flatbed trucks. "Our plan for rescue, if necessity arose, included sending the motor trucks to Peking, [and] seizing the Temple of Heaven where we would collect the Americans until we could evacuate them by truck and plane to Tien-Tsin and the coast. In case of an uprising against foreigners, we had arranged to shelter several thousand Americans in Tien-Tsin. We had provided cots, rations, food for babies and medical supplies."[23] Eighteen aircraft would provide cover for the relief column.

Butler made every effort to promote the good will of the Chinese. His airplane crews observed the movements of Chinese army units or warlords' troops, "so that when they came close enough to Tien-Tsin, we could go out and argue with them and persuade them to turn to the right or take the road to the left. That's what we did. We prepared thousands of circulars in the Chinese language to be dropped on them to explain that we were just ahead of them and to please not come any further but to take a road to the left or so off in that direction. Told them we wouldn't let them invade our area. If they persisted, a delegation of officers would call on them and discuss the situation. Perhaps receptions followed by review of the army would persuade the advancing army to change its course. At other times, the officers of advancing force were invited to Brigade Headquarters for a reception and a review of the brigade troops. There was no confrontation. Situations were handled diplomatically."[24]

On two occasions, the Chinese shot down two of the Brigades' planes. Again, diplomacy was required. Butler recalled, "A delegation was sent to

Top: Commanding General Smedley D. Butler reviews the Third Marine Brigade in Tien-Tsin, September 1928. (Marine Corps University Archives, Quantico, Virginia.) *Bottom:* Tien-Tsin, China, 14 September 1928. Tenth Artillery Regiment, Third Marine Brigade at review for General Butler. (Department of Defense [Marine Corps] photograph.)

call on Marshal Fu Chiang, Chief of Staff of the Advancing army of 20,000 cavalry. The delegation was splendidly received, the situation was clearly explained and he said, 'Why, we thought those were Japanese airplanes....' They gave our officers a fine reception and they reviewed the army, and the army got up and within twenty-four hours had moved fifty miles away. The officers of the army came in and had dinner with us, and the incident was entirely closed."[25] The whole idea was to settle matters diplomatically and get away from shooting.

The Marine airfield was located at Tangku next to the Standard Oil compound about ten miles from the mouth of the Pei-Ho River. Under the terms of the agreement with the Chinese, the brigade pilots were permitted to fly between Peking and the sea, in a zone about four miles wide. Although the flights were confined to this corridor, the Chinese often complained that the planes had strayed. Each time they lodged a formal complaint it was necessary to diplomatically soothe ruffled feelings. In reality, the Chinese officials often went so far as to admit that they felt safer with the American planes scouting around.

The Marine pilots flew Jennys on regular reconnaissance patrols over Chiang Kai-shek's army. "In a year and a half, the Marine fighter squadrons marked up 3,818 sorties."[26]

One of the Brigades' missions was to show the American flag conspicuously. In doing this, Butler made particular use of his aviation, which was still a novelty among all the armed forces in China, native or western. One of the General Butler's demonstrations had a spectacular climax:

> During an exhibition of stunting, Captain James T. Moore zoomed over the crowds, went into a spectacular climbing roll, lost both wings off his plane and parachuted into a moat in front of the stands. "Trust Smedley," a lady spectator commented. "He always puts on a wonderful show."[27]

All the duty was not dull garrison duty. On the day before Christmas, 1927, a fire broke out in the Standard Oil Company plant in Tien-Tsin. A large portion of the Brigades' gasoline, oil and other supplies were stored in the Socony plant warehouses. The fire, the most spectacular in the history of Tien-Tsin, nearly destroyed the $25,000,000 plant.

Within nine minutes after the alarm sounded, a battalion of Marines was on the spot to fight the fire. Said a *New York Times* report, "General Butler personally directed the troops, and the Chinese, British, French and Italian fire brigades in fighting the blaze...."[28]

In a biography, Butler later recalled:

I found two big warehouses blazing. Twenty feet away was another warehouse filled with gasoline. Near-by were six three million-gallon oil tanks. If they exploded, the destruction and disaster would have been terrific. I sent a hurry call for a thousand more Marines.

By the middle of the afternoon we had two thousand Marines fighting like — well, like Marines. They built a firewall sixteen feet high, of earth, empty drums, iron doors and other non-flammable material, between the burning warehouses and the stores of gasoline. They also removed all the cases of oil and gasoline from the adjoining buildings. By nightfall, the fire was under control. One hundred and fifty men continued to fight the fire, however, and one hundred guarded the gasoline and oil piled in open storage.

At three o'clock Christmas morning the main drain of the plant blew up and a giant stream of burning oil spouted forth and spread over the river. The Marines spent Christmas Day building a bulkhead around the mouth of the drain. At midnight an ice jam came down the river with the ebb tide and carried away part of the bulkhead. The river was again covered with burning oil. It was four days before the fire was put out.[29]

The *Times* reported, "The fire followed the explosion of a Chinese ammunition dump and two large fires in the British Concession the night before last, evoking theories of an incendiary campaign.

"The fire broke out in the company's candle factory, where thousands of tons of paraffin wax in wood cases burned all day yesterday and practically all night."[30]

During the heavy rains of 1928, one of the major bridges on the highway between Tien-Tsin and Peking was washed out. Since the highway was the planned evacuation route of the Americans in Peking, Butler sent Marine engineers to rebuild the bridge. "The Chinese were amazed at the speed with which the work was completed and delighted to have the bridge."[31]

To further promote good relations, the Marine engineers — using artillery tractors, homemade road drags and five hundred Marines — also put sixteen miles of road in good condition.

When the road was opened, hundreds of distinguished guests including the governor of the province attended the ceremony. Chinese General Fu Tso-yi reviewed the Marines and Butler in turn reviewed the generals' troops.

For this road work, the village elders conferred on Butler the "Umbrella of Blessings." The following report of the ceremony is taken from the *New York Times:*

"UMBRELLA OF BLESSINGS"
CONFERRED ON GEN. BUTLER

Commander of United States Marines Is First
Foreigner to Receive This Chinese Honor.
Tien-Tsin.

The ceremonial "Umbrella of Ten Thousand Blessings," accompanied by two "honorary banners," has been bestowed upon Brig. Gen. Smedley D. Butler, commander of the United States Marines in China, by the native citizens of Ta Chih Ku, a suburb of Tien-Tsin. The Umbrella with Banners has never before been conferred upon a foreigner.

According to immemorial Chinese customs, this honor can be bestowed only by unanimous vote of the residents of a city. Ta Chih Ku, which has a population of 40,000 people, put the question to a vote, and there was no dissenting voice raised. The award was made because of General Butler's service in promoting goodwill between China and America, and because of the assistance the American Marines under his command have given toward maintaining order in this region.

Sewn upon the Umbrella, a magnificent affair of red satin inscribed with complimentary characters, are 200 tags, each about an inch wide and six inches long, bearing the names of the 200 Elders of Ta Chih Ku who made the presentation. These Elders, in long ceremonial gowns, marched through the streets of Tien-Tsin with the Umbrella and Banners, and made the formal presentation at General Butler's headquarters.

The inscription on one of the banners says, "The Chinese love General Butler as they love China." The second banner is inscribed, "General Butler loves China as he loves America."

By an odd coincidence Ta Chih Ku, known as "The Boxer Village," was the scene of some of the most severe fighting between the Chinese and the Allies in the summer of 1900.

Recalling those days General Butler said, recently; An example of the way in which General Butler has earned the friendship of the Chinese occurred there days ago. Heavy rains had washed out a bridge on the motor highway between Peking and Tien-Tsin. General Butler sent some Marine engineers out to the place where the road had been cut, and in less than two hours, a new bridge was in place. The Chinese officials who watched the work marveled. "It would have taken us two months to build such a bridge," they said, "and now we have no money, so if the Americans had not built it the road would have remained useless."[32]

During his acceptance speech, Butler remarked that during the Boxer Rebellion of 1900 he had participated in an attack on their village.

The residents and merchants of Ta Chih Ku (Boxer Village) presenting the Blessing Umbrella to General Butler, September 5, 1928. (Department of Defense [Marine Corps] photograph.)

Afterwards Butler noticed five old men, standing with their hands up their sleeves, talking and smiling a little. "I turned to the interpreter who was translating my remarks. 'Have I said anything to offend them?'

"He went over to investigate, and came back laughing. 'Those old men were in the crowd of Boxers that shot you up in 1900.'"[33]

During the spring and summer of 1928, the Nationalist forces, under the command of Generalissimo Chiang Kai-shek, occupied Peking. The capital of China was then moved to Nanking. Peking was renamed Peiping.[34] This gave the Nationalists control over practically all of China.

On 25 July 1928, the United States became the first of the foreign powers to sign a tariff treaty with Chiang Kai-shek's government in Nanking. After Chiang became president of China on 16 October, China had quieted sufficiently to permit the return of the Third Brigade to the States.

In January 1929, the Third Brigade returned to its home country, leaving the protection of United States interests in China to a strengthened

General Butler and Blessing Umbrella, 1928. (Department of Defense [Marine Corps] photograph.)

Fourth Marine Regiment in Shanghai, the Fifteenth Infantry in Tien-Tsin and the Peking Embassy Guard in Peking.

The Third Brigade's mission was not only to protect the American citizens and their property, but to also promote good will. Apparently, the Marines did just that. "The Chinese children expressed approval by sticking up their thumbs and calling, '*Ding How.*' If they didn't like something they said, '*Boo How,*' with thumbs down. The Marines were in such good standing around Tien-Tsin that the children put up their thumbs and shouted '*Ding How*' every time they saw a Marine."[35]

When the Brigade left Tien-Tsin, "great electric signs were erected, flashing China's last word to us: "Good-by and Good Luck, Marines."[36]

Before Butler left China, he received a second "Blessing Umbrella" for preventing a bandit brigade from looting a village.

The Nationalist Government continued to strengthen its hold over the entire country, and except for the communist-bandit activities, there was peace in China until 1931.

11

The End of an Era—
The Old China Marine

The Nationalist Government grew stronger in all of China and, except for the communist-bandit activities, mainly in the north, there was a better prospect for unity and peace by 1931 than at any time during the previous ten years.

Japan, however, continued to be a thorn in China's side. It probably can be said that their trouble started in 1910 when Japan annexed Korea during World War I. In addition, once Germany became involved in World War I, she lost her concessions in China as well as her island colonies in the Central Pacific. With Germany involved elsewhere, Japan not only took over the German Concessions in Shantung Province but also Germany's islands in the Pacific. The Allied Powers engaged in World War II were not prepared to stop the Japanese. Later, after China bowed to Japan's Twenty-one Demands in 1915, it was too late, a new era had opened up in Asia. Japan, hungry for an empire, was in the position to exploit all the advantages gained during World War I.

Using Korea as a base of operations, Japan seized Manchuria in September 1931, and made it a puppet state called Manchukuo. Manchukuo became the stamping ground of the warlord Chang Tsu-lin. Japan, ignoring protests from the League of Nations, eventually dropped out of the League in March 1933. The United States did not intervene to stop Japan's aggression.

The separating of Manchuria from China aroused strong anti–Japanese feelings throughout China that resulted in the Chinese boycotting Japanese goods. This, in turn, led to mobs against the Japanese businesses and her citizens. Eventually, there was a confrontation between the Chinese and the Japanese armies in the Chapel District in Shanghai in January 1932. The Chinese army stoutly resisted the Japanese, forcing the Japanese to bring in some 50,000 troops to face the Chinese opposition. Finally, the Chinese were forced to retire on 3 March, which put an end to hostilities. The Japanese, however, continued to dominate the area.

During this conflict, the foreign powers brought in reinforcements to protect the International Settlement in Shanghai. For their part, the Fourth Marines, reinforced by 334 Marines from the Philippines, the Marine detachment from the USS *Houston* and the Army's Thirty-first Infantry, helped other foreign powers defend the International Settlement.

The emergency ended in June 1932, the reinforcements in the Shanghai were withdrawn and the situation returned to normal. During this conflict, very little unrest, if any, affected the legation guards in Peiping.

In fact, the Marines had settled down to garrison duty. They had plenty of time on their hands and life was comfortable. Each squad of men had a roomboy to keep their quarters ship-shape, press their uniforms, shine leather goods and take care of other personal duties. For the services

Colonel Presley M. Rixey, USMC, commanding, reviews the guard detachment. The parade takes place at the Polo Field or French Glacis, as it was called. Hata Men Street is in the background. Peiping, circa 1934–35. (Department of Defense [Marine Corps] photograph.)

of the roomboy and laundry, each man of the squad was charged about a dollar a month. The company clerk collected the dollar at the pay table at the beginning of each month. As for the other mundane chores, such as mess duty, cooking, baking, keeping the compounds clean, and like duties, the Marine Corps employed Chinese. Qualified Marines supervised these Chinese laborers. The only thing required of a Marine was that he take care of his rifle and other military equipment, make formations and parades, perform guard duty, and compete in athletics and training.

Liberty was the best. Besides sight seeing, the Marines' main source of entertainment was visiting cabarets. Each cabaret had its own bevy of taxi dancers. The taxi dancers were usually Chinese, Korean, or Russian girls. The Russian girls were all descendants of people exiled from Russia after the Revolution. In China they were referred to as "White Russians" because that was the faction that opposed the Red Communists. For the young Marines serving on a twenty-four month tour of duty, the girls in their long, svelte tunics slit up to the knee, sitting at tables delicately nibbling at dried melon seeds, helped to relieve the boredom of military duties.

In Peiping, another place the Marines patronized was Hemple's Restaurant located on Hataman Street. The restaurant was advertised as "Hemple's Hotel and Restaurant, Butchery & Sausage Factory. The only foreign butchery in Peiping." A big red jug sign hung outside the front door. Underneath the sign was written, "You can't beat Hemple's meat on Hataman Street."

A German named Hemple originally owned the restaurant. As time passed, however, Pa Hemple died and Frank E. Gowen, an ex–Marine that had married Hemple's daughter Olga, bought the restaurant. Later, in 1935, A.J. Herrick, another ex–Marine, bought half interest in the restaurant. But all that history really has nothing to do with the Round Table.

When you entered Hemple's you might think you were in a butcher shop. Walk through the butcher shop and you emerged into a cozy, cheerful little bar and eatery that might have been lifted out of San Francisco.

Marines went there to drink beer or anything else they could pay for; it was a well known hang out for a select few noncommissioned officers of the legation guard who met there twice a week in camaraderie to guzzle the suds in good cheer. There men gathered around a round table in a back room that eventually became known as the Round Table. Frank Gowen served as keeper of the Round Table on behalf of the men, who were known as the Knight of the Round Table. As time passed, a constitution with bylaws was drawn up. Membership was by invitation only. Consequently, the Knights of the Round Table became known throughout the Marine Corps. As specified by the constitution, once a Marine became a member of the club, a silver nameplate was set into the surface of the tabletop. When a member died the silver nameplate was replaced with a gold one. In those days the *Leatherneck* magazine published a list of all deceased Marines. The members stations in Peiping monthly scanned the *Leatherneck's* list of deceased Marines to determine whose nameplate needed to be changed. When the silver nameplate was changed to a gold one, the members toasted the departed with steins of beer. After the first toast, there would be another and another. It made no difference if the departed was a nice guy or an S.O.B.; he was remembered and toasted anyway. A list of the Knights of the Round Table with the years of their deaths can be found in Appendix K.

The typical pay for a private was $21 a month. A Marine could buy a steak for about ten cents, a fifth of Johnny Walker Black Label for less than a dollar, and beer was two cents a quart. The duty in North China, like that of the Fourth Marines in Shanghai, was considered one of the best posts in the Marine Corps.

In North China, civil war between the Nationalist Government and the Communists continued. Warlords in Western China grew stronger and gave Chiang trouble. This internal strife prevented China from presenting a united front against Japan. For the legation guards, these incidents were more a nuisance than anything else.

After Japan succeeded in cutting off Manchuria from China in 1931–32, she kept continuous pressure against North China to bring the area under her control. The province of Jehol was separated from China in 1933, Chahar Province in June 1936, and later, four other provinces were dominated. Chiang, busy with his civil war with the Communists, was not able to confront the Japanese and left them in control of Manchuria and the northern provinces.

Early in 1936, Japan walked out of the Second London Conference on naval strength and in November Japan signed a treaty with Nazi Germany.

The following month, some of Chiang's own military colleagues kidnapped and held him until he agreed to end the civil war with the Communists and fight Japan on a united front. Ironically, the man who negotiated for a common front against the Japanese was the Communist leader Chou En-lai.

It might be said that the Second Sino-Japanese War started at the Marco Polo Bridge near the small town of Lukouchiao outside Peiping on the summer night of 7 July 1937, when the Japanese troops on field maneuvers clashed with Chinese troops.

The serious clash between Chinese and Japanese troops on the outskirts of Peiping called attention to the extraordinary situation that made it possible for Japanese army maneuvers near the capital of North China.

On 16 January 1901, China signed a protocol containing twelve articles, one of which acknowledged the right of each foreign power to maintain a permanent guard for its legation, while denying the Chinese the right to reside in the Legation Quarter. These provisions were then included in the September 1901 Boxer Protocol, along with other military related articles. A note of 15 July 1902 elaborated on the Protocol of 1901, adding that foreign troops would have the right to carry out field exercises and rifle practice without informing the Chinese government.

By the subsequent Hopei-Chahar agreement with the quasi-autonomous Provincial Government, the Japanese were also permitted an army headquarters at Tien-Tsin.

While the Nationalist government in North China was weakened by the unrest in the south, Japan capitalized on these agreements and increased their armed forces in the North China to some 10,000 men. This increase of Japanese troops near Peiping was similar to that in Manchuria before the Mukden incident in 1931.

The Twenty-ninth Chinese Army prepared to defend the city of Peiping to the last man. The gates leading into the city were barricaded and sandbag machine gun emplacements were erected. Machine gun emplacements were also erected at critical street intersections throughout the city. Although the Chinese General Sun Cheh-Yuan stated he could handle the Japanese outbreak, without reinforcement he was unable to do so.

The foreign legation guards in Peiping found themselves in the midst of fighting around the city but successfully avoided being drawn into it.

Coupled with the fear that the Japanese might bomb and take the city of Peiping by force was also the fear that the Chinese army might also take action against the Japanese in the Legation Quarter.

Colonel John Marston, who had relieved Colonel Alexander A. Vandegrift on 6 March 1937, was in command of the legation guard detachment when the hostility broke out. Colonel Marston handled the coming situation, which was similar to no other in the recent history of the Marine Corps, with the good old Marine Corps "Situation Well in Hand" spirit.

In the Marine compound the morning following the fighting at Marco Polo Bridge, there was talk of the fighting but no one knew how serious it was. The enlisted men first realized that something was amiss when liberty was curtailed. For the next few days there was no liberty except in the Legation Quarter or on Tartar Wall, which was adjacent to the Marine Compound. Tartar Wall overlooked the railroad station and the Chinese

City and was an excellent observation point for what was going on outside the Legation Quarter.

The Legation Quarter immediately assumed a "state of preparedness." In addition to the regular guard posts, Marines, according to plans, manned the walls and gates of their sector of the Legation Quarter.

The British, French, Italians, and Japanese embassy guards also manned their sector of the Legation Quarter Walls. Each nationality assumed command of their sectors. There was, however, a senior ranking officer and his staff in overall command. The Japanese, naturally, exercised a stricter routine than the rest of the legation guards. Everything was friendly, however, and there was no discord in carrying out the plans for the defense of the Legation Quarter.

During this period, there was much activity in the Headquarters Company. Scuttlebutt had it that the American nationals were going to be "called in."

At the time there were some 800 American nationals living in Peiping. According to preexisting plans, the American nationals would be informed of a "call in" by hoisting signal flags to the top of the 300-foot radio tower by day, to be replaced by signal lights at night.

With preparation complete, on the morning of 28 July, it was considered well to "bring in the nationals." For the first time since the Boxer Rebellion, the flags were run up on the radio tower, and trucks and the members of the Mounted Detachment went out in the city to do their prearranged work.

One incident marred what would have been a flawless operation. During the morning a small mounted detachment was proceeding along the streets of the city when a newly arrived detachment of Chinese troops, entrenched behind sandbags on one of the main streets, failed to recognize the American uniform and opened fire. The patrol turned aside, but before they had filed off the street a stray bullet struck Private Julius F. Fliszar in the thigh. Fliszar was brought to the sick bay and treated. A military magazine reported, "Now he is running around as though nothing had ever happened. In fact, he recently extended his enlistment in order to stay in Peiping."[1]

After this incident, American flags were prominently displayed on all official and civilian vehicles, including bicycles, rickshas and coal carts pulled by donkeys. To prevent a reoccurrence of such an incident, the Mounted Detachment proceeded in trucks to carry out their duties.

According to an article in the January 1938 issue of *Leatherneck*, "The 28th was a busy day. The bandsmen erected tents for themselves on the western compound lawn, and moved into them to leave their own barracks for occupation by civilians. The entire east barracks were vacated by the Headquarters Detachment.... Tents were erected in the eastern part of the compound lawn, and in all sections of American Embassy Compound." Also, various billets were made available in the Legation Quarter, mostly in the private homes of members of the diplomatic corps, or of officers of the detachment. Trucks, automobiles, carts, rickshas, bicycles—all these came in with our nationals.

Old people, young people, men and women, children, babies, missionaries, Eurasians, Chinese and Russian wives of Americans, amahs [nannies for western children], servants—all these came in. One man and woman brought nine children and a goat to give milk for the youngest. All had to be taken care of and fed.

About 435 American people moved into the Legation Quarter, of whom 350 were quartered in the Embassy and Guard Compounds proper, or elsewhere, but under control of the Billeting Officer.

The busiest place in the Marine Compound that morning was the Billeting Office. Company clerks augmented the regular staff of Major James L. Denham, the Pay Officer, and Mr. George W. Stahl, Chief Pay Clerk, who were the designated Billeting Officers. Because of earlier preparations, billeting went smoothly, the nationals found their quarters, and by nightfall things gradually settled down.

Thereafter, there was a change in the life in the Marine Compound. No longer was it a military compound. Now, an air of festivity prevailed. American Nationals in civilian clothes paraded about the compound. Children played on the glacis (an open area adjacent to the Marine compound that provided a field of fire if the compound came under attack) where Marines once drilled and trained. In Johnson Hall, the Marines' gymnasium and movie palace, clotheslines were draped with drying children's wear and feminine attire. Chow formations were shared with civilian men, women and children.

Gradually the Marines became acquainted with these changes and settled down to enjoy the discomfort of living in tents. Later, one Marine wrote:

> We gradually became acquainted with some of the people, and everyone seemed to enjoy the stay. In the evenings the band would play concerts, and later in the evening we would group around the bandstand, lolling on the lawn and have an informal good time, to the accompaniment of the accordions, violins, guitars, that various of the men would break out for the enjoyment of the crowd. These little informal "carryings on" in the long, warm evenings were something we shall never forget. They showed that Marines could have a helluva good time even if there were no liberty! And, after all, we did

Saturday Parade. Battalion in mass formation, circa 1938–39. (Department of Defense [Marine Corps] photograph.)

become acquainted with some of the charming young American girls! And there was always the moonlit glacis (field, to you) about which to walk with the right companions. And chairs here and there in which to rest, talk, and sip cool drinks. No, we didn't have such a bad time at all, we Peking Marines, during those "Days of the Nationals." Also, the weather was perfect—a trifle on the hot side, perhaps, but with splendid long twilit evenings when just the right sort of cool breezes came along. And the swimming pool was going full blast, with a swimming meet being put on the 2nd of August.[2]

During this time, the Marines' sector of Tartar Wall was frequented more by Marines than during any other time. To get away from the close confinement of the Compound, Marines often took walks along the top of the wall. Tartar Wall was some fifty feet wide with a stone road running down the middle. The road was wide enough for a horse and carriage. Grassy borders on either side were wide enough for a couple of squads' fronts, standing in line. Dodging a few cattle that were sometimes taken there to graze, and the lone goat, which had come into the Compound along with the baby for whom it furnished milk, they were able to get in sorely needed physical exercise.

All was not beer and skittles for the Marines.[3] During this time the Marines had been in the "state of preparedness." Various military plans for the defense of the Legation Quarter required extra guards and guards on post that had not previously existed. There were the Legation Quarter gates under the American sector to be taken care of, Tartar Wall as a vantage point for observations, the radio station, and other places that had to be kept under special watch.

The Naval Radio Station handled thousands of word groups for both officials and civilians. For the period of July–August–September, the station handled 1,331,653 words, six times the normal traffic for the detachment. During the time the Chinese telegraph system was not available, members of the detachment as well as civilians were permitted to send messages to their families in the States. The station also handled dispatches for American correspondents during the crisis. For one twenty-four hour period, the radio was the only communication channel out of Peiping; this included other foreign detachments.

"Captain John F. Hough and Chief Radio Electrician Mars W. Palmer, and every one of the signal men deserve great credit for their performance of duty under stress."[4] The Radio Detachment, Station NPP, had three circuits. The first circuit was a "High Frequency–Short Wave" circuit and was in communication with NOP, Cavite, Philippine Islands.

The second circuit was known as the "Intermediate Frequency" and it communicated with the ships of the Asiatic Fleet. The Third Circuit, a "High Frequency–Short Wave" was known as the CinC Circuit. It was used for training radio operators and was manned continuously. The operators copied all messages heard on the frequency as well as press matters. It was from this circuit that the legation guards received the daily news and sports scores.

The fighting for North China took place outside the walled city of Peiping. While the rumble of artillery and the sharp report of small arms fire were heard, the city remained relatively quiet. Although the city was crowded with refugees fleeing the fighting, the Twenty-ninth Chinese Army, which had occupied Peiping at the outset of the struggle, kept order in the city.

In fact, according to the *New York Times*, "The Japanese military authorities assured the United States Embassy today that the Japanese Army under no conditions would bombard Peiping either by artillery or from the air, thus alleviating the fears of American officials for the safety of their nationals."[5]

During this time, the Nationalist Government did not send reinforcements from the south. After several days of fighting, the Chinese began to use their policy of "retreat to win" and gradually withdrew from the city and North China.

On 8 August 1937, Japanese General Kawabe Shozo at the head of some 3,000 troops entered the city and took command. Consequently, with a comparatively small force, Japan took possession of the Peiping–Tien-Tsin Railway. With reinforcement brought down from Manchuria, Japan set up a military rule in North China and began to extend their conquest to the west and south.

When the Twenty-ninth Chinese Army marched out of the city and the Japanese Army replaced them, there was some apprehension on the part of the foreign population as to what would take place next. Although the Japanese treated the Chinese badly, there were few restrictions on the foreign westerners.

Finally, it was deemed safe enough for the American nationals to return to their homes. With the departure of the last of the American nationals at 1400 hours on 3 August 1937, the Refugee Camp was closed.

Gradually the Marine Detachment resumed normal routine. Liberty, expiring at nine or ten o'clock, was granted to fifty percent of the command, however, the privilege of wearing of civilian clothes was withheld. As one Marine wrote, "The city is so nearly normal —'the safest place in China'— that we hope that privileges will shortly be restored."[6]

The winter training hikes to the rifle range were resumed. These were not only conditioning hikes but they also permitted training in squad tactics. With the resumption of normal duty, the athletic programs again got underway. The event most looked forward to was the competition against other legation guards in the yearly International Track and Field Meet. On 15 September, the Marine detachment held its Inter-Company Track Meet to select the athletes who would represent them in the track meet. Upon completion of the inter-company meet, the Marines were confident they had the International Meet "in the bag." The Marine detachment met the British, French and Italian legation guards in the International Meet on 17, 18, 19 October. Despite the fact that training had been hampered by the recent conflict, the games proved to be interesting and exciting. The Marines took the 1937 meet handily.

The rifle range in North China was normally opened from May until October, inclusive. Before and after those months there was both too much wind and dust, or too biting a cold. In this short range season, it was necessary to prepare and train the men to qualify with the rifle. Despite the recent conflict between the Japanese and the Chinese, the Marines managed to prepare and train three line companies and what was probably one of he largest Headquarters Detachments in the Corps. On completion of

Marines returning from a conditioning hike through the back gate of the Marine Compound, 1941. Note field scarves (ties). In the background are the Tartar Wall and the ammunition magazine. To the left is the Quarter Deck, where rank and file checked out on liberty. The post brig was also located there. (Photograph from the author's collection.)

the range season, the command as a whole had 103 Expert Riflemen, 211 Sharpshooters, 170 Marksmen, and 30 unqualified, out of a total of 514 men. The detachment was quite proud of this record.

Although the detachment managed to squeeze in their rifle qualifications, they could not manage the annual field maneuvers at Peitaiho Beach. Normally during the summer, each company spent about three weeks at Peitaiho Beach, which was adjacent to the Army's Camp Burrough (sometimes spelled Barrows) near Tien-Tsin. The Marines used it for training in field maneuvers and healthful recreation. The terrain of sandy hummocks was excellent for field maneuvers. Hiking around the bay to Camp Burrough, the Marines fired the 37mm howitzer with which they were armed. The first company to arrive set the camp up and at the end of the season, the last company dismantled the camp.

Because of the growing political tension in the Far East, early in 1938 the United States relieved the Army Fifteenth Infantry of its duties in Tien-Tsin and returned it to the United States. The regiment was replaced with

Top: Tien-Tsin, China. Changing of the Guard. A Marine relieves a soldier on post at the main entrance of the Marine Compound. *Bottom:* Marine Detachment Compound in Tien-Tsin. When the Marines relieved the Army, they took over the former Army quarters. (Marine Corps University Archives, Quantico, Virginia.)

a headquarters detachment and two companies of Marines. At the time, the Fifteenth Infantry's strength had been reduced from over a thousand men to less than nine hundred.

On 1 March 1938, Charlie Company from Peiping arrived in Tien-Tsin and took up quarters in the Fifteenth Infantry Compound. The next morning at 0400 hours the company took over the guard from the Fifteenth Infantry. Lieutenant Goen was the first Officer of the Day and Private B.B. Collins was credited as the first sentry posted. Captain William W. Orr commanded the company and Lieutenants Roger W. Beadle and Odell M. Conoley were the company officers. Charlie Company was a line company with 37mm howitzers and 60mm Stokes Trench Mortars as auxiliary weapons.

Dog Company came into being with the departure of the Fifteenth Infantry from Tien-Tsin. The first platoon of Dog Company was made up from men taken from Able and Baker Companies in Peiping. The second platoon was formed from the famous Mounted Detachment, which was disbanded at the time, as well as men from Able and Baker. At its formation, Dog Company was under the command of Lieutenant Trachita with Platoon Sergeant "Jim" Garris as acting first sergeant. Later, Captain Kirk took command with First Sergeant Henderson as "Topkick." Lieutenants Trachita and Chidester were platoon leaders of the first and second platoon respectively. Although a line company, Dog Company's auxiliary weapons were the Browning water- cooled heavy machine guns.

With the Headquarters Detachment, the Marine Detachment in Tien-Tsin totaled some 200 men and officers. Captain Bean first commanded the Tien-Tsin Detachment. Later, Lieutenant Colonel William C. James relieved Captain Bean, who returned to Peiping.

Arriving in Tien-Tsin, the Marines from Peiping expected to see a city much like the city they just left — an ancient city of "Old China." Instead, they found a modern city — theaters, roller skating rinks, *hai alai*, taxi cabs and many other modern conveniences— just like Stateside. It was a great change from the old walled city of Peiping.

When disbanded, the famous Mounted Detachment made the headlines in the *New York Times.*

American "Horse Marines"
at Peiping Are Disbanded

by the Associated Press

PEIPING, China, Feb. 22.— This world's only "horse Marines" passed out of existence here today. This mounted detachment of the United States Embassy Marine guard passed in review before a record

The last Blue Parade of the Battalion and Mounted Detachment, February 22, 1938. The ice skating rink in the background was constructed of poles, grass mats and ropes. No nails were used in its construction. In the far background is Tartar Wall with the Chien Men Pagoda. (Marine Corps University Archives, Quantico, Virginia.)

crowd of Americans and other foreigners at Breckenridge Field before disbanding forever. The "horse Marines," thirty expert sabermen, all crack pistol and rifle shots, organized in 1912 to protect Americans outside the embassy quarter in Peiping. It has been decided to split the Peiping embassy guard, transferring half its personnel to Tien-Tsin to replace the departing Fifteenth Infantry. The men will be absorbed into other regular Marine combat units. Some of the stocky Mongolian ponies will be retained here and at Tien-Tsin. The rest will be sold to American officers and other non–Chinese for riding....[7]

MARINES ON HORSEBACK

Sad as it may be, the old order changeth, giving place to new. It must have surprised many to learn that the United States Government has just abolished its Horse Marines, a military body which was generally thought to be mythical. But we had them and, of all places, in Peiping, China.

In 1912 thirty of the Marines stationed there were mounted to give quick protection to Americans living outside the embassy zone.

All were expert sabermen and crack rifle and pistol shots, and it is a safe bet that their commander, what-ever his name may have been, was called Captain Jinks. It may be that the need for them has passed, and it may be that this undeclared war in China has exhausted the supply of corn and beans for Captain Jinks' horse.[8]

To First Lieutenant David M. Randall fell the honor of being the first commander of the Peiping Mounted Marines. To Second Lieutenant DeWolf Schatzel fell the honor of being their last. In between these two, several officers, some who later became legends in the Corps, held the command.

CAMP HOLCOMB

The Tien-Tsin Marine 1940 Annual described the Marines' camp. Camp Barrows, U.S. Army, Chinwangtao, China, was taken over by the U.S. Marines in March 1938, and renamed Camp Holcomb in honor of the Major General Commandant. Platoon Sergeant Crecion with of twenty men from the Legation Guard, Peking, took possession. Since that time, Lieutenant K.F. McLeod and Second Lieutenant R. L. Vroome have been commanding officers.

The Camp occupies a stretch of sandy ground on the shores of Chihli Bay, it is owned by the Kailan Mining Administration and is about three miles from their docks. The excellent rifle range boasts a 1,000 yard firing point. The permanent detachment barracks and mess hall are of brick construction. In the summer, the single stone house is used as a club for officers and their families. In winter, it is the C.O. hermitage. A group of about twenty-five cottages house officers and their families. Visiting details live in tents in an area provided for that purpose.

The Tien-Tsin Post Exchange maintains a branch at the camp during summer, which often proves more profitable than the home store. Mr. Wa runs a restaurant on the reservation. His star performer is the famous "one armed bandit", but bull sessions and beer drinking are also poplar. The native city of Chinwangtao is out of bounds but those who must make a liberty provide themselves with general merchandise and ship supplies at T.T. Wang's Emporium. The men have the freedom of the K.M.A. City and are invited to their club twice a week for movies.

The Navy has priority in the use of the range, but the Fourth Marines actually use it most. Moreover, the Permanent Detachment is under Tien-Tsin Command. Company "C" furnishes the complement. Camp Holcomb is variously known as the Co. "C" Beach Club, sanitarium, or concentration camp depending on one's viewpoint and the season of the year.[9]

The Tien-Tsin Flood

The Marine Detachment had not been long in Tien-Tsin before disaster struck. For several weeks before the flooding of Tien-Tsin on Sunday, August 10, 1939, there had been heavy rains in the watershed region north and west of Tien-Tsin. At the same time, Tien-Tsin proper had been experiencing one of the driest summer seasons in years. The excessive water from the back country seemed to be effectively controlled by the protective dikes to the south and west of the city. The floodwater was being carried off by the Hai Ho River, which passed through Tien-Tsin. In fact, on Saturday, August 19, it had been reliably reported that these dikes would hold and that the conditions of the Hai Ho River were not alarming.

At about 0700 hours Sunday morning, August 20, Colonel William G. Hawthorne, the commanding officer, received a report that the dikes outside of the city were giving way and that the flood waters would probably be two or three feet deep in the vicinity of the Marine Compound. Liberty was canceled, all officers were called into the compound and steps were taken to prevent damage to government property.

Work was started to move stores and equipment in basements to second floors of buildings in the compound. Chinese masons were hired and Marines that had previous experience in brick laying began building barriers to block all entrances to the compound. A reliable gauge to the seriousness of the situation was the continuous stream of Chinese refugees passing the Marine compound, seeking safety on the high ground in some of the foreign concessions.

When the noon mealtime approached, no regular mess formation was held. All working parties were needed to save the property in the compound. Instead, working parties ate during intervals when they could be spared from their labors. By 1300 hours, to protect the power plant and ice plant, a barricade some three feet high had been built to keep the water out.

All available containers were filled with water and stored in safe places as a precaution against the possible contamination by the floodwaters.

From 1300 to 1500 hours, work details labored constructing barriers at the entrances to the Marine compound. As water continued to rise on "Can Do" Field, it was necessary to move twelve steers and twelve calves, corralled there as a reserve meat supply, into the main compound, as well as six horses owned by officers. Later, the horses were moved to high ground elsewhere in the city. The steers and calves along with their fodder were later moved into the second floor of one of the barracks.

When the floodwaters continued to rise and it appeared that the bakeshop would be flooded, the bakers filled the ovens with bread. Fortunately, they were able to complete baking the bread and storing it in the mess hall before the flood waters reached a level that made it necessary to pull the fires in the ovens.

As the water continued to rise, the supply of 1,500 gallons of gasoline in five-gallon tins, stored in the quartermaster building as a reserve in anticipation of further Japanese restrictions at the barricades, was removed from the basement and stored at a higher locality.

By 1630 hours, water in the street outside the Marine compound had reached a depth of about one foot. While barricades at the entrances were keeping an influx of water from entering the compound, water had begun to seep through the porous ground and force its way into the compound. It was apparent that it would be only a matter of time before the entire compound was flooded.

Work continued throughout the night to move supplies and equipment into second floors. Details moved the ammunition from the magazine to the second floor of the administration building. As the water seeped into the compound, extra effort was made to save the power plant and the cold storage installations. By 1800 hours, the water outside the compound had reached a level of two feet. Because of seepage, the water inside the compound continued to rise. A portable gasoline pump was floated on a raft to the power plant where the steam pumps were working to empty the water that was coming up through the brick and cement floor.

As night fell, it was noticed that there was no electricity in the British Concession. The Marine compound still had electrical power supplied by the First Special Area, which was controlled by the Japanese.

By 2115 hours, the water in the compound had reached the depth of about two feet and had reached the two lower boilers in the power plant. The fires in these two boilers had to be pulled. The third boiler, which had a slightly higher grate, was lighted off to keep the steam pumps going. This pump would operate the cold storage installation which contained about 7,000 pounds of fresh beef and other stores.

To prevent a possible shorting of the electrical system, which was in subterranean conducts, the lights in the compound were shut off shortly after midnight on 21 August, but work continued by kerosene lanterns.

The vehicles in the compound, including three privately owned automobiles belonging to officers of the Marine Detachment in Peiping, were raised by jacks well above flood level and placed on platforms built of six-by-six timbers. Most of this work was done under water and without adequate lights.

Shortly after midnight, one third of the detachment was released from work details and permitted to get some rest. The remainder of the men did not get to sleep until around 1600 hours on 21 August.

At midnight on 20 August, the water level at the guard house gate was thirty-three inches.

During the night the radiomen moved the radio equipment to the second floor of a building in the compound and set up the emergency radio equipment. Later the regular radio receivers and transmitters were placed in operation using a heavy-duty gasoline engine to furnish power. The radio station no longer had to rely on outside electrical power.

By 1600 hours on 21 August, the water level in the compound had reached the same level as that at the main gate guardhouse. The effort to save the water pumping station failed when water seepage flooded the motors. When working parties were forced to pull the fires in the last boiler, and the power plant and refrigeration installations were shut down.

With some three feet of water in the compound and more outside the main gate, working parties set to work building flat-bottom boats with a six-man capacity. This enabled the Marines to move about the compound without wading in the floodwaters. During the flood, a dozen or more of these flat-bottom boats were built. In addition, the Quartermaster hired two Chinese sampans to facilitate moving about the city.

During the flood of August 1939 in Tien-Tsin, all Marine activities moved into the second floor of their barracks. Catwalks were necessary to move about the compound. This photograph shows a Marine on watch at the main gate of the compound. (Marine Corps University Archives, Quantico, Virginia.)

To reduce to a minimum the amount of time that personnel had to spend in the floodwaters, working parties also constructed ramps connecting various buildings within the compound.

The floodwaters were rapidly becoming contaminated. The guard at the main gate of the compound reported that corpses and coffins from the nearby cemetery were floating by the gate.

Following breakfast on 21 August, the routine of the day became flood damage prevention. This routine continued until the flood subsided.

To safeguard the supply of drinking water, the 800 to 1,000 gallons of distilled water in the ice plant tanks was designated as a last reserve and to be used only on orders of the commanding officer. The medical officer established a water-purifying center in the galley to maintain a constant supply of fresh, pure water for the detachment. Later, the galley combined the operation of baking bread and purifying water at night to conserve fuel.

While drinking water was not rationed, water for bathing was. Instead of showers, the men were instructed to take sponge baths from buckets.

With the cold storage facilities closed, and only enough ice for some forty-eight hours, the galley hard-boiled 10,000 water-soaked eggs. Later some 8,000 of these eggs were pickled to prevent spoilage. Several hundred

The Tien-Tsin Flood of 1939. The Marine Compound at this stage of the flood was under about four feet of water. Catwalks and boats of sufficient quantity and capacity had been built. Marines were ordered to stay out of the water, which by this time had reached a filthy state. (Marine Corps University Archives, Quantico, Virginia.)

pounds of fresh beef were also cooked. As the mess hall could use only a small portion before spoilage, the commanding office offered all the beef in excess of the requirements of the command to the British Municipal Police, American nationals, other nationals including Chinese and other relief organizations. It was at this time that the Marines began to provide the Chinese employees their meals, which consisted of rice and beans.

Colonel Hawthorne also offered to furnish inoculations, cooked meals and a supply of fresh water to any American nationals who would come to the compound for these services. Some Americans took advantage of his offer.

By noon on 22 August, the floodwater had reached a depth of 44 inches. Morning and evening colors, using boats, were the only ceremonies that could be performed. Boats were assigned to the guard of the day for posting sentries.

The electrical and telephone lines were no longer serviceable because they were in flooded subterranean conducts. Late in the afternoon of 21 August, the electricians set to work to restore the electrical power to the compound. They strung overhead power lines and connected them to the

Evening colors at Marine Detachment, Tien-Tsin, China, during the flood of August 1939. (Marine Corps University Archives, Quantico, Virginia.)

First Area System, which was still functioning. Once connected, the compound had lights again.

Following suit, the communication personnel, using overhead lines, installed an emergency telephone system connecting all buildings within the compound. Later, the system was extended to the American Consulate in the National City Bank Building on Victoria Road.

Because of the contamination and disease borne by the floodwaters, Marine and naval personnel were given smallpox vaccinations and inoculations against cholera and typhoid.

When the flood conditions were reported to Peiping, the Commanding Officer, Marine Forces in North China, immediately offered to furnish any assistance possible to the Tien-Tsin Marines as well as the American Nationals residing there. This, however, proved easier said than done. To do so, the Commanding Officer, Marine Forces in North China, had to take up the matter with the Japanese Military Authorities in Peiping. Permission was granted to ship relief supplies. However, a note from Japanese Headquarters to the railroad officials certifying the supplies were for relief purposes had to accompany the shipments.

Some medical supplies were sent from Peiping by courier on 21 August. The Peiping Marine detachment later reported by radio that the railroad authorities were allowing only medical supplies and clothing to be sent. The Japanese, through red tape, slowed the shipment of much needed relief supplies. Later, however, the detachment at Peiping was permitted to ship two tons of ice together with fresh fruit and vegetables every other day.

On 21 August, a dispatch was received from the USS *Black Hawk* off Taku Bar. The Commander in Chief of the Asiatic Fleet directed the *Black Hawk* to render assistance to the Marine Detachment at Tien-Tsin. The USS *Finch* and USS *Bitten* also arrived carrying all the rice, sugar, potatoes and other supplies that could be spared by the destroyers at Chefoo.

On 26 August, the USS *Chaumont* arrived with a load of relief supplies. These supplies were transferred to the *Black Hawk*. Once the supplies were transferred, the *Chaumont* returned to Chinwangtao.

On 25 August, Lieutenant W. F. Graf, USN, from Destroyer Group Five, reported to Colonel Hawthorne to coordinate the movement of relief supplies ashore. Meeting with Colonel Hawthorne, plans were developed for moving the relief supplies from the naval ships at Taku Bar to Tien-Tsin.

The Marine Quartermaster negotiated a lease for a godown (warehouse) in the French Concession capable of holding about 20,000 cubic feet of supplies. Relief supplies would be moved to the godown by truck from either the railroad station or the river port. Later, the supplies would be relayed to the Marine compound by sampan. Several trucks were hired to move the supplies once they arrived.

Because the railroad was washed out between Chinwangtao and Tien-Tsin, it was felt the best way to move the relief supplies was up river by boats. The Commander of Destroyer Squadron Five notified Colonel Hawthorne that because the current in the river was from five to seven knots, ship's boats could not be used to move the supplies. Despite the river traffic being subject to gunfire by refugees on the river bank in an attempt to hold up shipping and seize food, Butterfield and Swire Tugboat officials agreed to move the supplies. Butterfield and Swire, however, required armed naval guards be provided to safeguard the supplies in transit. They acknowledged that the armed guards would probably be subjected to gunfire from the riverbanks. The use of armed guards aboard their tugboats would require authorization by the British Consul. After some delay, the British Consulate authorized the armed guards.

The squadron commander further pointed out that the Japanese halted all vessels at Ku Ku Beach about halfway to Tien-Tsin, where the vessels were required to remain overnight for inspection and search; routine customs clearance was also required at Tangku and Tien-Tsin. Because of river hazards and delays, the commander further recommended that forwarding of supplies be withheld until the Marine detachment made arrangements with the Japanese authorities to ensure expediting the movement of supplies from Tankgu to Tien-Tsin without stoppage, search, or delay by the Japanese.

Lieutenant General Homma, the Japanese general commanding the area, assured Colonel Hawthorne that relief supplies would be permitted to come up the river to Tien-Tsin; if shipments were made in foreign bottoms, and with both United States and foreign flags being flown. The general further specified American armed guards must be in each boat. He also wanted to be notified as soon as possible the time the boats departed from Taku Bar and the number of boats making each passage. While assuring that no inspection or search would be made at Ku Ku Beach and Tien-Tsin, he could not guarantee such for Tangku, as that port was under the jurisdiction of the Japanese Provisional Government. He would, however, recommend to that office that any inspections at Tangku be made as speedily as possible. General Homma also authorized the shipment of relief supplies from Chinwangtao. Because the railroad was washed out between Tangku and Tien-Tsin, which would necessitate the transfer of shipments to boats at Tangku, he advised that it was better to ship the relief supplies by boat.

Finally, after many conferences to coordinate authorization from various offices, the shipment of relief supplies got underway.

Once the details were settled, Lieutenant Graf returned to the *Black Hawk* with passes from General Homma, which would ensure there would be no delays of relief supplies at Ku Ku Beach or Tien-Tsin.

By midnight on 26 August, the water level was fifty inches. In the days to follow, the water level would not rise any higher.

The weather continued to be hot and humid. Intermittent showers added to the discomfort caused by the continued hot weather and flood conditions. Clouds of mosquitoes and other insects were everywhere.

Despite the struggle to keep the compound afloat, the command found some time for relaxation. On the night of 22 August, around 2200 hours, a movie was shown in the recreation hall, thereby furnishing the command the first recreation since the flood began. It was well that the command had that short period of relaxation, because on 23 August, the electrical power from the First Special Area was shut off and kerosene lanterns again lighted the compound.

While the negotiations for the movement of relief supplies were going on, means were discussed for the probable evacuation of American citizens to Peiping, Peitaiho and Chinwangtao. Mr. Berger, the American Consul, provided a list of Americans residing within the city. Marine officers were dispatched by sampans to learn who intended to leave and who was going to remain in Tien-Tsin. The officers were also to ascertain the needs of those that remained in the city.

While the official measurement of the water in the city was some fifty inches, elsewhere in some sections the water was eight to ten feet deep. With the primitive sampans or flatboats, it sometimes took officers all day to contact the civilians in their assigned area.

In the majority of the cases, the Americans were well supplied with food. In anticipation of earlier Japanese barricades, which prohibited movement throughout the concessions, food had been collected and stored. A considerable percentage of Americans had received inoculations and vaccinations of one kind or another within the past year. Many were found to have left Tien-Tsin before the flood, and others had moved from the deeply flooded areas to hotels in the higher, drier parts of the city. Only about eleven percent of the Americans visited needed food, which was furnished them.

On 27 August, electrical power was restored to the compound and again the kerosene lanterns were put away. With the electrical power restored, it was again possible to show movies in the recreation hall. The medical department again had power to operate their equipment and refrigeration for medical supplies.

On 28 August, a much need emergency laundry was set up in an empty building adjacent to the mess hall. Up until this time, the rationing of water, except of drinking and cooking, did not permit the washing of clothing. Since the water level had dropped to 45½ inches and was consistently dropping, it was felt that some water could be spared for the laundry.

Colonel A.H. Turnage, Commanding Marine Forces in North China, arrived in Tien-Tsin for a tour of inspection and a conference with Colonel Hawthorne. After two days on post, he returned to Peiping on 30 August.

During the early stages of the flood all the command's efforts were concentrated on maintenance of the Marine compound and assisting American nationals. With the flood at its crest, the Commanding Officer felt that men could be spared for some military training. Consequently, he authorized a twenty-man detail to depart for Peiping on 30 August to fire the rifle range.

On 30 August, the Peiping and Tien-Tsin home-going detail went down river on the Butterfield and Swire tugs where they embarked on board the USS *Chaumont* to return to the States. On 3 September, a portion of the incoming draft which had debarked from the *Chaumont* several days earlier left Chinwangtao by train to Tangku, where they transferred to tugs for the trip to Tien-Tsin. (The railway was still out between Tangku and Tien-Tsin.) Arriving in Tien-Tsin, the Tien-Tsin replacements reported to the Marine compound while the remainder of the draft transferred back to the train for the trip to Peiping.

On 1 September, to prevent further outages, the compound's electrical system was adjusted so that electricity could be received from either the Special Services Area lines or the British Concession lines. Once a source of electricity was assured, movies were shown nightly in the recreation hall.

Saturday, 2 September, was payday, the first since the flood. As many men as possible were given liberty. The height of the floodwaters precluded liberty after sunset.

The Enlisted Men's Club, located across the street from the Marine compound, opened on 3 September, for the first time since the flood started some two weeks before. A sampan ferry operated by the club provided transportation from the barracks to the club and return.

The remainder of the incoming *Chaumont* draft came through from Chinwangtao by tug and train and followed the same schedule as the detail on the previous day.

Monday, 4 September, being Labor Day, holiday routine was in effect.

Because of the flood conditions, however, Post Headquarters, the Quartermaster, Sick Bay, Mess Hall and Radio Station followed the same routine as on preceding days.

At noon on 4 September, the water level was 37½ inches and by midnight, it had dropped to 36½ inches.

During the last days of the flood the water level fluctuated up and down each twenty-four hours. For example, at noon on 2 September, the water level was 34½ inches. By midnight, it was 40 inches. At noon on 3 September, it was 36 inches and at midnight, it was 39 inches.

As the floodwaters continued to drop, the Marines "turned to" to restore the compound to its original pre-flood condition. By 1 October, the water had gradually receded to the extent that activities in the compound were again carried on normally.

The only reminder of the flood was the water lines on the buildings inside the compound and the plaque on the commissary building commemorating the crest of the flood.[10]

The Final Days

After the flood, routine for the North China Marines, in both Tien-Tsin and Peiping, settled down to normal garrison routine. Because of the political situation, conditioning hikes out into the country around Peiping as well as training at Peitaiho Beach were discontinued. The rifle range, however, opened on schedule and men from both Tien-Tsin and Peiping fired for records.

On 22–27 August 1940, the Asiatic Division Matches were held at the Rifle Range in Peiping. Shanghai's Fourth Marines swept all honors in the Asiatic Division Competition in Rifle and Pistol and the Triangular Rifle and Pistol Team matches by winning three trophies and two cups. These were in addition to the gold, silver and bronze medals awarded to individual Marines.

Because of the formation of the Tien-Tsin Detachment, which had cut the strength of the Peiping Detachment in half, the ice skating rink, which was normally built in the winter, was not built in the winter of 1940. Therefore, the company competition in ice hockey was dropped from the athletic program. Marines, did, however, skate on the lake at Central Park that was adjacent to the Forbidden City.

Sports, which had always been a mainstay in North China, were still pursued. There were intramural athletic competitions between the Marine detachments at Tien-Tsin and Peiping. While bowling and swimming

A Marine goes on liberty after the flood subsided. (Marine Corps University Archives, Quantico, Virginia.)

competition was confined to Marine personnel, Marines competed against students from the Yen Ching University, the Catholic University and other local teams in basketball, baseball and track.

As the political situation worsened with Japan and the war in Europe escalated, other foreign legation guards were withdrawn. With their departure, the International Track Meet was discontinued. In July 1940, the Marines at Peiping met the students from the Yen Ching University in a track and field meet. The Marines won the meet handily.

In the summer of 1940, changes began to occur that indicated that all was not well in North China. In July, the amateur radio station was taken off the air. Located in Johnson Hall, it ceased operation by order of Col. Allen H. Turnage because the Federal Communications Commission had forbidden American amateur stations from communicating with foreign stations. It was a small change, to be sure, and one that did not greatly affect the detachment, but it was a forerunner of things to come.

On 9 August 1940, the British War Office announced that it was withdrawing the last of its military forces from the International Settlement in Shanghai and North China where Britain had maintained garrisons under international protocol since the close of the Boxer Rebellion in 1901.

On 12 August 1940, the British Embassy Guard of thirty men from the East Surrey Regiment marched down Legation Street in full summer kit, topees, and shorts, with their helmets slung over the shoulders. They were led by their commander, Capt. C.O. Wallis, and accompanied by many of the British residents. As they marched briskly along, they sang wartime songs. When they reached the American embassy where a Marine guard of honor was drawn up, the Marines smartly presented arms as the British passed and the British responded with "eyes left." With that, the Marine band struck up the strains of *Auld Lang Syne*. The troop continued to the railway station. Before boarding the train, the Tommies gave three cheers for those who were left behind and the British civilians remaining responded with three cheers of their own.

On 14 August, at 0600 hours, 172 members of the British garrison in North China boarded a tender and went downriver to Tangku, where they boarded the British liner *Tehsheng* and at 1600 hours departed for Hong Kong on the high tide. With the departure of the garrison, a few radio men remained behind for duty with the British embassy.

The Germans and Russians had long since withdrawn their garrisons from the legation quarter in Peiping. The Italians had withdrawn their

The British Tommies leave Peiping, 1941. A U.S. Marine honor guard lines the sidewalk along Legation Street. (Photograph from the author's collection.)

legation guards also. French forces had been reduced in December 1939, when the French Concession garrison in Tien-Tsin sailed for Indochina. In North China, only a few Italians and Frenchmen remained behind as radio men for their embassies. The French did have a small detachment of Annamese (Vietnamese) that guarded the French embassy.

The British departure from China left some 1,200 Marine officers and enlisted in Shanghai and about 500 officers and men in North China. This placed the United States in an almost untenable position, especially after a Japanese embassy spokesman said the Japanese were "very pleased over the British decision to withdraw."[11] The spokesman recalled that "Japan has suggested that the forces of belligerent powers be removed from China to prevent clashes there, and he expected belligerents would follow [the] British's example."

This was wishful thinking on the part of the Japanese because on August 10, Acting Secretary of State Summer Wells announced that "American Marines in Shanghai and in North China will remain there, at least for the present, regardless of the British withdrawal from those points."[12]

The situation was tense. One reporter wrote, "No one imagines that any nation would risk war to maintain integrity of Shanghai's International Settlement."[13] The United States accepted the untenable position. Life at the Marine detachments continued the same as always.

While some phases of the Marines' training was discontinued, qualifying with the '03 Springfield rifle went on. The rifle range opened on schedule and continued to do so through the summer of 1940. Men from the detachments at Tien-Tsin and Peiping spent some two weeks at the range re-qualifying.

While at the rifle range, which was located several miles from the city, the Marines were not authorized liberty in the city. After spending the morning on the range, the men could either ramble around the countryside on rented small donkeys or sit in the cool of the giant cedar trees that shaded the camp area drinking beer and playing pinochle, acey-deucy, backgammon, chess or cribbage. Many a sea story was spun the shade of those ancient cedars by men who had served on many posts and stations throughout the world as well as with the fleet. These men could hold an audience for hours, especially if the audience bought the beer.

While at the rifle range the men were quartered in tents. The only permanent structure at the range was the Post Exchange.

Since June 1939, the British and French Concessions in Tien-Tsin had been barricaded from the surrounding areas by barbed wire entanglements erected by the Japanese Army. Movement of people, especially Chinese, into and out of these a two concessions as well as the transportation of all

Top: Firing at the rifle range, 1941. The shooter is wearing a shooting jacket with padded elbows and shoulders and a shooting glove. Everyone in the guard detachment owned a shooting jacket and glove and wore them while firing the range. *Bottom:* Marines exploring the country around the rifle range. Left to right: The author, Pfcs. Beavers and Pittner, and Cpl. Andressen. (Photographs from the author's collection.)

merchandise through the barricades were subject to severe restrictions by the Japanese authorities. This led to many confrontations with Japanese authorities. Representative of such was an incident in which an American woman was detained at a barricade and searched. During the search, the sentry slapped the woman. When the American diplomats demanded and explanation, the Japanese explained that the woman was arrogant with the sentry.

Despite incidents such as these, the racecourse at Paomachang opened for the fall meet in November. Races were held at Peiping twice a year, once in mid-spring and again in the fall. These races were unlike Stateside races, but they were interesting to attend. The horses were all small Mongolian ponies groomed to perfection. Despite their smallness and lack of speed, the ponies' performance equaled the thoroughbreds of Churchill Downs. Horses with names of Lady Be Good, Gobi Girl, Sze His and Summer Wind running clockwise on a short dirt track gave a good account of themselves. Betting was the same as Stateside. The races created a diversion in the garrison life of the Peiping Marines and were always looked forward to.

With the dependents of the officers and senior noncommissioned officers present, the Marine compounds in both Tien-Tsin and Peiping had the feel of a Stateside post. Most of the officers and all of the enlisted with dependents lived outside the Marine compounds. Dependents shopped in the Post Exchange, used the library and attended the nightly movies shown at the recreation hall in the compound. Adult dependents as well as special guests of the commanding officers always attended the Saturday morning inspection and parade. Women and children were not entirely absent from the Marine compounds.

All that changed in October 1940, when President Franklin D. Roosevelt ordered all dependents of the United States employees evacuated. While diplomatic negotiations between Japan and the United States were being held, the tension in the Orient had not abated. If anything, it had increased, especially since the United States would not lift the imposed embargo on aviation gasoline, which Japan sorely needed.

By mid–November the dependents were gone. While the rank and file had very little contact with the American dependents, their presence was missed. The posts became all male.

The fall of 1940 also saw another change. That was the downsizing of the detachments in both Peiping and Tien-Tsin. Formerly, the rotation drafts brought in as many replacements as the home-going draft returned to the states. This fall, however, while the specialist rating personnel, like radio operators, cooks, bakers, and motor transport, were more or less on a one to one exchange, the line companies were not. This was the beginning of the reduction of forces in North China. This reduction continued until the fall of 1941, when the once almost battalion-strength force of some 500 men was reduced to some 200 men and officers. After that, duty in North China intensified. Guard duty went from one day in four to every other day. Most training was suspended.

In December, the cold winter winds swept down from the north and across the Gobi Desert to bring the extreme cold and, at times, a fine dust that sifted into everything. At times the dust storms were so severe that visibility was limited to ten or fifteen feet. At these times the sentries wore goggles and heavy storm coats while on duty. When the temperature dropped to well below zero, watches were shortened to a one-hour duration. The dust storms lasted only a day or so. Then, the sky was clear once again, leaving a fine film of dust over everything. The snow became dingy and remained so until the next snowfall. It took several days to clean up the barracks and equipment. While there were room boys to clean the barracks and coolies to keep the compounds clean, the Marines had to spend extra hours in the gun sheds and armory cleaning weapons.

Although tension was mounting, the Marines were still authorized to wear civilian clothing on liberty. The commanding officer felt that Marines in civilian clothing would attract less attention from the Japanese. Conflicts with the Japanese were mounting by the fall of 1940 and throughout the summer of 1941.

On the morning of 31 December 1940, the following article appeared in the headlines of The *Peking Chronicle*.[14]

Japanese and U.S. Marines in Cabaret Row

The trouble started, it is reported, when a Japanese gendarme in plain clothes, on his usual round of duty at the International Cabaret, had his pipe abruptly snatched away by an American Marine. The two interpreters tried to reason with the American but only succeeded in causing the incident to assume unexpected proportions when other Marines interfered.[14]

As a result, Cpls. George Petroff and Francis A. Barber along with Pfcs. Walter G. Allen, Hurbert Sims, and Merlin W. Ankron were severely beaten and confined in the local jail. After a full investigation and some seventeen hours of imprisonment, the Marines were released and returned to Marine control.

The investigation revealed the Japanese had staged the event with the intent of creating an international incident. The Japanese had their incident, but it did not become the international one they expected. Locally, it was played up in The *Peking Chronicle*, whose headlines read,

"Peking Cabaret Brawl Unsettled" and "Turnage Quiet on Dec. 30 Incident"[15] The incident did make the *New York Times.* On January 2, 1941, page 2 in an AP release, the following headline appeared: "Japanese Injury to U.S. Marine Charged; Peiping Commander to Demand Apology." On January 4, 1941, the incident again received attention in the *New York Times:* "Japanese in Peiping Accuse U.S. Marine." The first article printed the Marine version of the incident. The second article printed the Japanese version. The lateness of the Japanese version was explained as "undoubtedly delayed by North China censorship."[16]

On 27 January 1941, in an oral and written statement, Ambassador Joseph C. Grew in Japan brought the incident to the attention of the Japanese Minister of Foreign Affairs Matsuoka. In the statement, he set forth the facts as revealed by the American investigation and concluded with the statement,

> If the attitude of the Japanese military authorities at Peiping accurately reflect the attitude of the Japanese Government, my Government can only conclude that there does not exist a disposition on the part of the Japanese Government to make any real effort toward settlement of the incident. Under these circumstances my Government is forced to assume that no useful purpose would be served by further discussion of the matter and it therefore will have to add this case to the list of unsettled cases involving infringement by Japanese agencies of American rights and interests in China, of willful abuse by the agencies of American citizens and of affronts of American official agents.[17]

With that statement, the International Cabaret incident was laid to rest. If the Japanese did instigate the incident, and there was little doubt in the commanding officer's mind that they did, it did not gain the notoriety they expected. It did, however, restrict the movements of Marines in Peiping for several months.

Tension remained high in Peiping and for several months; Marines going on liberty were restricted to their clubs and the YMCA. Even then, all Marines were required to go on liberty in pairs and check in the same way. There was no overnight liberty.

The incidents in Peiping did not affect the Tien-Tsin Marine detachment in any way. They had their own problems with the Japanese. Barriers, inspections and similar harassments hampered their movements between the various concessions.

Early March 1941 saw many changes in the strength of the Marine detachments in Peiping and Tien-Tsin. With the downsizing of the detachments in Peiping, Able and Baker companies were combined. Able

Top: The west end of the Marine Compound in Peiping, 1941. At the back of the barracks is the glacis used as a parade ground and drill field. *Bottom:* North side of the Marine Compound as viewed from Tartar Wall, 1941. From left to right: corner of barracks, sick bay, offices, officers' quarters. The Russian Glacis is in the upper right hand corner. To the right is the American Embassy Compound. In the background is Forbidden City and Coal Hill. (Photographs from the author's collection.)

Top: Wall Street and the Marine Compound as seen from Tartar Wall, 1941. Chien Men Tower is the building astride Tartar Wall. *Bottom:* The American Embassy Compound, 1941. (Photographs from the author's collection.)

The back gate to the Marine Compound, 1941. Tartar Wall is in the background. The ammunition magazine is seen through the gate. From reveille to taps, the ship's bell was sounded on the hour and half hour designating the time of day. (Photograph from the author's collection.)

Company now had a strength of some three officers and 103 enlisted men. After the departure of the May 1941 draft, a dozen men were transferred to Peiping. This reduced the Tien-Tsin detachment to a strength of around 60 men. The band which had been stationed in Peiping for some thirty-one years returned to the States with the May Draft. The Marines in North China had now been downsized from a combat battalion to detachments that were little more than pawns in an international game of chess.

Rumors began to circulate about this time that the Marine detachments in North China were about to be evacuated to the Philippines. For the Marines, this was preposterous. On 21 May, Secretary of State Cordell Hull announced "that extraterritoriality for Americans in China existed" and "he intimated that the time had not come to dispense with the protection that American forces stand ready to accord to American citizens there."[18]

Japan had now pushed its armies westward into the interior of China. By 1939, Japan had conquered most of eastern China, and had forced Chiang Kai-shek to move the capital from Nanking to Chungking. Although Japan had a firm grip over the area they controlled, guerrilla activities continued to plague them. Certain areas in North China were now restricted because of guerrilla activities and travel was not permitted.

During all this time, the Marines in North China continued to walk a fine line, avoiding any situation that might develop into an incident that would cause embarrassment to the United States. The tension, however, between the Marines and the Japanese never abated. While there were no more incidents during the long, hot summer, the Japanese got at the Marines by harassing the rickshaw boys the Marines patronized and the girls from some of the cabarets where they went on liberty.

This kind of harassment led to another incident on 21 September 1941. At around 2245 hours, First Lieutenant George R. Newton, commanding officer of Baker Company, was on his way to the Marine Club to join the military police for a tour of the city. As his rickshaw pulled up in front of the club, he saw two Japanese beating up a rickshaw boy. When he interfered, one of the Japanese struck him across the mouth. The military police were called from the club and after a brief scuffle, in which several Japanese bystanders became involved, everything was brought under control. Captain James R. Hester and Major Munson, military attaché, had to be called in to help settle the matter. Since the incident occurred inside the legation quarter, the Japanese gendarmes were not involved and nothing further was heard of the incident.[19]

In August, the United States embassy in Peiping "made strong representations against Japanese restrictions imposed on Americans' travel in North China." Attention was also called to Japanese detention of American luggage and instances of mail censorship.[20]

The last major incident occurred around 0015 hours on October 28, 1941. It happened on Post No. 1, at the embassy gate. Pfc. Douglas A. Bunn was posted as sentry at the embassy gate. He was armed with the '03 Springfield rifle. He carried two clips of .30 caliber ammunition in a little leather pouch that was attached to his leather belt. All sentries on duty carried unloaded weapons. There was little traffic on Legation Street at that time of night, and what little there was, was usually legation personnel returning home. Those were the conditions on that night.

A rickshaw came down Legation Street and turned up Rue Linevitch, which intersected Legation Street almost directly opposite the embassy gate (see Map 11, next page). Once the rickshaw turned into Rue Linevitch, it stopped in the shadows of the trees that lined the street and the passenger dismounted. Bunn did not pay much attention to the rickshaw. He did notice that the man was in civilian clothes. Once the rickshaw left the

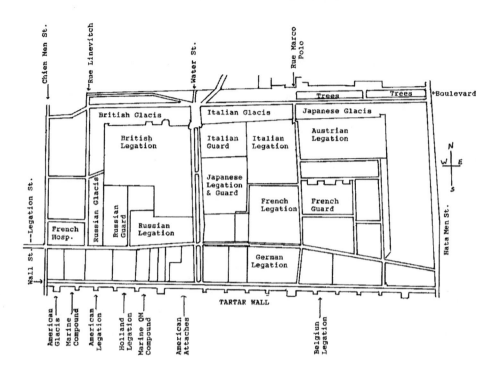

Map 11. Diplomatic Quarter, Peiping, China.

scene, the unknown assailant opened fire on Bunn from about five yards. When the assailant opened fire, Bunn had just reached the limits of his post and had done an about-face. His back was toward the assailant. One of the shots hit Bunn in the right foot, knocking him down. Although injured, Bunn loaded his rifle and fired five rounds in the direction of the unknown gunman. After firing, the assailant fled up Rue Linevitch. Bunn was positive the gunman did not leave the legation quarter, that he entered one of the residences on the street. Chief Marine Gunner William A. Lee was officer of the day. He turned out the guard of the day and a thorough search was made of the area. His search was limited because he did not have the authority to enter any of the residences that lined Rue Linevitch. While the assailant was not found, Pfc. Walter F. Freiberger did find four cartridge cases and one steel-jacketed bullet used in the attack. Pfcs. William J. Dees, Freemont F. Sheet, and Wade H. Armstrong reinforced the guard on Posts No. 1 and No. 2 for the remainder of the night.[21]

Bunn was removed to the hospital, where the fragments of a .32 caliber bullet were removed from his foot.

The next morning The *Peking Chronicle* carried a news article on one of the inside pages. Under a short heading, "U.S. Marine Wounded," it carried a brief account of the incident that ended with, "The United States Embassy has written to the Japanese Embassy protesting against the assault and asking that the assailant be found."[22]

A similar account of the incident appeared in the *New York Times* that ended with, "The American protest demanded that strong measures be taken to apprehend the assailant and offered the cooperation of American authorities in the investigation. No trace of the assailant has been discovered today."[23] The incident ended that way. The assailant was never found. It was the consensus of the detachment that this was another Japanese-instigated incident. As a retaliatory measure, all sentries thereafter carried loaded weapons while on duty and were ready to use them.

Admiral Thomas C. Hart, commander of the Asiatic Fleet, advised Washington on 28 August 1941 that he saw no advantage to keeping Marines in Peiping. In fact, he stated, "In the event of war with Japan, they would be quickly contained and destroyed, probably without being able to inflict even a comparable loss to the enemy."[24]

The policy makers in Washington, however, disagreed, believing a complete withdrawal of the Marines would put American interests at the mercy of Japan.[25] Obviously, the Marines in China were in a precarious position, yet they had no instructions regarding possible action in the event of war.

On November 10, the Marine Corps' birthday, Admiral Hart ordered the withdrawal of the Marine forces from China. Col. William W. Ashurst, commanding the Marine forces in North China and the legation guard at Peiping, was asked how much time would be needed for the complete evacuation. Major Luther A. Brown, commanding the Marine detachments in Tien-Tsin and Chinwangtao, answered ten days. Because of the distance between Peiping and Tien-Tsin, Col. Ashurst said at least a month.[26]

It was planned to evacuate the North China Marines first, but as the political situation between the United States and Japan rapidly deteriorated, the Fourth Marines in Shanghai, some 1,200 strong, received priority.

The Japanese controlled the railroads in China. In the past, when the Marines requested freight cars, the Japanese promptly authorized the requests. However, when evacuation commenced, the command in Peiping had trouble in securing freight cars for shipping of Marine equipment and supplies to Chinwangtao. The Japanese gave no explanation why the freight cars were not available. Although the Marines were leaving China as Japan desired, it appeared that they were going to make it difficult for them to do so.

Finally, Major Brown interceded directly with Lt. Gen. Kyoju Tominogo, commanding the Japanese forces in Tien-Tsin, and received the necessary authorization for the required railroad cars. After that, evacuation moved smoothly.

During the last weeks of November, while the North China Marines were packing and shipping their equipment to Chinwangtao, the President liners, SS *Madison* and SS *Harrison* moved into the Whangpoo River at Shanghai and embarked the Fourth Marines, their destination Manila.

By the first week of December, the Fourth Marines had joined General Douglas Macarthur's forces in the Philippines. With the SS *Madison* sailing eastward to the United States, the SS *Harrison* reversed course and was back at sea. She was scheduled to arrive in Chinwangtoa on December 9 and embark the North China Marines on December 10.

While the President liners were evacuating the Fourth Marines from Shanghai, the North China Marines were busy packing all their military equipment and supplies and disposing of all other material. Every few days, under guard, military equipment and supplies were dispatched from Tien-Tsin and Peiping to Chinwangtao, where they were received and unloaded by the Marine detachment stationed there. By Sunday night, December 7, 1941, the Marine compounds at Peiping and Tien-Tsin had been stripped. The Marines were scheduled to embark on 9 December aboard the SS *Harrison* and depart North China on 10 December.

For the North China Marines, the morning of 8 December 1941 was like no other they had ever experienced. When they awakened both the compounds in Peiping and Tien-Tsin were surrounded by Japanese troops. During the night Pearl Harbor had been bombed and a state of war existed between Japan and the United States.

Col. Ashurst sent the following message to Major Brown, commanding the Marine detachment at Tien-Tsin, "I am complying with the demand of the Imperial Japanese Army and advise you do likewise."[27]

Major Brown surrendered his detachment to a Japanese lieutenant and thirty men.

At first, the 21 man detachment at Chinwangtao under the command of Second Lieutenant Richard Huizenger and Chief Marine Gunner William A. Lee had other ideas. When it was learned that a state of war existed and Japanese surrounded their compound, men were sent to the railroad siding to off-load Browning .30 caliber, water-cooled, heavy machine guns and ammunition.

These weapons had been packed in cosmoline (rust-preventive grease) for shipment to the Philippines. The weapons had been stored in crates in boxcars and the severe cold had hardened the cosmoline to the consistency of tar. To remove the heavy grease, the machine guns were hurriedly washed down with hot water in the showers. Once clean and a light coat of oil applied, they were placed in defensive positions. While all these preparations for defense were being made, Japanese troops that surrounded the area had not made any hostile moves against the Marine detachment. Despite the overwhelming odds, the Marines at Chinwangtao were prepared to defend themselves.

Lt. Huizenga sent the following radio message to Major Brown in Tien-Tsin: "Have set up machine guns and think we have a chance to stand them off. Request instructions." Major Brown sent Huizenga the following urgent radio in reply: "Do not repeat not resort to fire except in self defense. Comply with demands of Japanese Army Forces."[28] Huizenga complied with those orders.

The Japanese authorities in Peiping demanded a formal surrender. Col. Ashurst complied with the request.

At 1300 hours the command fell out under arms on the company street. Once in formation, the field music sounded Recall. A few minutes later the sentries who were on duty at the compound gates joined the formation.

As the sentries came in, a company of Japanese soldiers followed them. The Japanese company halted in front of the Marine formation, executed a right face, and brought their rifles to order arms. Their baggy, mustard colored uniforms with wrapped leggings and earflap caps contrasted sharply with the trim forest green uniforms and Russian-style fur caps that were so distinctive of the North China Marines. They stamped their feet to keep warm. The temperature was around zero. The Marine companies stood there facing the company of Japanese soldiers, waiting.

The color guard accompanied by the field music took its place at the base of the flag pole in preparation for lowering the American flag. There was a long pause. The silence was deafening. Then Col. Ashurst gave the command, "Sound Retreat."

Cpl. Carroll W. Bucher, the field music, placed his bugle to his lips, and the sound of Retreat floated out across the compound.

The American flag that snapped in the brisk breeze started its slow descent. At last note of music died away, Bucher lowered the bugle from his lips. The color guard received the colors, slowly folded them, and took them to Col. Ashurst. The colonel received the colors and looked at them sadly for a moment before passing them to the Japanese officer in charge of the surrender ceremony. The Japanese officer held the folded colors in his hand and looked thoughtfully at the Marine colonel. After a long minute, he returned the colors to Col. Ashurst.

Col. Ashurst gave a nod of appreciation and passed the colors to his adjutant, who tucked them under his left arm, holding them securely with his forearm. The Japanese color guard came forward and, to the blare of a bugle, ran their colors to the peak of the flag pole and secured them.

The order was given to "stack arms." Silently the men stacked their rifles, unhooked their bayonets from their belts and dropped them beside the stacked rifles. When the rifles were stacked, the staff NCOs moved forward unbuckled their .45 automatics and dropped them on the stacks of bayonets.

When the command had been disarmed, the terms of surrender were read by the Japanese officer and translated into English by an interpreter.

Finally the ceremony was over and the order given to fall out and return to the barracks. As the men entered the barracks, they passed armed Japanese guards posted at the entrances of the barracks. Now they realized they were prisoners of war. Knowing the Japanese considered surrendering an act of dishonor, their future looked bleak.

Many of the 204 men taken prisoner in North China that day would remember the words Admiral Hart uttered on 28 August, "In the event of

The Marine Detachment as prisoners of war march through Chinese City en route to the railroad yards, 1941. (Photograph from the author's collection.)

war with Japan, they [Marines] would be quickly contained and destroyed, probably without being able to inflict even a comparable loss to the enemy." How true those words proved to be.

On 8 January, the Marines from Peiping joined the Marines at Tien-Tsin. On 28 January 1942, the combined detachments were moved south to Shanghai where they entered the Woosung Prisoner of War Camp. The survivors of Wake Island had established the Woosung camp some two weeks earlier.

With their departure from Tien-Tsin, the North China Marines, the last of the "Old China Hands" ended an era of some forty years.

At the end of World War II in 1945, two divisions of Marines, the First and Sixth Divisions of the III Amphibious Corps, would return to North China to disarm and repatriate the defeated Japanese troops and civilians and help the Chinese Nationalists build a stable government. These Marines, however, would be a new breed of Marines. The men known as "Old China Hands" were no more.

Epilogue

On December 8, 1941, there were 204 Marines and naval personnel serving in North China. After becoming prisoners of war of the Japanese, they were confined in labor camps located in China and Japan. Of that number, 184 survived the rigors of the prisoner of war camps and returned to the States.

It is interesting to note that more than 90 of the surviving members of the North China Marine Detachments remained in the Corps until retirement. Of the enlisted men who chose the Corps as a career, 32 were promoted to the officer ranks between 1946 and 1951.

APPENDIX A

Chronology

1655   The Dutch ambassador travels to Peking.

1793   The British government sends Lord McCartney to Tien-Tsin to negotiate trade treaties.

1796   The *I Ho Ch'uan* or Fist of Righteous Harmony, known as the "Boxers," is founded during the reign of Chia Ch'ing.

1816   Lord Amherst arrives in Tien-Tsin to improve trade treaties.

1831   Karl Gutlaff, German missionary, arrives in Tien-Tsin.

1858   Following the Opium War in South China, the French and British begin the first foreign military operation in North China. The Treaty of Tien-Tsin is signed.

1859   After being denied entry, British naval forces try unsuccessfully to force passage for a British ambassador en route to Peking.

1860   Lord Elgin and Baron Gros, commanding an expeditionary force, invade North China, capturing Tien-Tsin and Peking.

1894   Under the Command of Captain George F. Elliott, Marines from the USS *Baltimore*, flagship of the Asiatic Squadron, are ashore at Tien-Tsin, China.

1898   Awakened by political activists after nearly a century of slumber, the *I Ho Ch'uan* or Fist of Righteous Harmony again becomes active. Marines from the USS *Boston*, USS *Raleigh* and USS *Baltimore* are ashore in Peking and Tien-Tsin as legation and consulate guards.

1899   The Boxer movement intensifies when the Catholics purchase a temple and replaced it with a church.

1900   The kidnapping and decapitation of the Reverend Brooks focuses the attention of the world on the Boxer Rebellion.

May 27, 1900	In response to a request from American Minister E.H. Conger for Marine legation guards, the USS *Newark* and USS *Oregon* arrive at Taku Bar forty miles down the Pei-Ho River from Tien-Tsin.
May 28	Boxers attack the Belgian railroad between Peking and Paotingfu and Peking–Tien-Tsin Railroad junction at Fengtai. Alarmed foreign ministers in Peking request legation guards.
May 29	American Marines and sailors disembark and proceed to Tien-Tsin.
May 31	American Marines and sailors depart Tien-Tsin for Peking as legation guards. They are followed by British, Russian, French, Italian, German, Austrian and Japanese legation guards.
June 2	Captain McCalla, USN, commanding American ground forces in North China, returns to Tien-Tsin.
June 5	Railroad lines and telegraph lines between Peking and Tien-Tsin are cut. Peking is under siege.
June 8	Foreign Ministers in Peking formulate plans for the defense of the Legation Quarter.
June 9	The international force to relieve the besieged legations in Peking are organized under the command of Admiral Edward Seymour. In Peking, Boxers burn the grandstand at the race course.
June 10	The Seymour Relief Column departs Tien-Tsin with American and British Marines in the vanguard. In Peking, Capt. John T. Myers detaches ten men to defend the Methodist Mission. The French and Italian detach forty-three men to defend the Catholic Peitang Cathedral.
June 11	The Seymour relief column reaches Lang-Fang some sixty-five miles from Peking. The advance is decisively checked. In Peking, Japanese Chancellor Sugiyama is murdered by Chinese soldiers while en route to the railroad station to check on the arrival of the relief column.
June 13	Marines from the Methodist Mission garrison in Peking disperse rioting Boxers threatening the mission.
June 15	The Seymour Relief Column's lines of communication and supply are cut. Peking — Boxers torch the Nan T'ang Catholic Mission and slaughter Chinese converts. A sortie of American and Russian Marines rescue the converts. Other foreign powers follow suit.
June 16	The Seymour column falls back on Yang-Tsun.
June 17	Allied naval forces capture Taku Forts. In Peking, Boxers fire on the Marine barricade on Legation Street and probe the Legation Quarter defense lines.
June 18	The Seymour column slowly retreats toward Tien-Tsin. In Peking, after three days of rescue work, Capt. Myers halts the

work because of troop exhaustion. Other foreign powers follow Myers' lead.

June 19, 1900   Marine detachments from the USS *Solace* and USS *Nashville* under Major L.W.T. Waller are ashore at Taku and depart for Tien-Tsin. The Chinese government declares war on the Allied Powers. The Tsung Li Yamen (foreign office) demands that the Legation Quarter be evacuated by 1600 hours on June 20.

June 20   Twelve miles from Tien-Tsin, Waller's advance is blocked by Boxers. Tien-Tsin — James Watts and three Russian Cossacks slip through the Chinese to Taku seeking help for besieged Tien-Tsin Concessions. Peking — German foreign minister Baron von Ketteler is murdered by Chinese army troops while en route to Tsung Li Yamen. The Methodist Mission is abandoned. All Europeans take refuge in the Legation Quarter. At 1600 hours the Boxers and Chinese army troops open fire on the Legation Quarter defense lines. The Legation Quarter is under siege.

June 21   Waller joins forces with Russians and again advances on Tien-Tsin. Once again his entrance into Tien-Tsin is denied by Boxers. In Peking, the first attack in strength is made by Chinese forces on the Legation Quarter.

June 22   The retreating Seymour column captures the Imperial Hsiku Arsenal 8 miles from Tien-Tsin and digs in to await relief. Austrian Marines in Peking abandon their legation. Legation defense lines are shortened. Erroneously, all legation guards withdraw from defense lines. Later they return without a struggle.

June 23   Waller joins a 600-man British naval force and reaches Tien-Tsin. Peking — Hanlin Library is fired upon by Boxers. Gen. Chang Foo Shiang's soldiers attack the legation defense lines. Marine quarters are burned.

June 24   American and German Marines in Peking establish permanent defensive barricades on Tartar Wall overlooking the Legation Quarter. Buildings in the Empress Dowager's Carriage Park are fired in an attempt to burn the British Legation. Capt. Myers leads an unsuccessful Marine attempt to capture the Chinese barricade on Tartar Wall.

June 25   Peking — Supply of beef is exhausted. Horse meat is issued.

June 26   The relief column from Tien-Tsin rescues the besieged Seymour column.

June 27   Tien-Tsin — The Russians' attempt to capture the East Arsenal fails. Reinforced by American and British Marines, a second attack captures the arsenal. Peking — The Chinese unsuccessfully storm the Marine barricade on Tartar Wall.

June 28   Peking — The Chinese shell the Japanese position in the Fu with a 3-inch Krupp gun.

July 1,   The Chinese overrun the German barricade on Tartar Wall in Peking,
  1900   forcing Marines to retreat. Reinforced by British Marines and Rus-
              sian sailors, the barricade is retaken. The German barricade is aban-
              doned. Marines build and man a second barricade to the east to
              protect their rear.

July 2   Marines are forced to withdraw from their barricade on Tartar Wall.
              The walls of the French Legation is breached by Boxers.

July 3   Marines reinforced by British Marines and Russian sailors retake the
              barricade and capture the nearby Chinese barricade. Capt. Myers is
              wounded.

July 6   Ninth U.S. Army Regiment lands at Taku and proceeds to Tien-Tsin.
              Peking — Shell fire destroys the American flagpole. The flag is imme-
              diately hoisted to the top of a nearby tree. A sortie by Japanese
              Marines, supported by Gunner's Mate Mitchell and the Colt machine
              gun, make an unsuccessful attempt to capture the cannon that is bat-
              tering the Fu.

July 7   Gunner's Mate Mitchell builds a cannon from an old relic.

July 8   The cannon, named "The Old International," also known as "Old
              Betsy," is successfully test fired.

July 9   Japanese Marines foil the Boxer attempt to build a barricade along the
              north wall of the Fu.

July 12   The Chinese troops' attempt to take the British breastworks near the
              destroyed Hanlin Library is thwarted. Col. Meade and a regiment of
              Marines are ashore at Taku. Gunner's Mate Mitchell, reinforcing the
              British lines with "Old Betsy," captures a Chinese battle banner.
              Marines advance their east barricade atop Tartar Wall 50 yards.

July 13   Allied forces attack the walled city of Tien-Tsin.

July 14   Tien-Tsin is captured by allied forces. Peking — Marines advance the
              east barricade atop Tartar Wall to Water Gate. Foreign ministers
              receive a letter from the Tsung Li Yamen requesting all legation
              personnel to move to the Yamen. All military personnel will be dis-
              armed.

July 15   Peking — Marines and Russian sailors clean out snipers in the com-
              pound outside the legation defense lines. Marines advance the east
              barricade atop Tartar Wall another 200 yards.

July 16   American Minister Conger in Peking receives a message from the State
              Department.

July 17   An uneasy truce begins.

July 18   The Chinese build new barricade on Legation Street in Peking. "Old
              Betsy" is brought up and destroys the Chinese barricade. The first
              news from the outside is brought in by a Chinese courier.

July 19, 1900   As a sign of good feelings, the Tsung Li Yamen sends in a few carts of fresh vegetables and fruit for women and children.

July 27   The Tsung Li Yamen sends in fifteen carts of vegetables, flour and ice for women and children.

July 28   A second courier arrives in Peking with news from Tien-Tsin.

July 30   Maj. Gen. Adna R. Chaffee, USA, takes command of American forces in North China. Fourteenth Infantry, Sixth Cavalry and Reilly's Battery, Fifth Artillery, arrive at Tien-Tsin.

Aug 1   Peking — Many letters arriving by courier bring encouraging news.

Aug 3   Major William P. Biddle, USMC, is ashore in Tien-Tsin with a battalion of Marines.

Aug 4   The International Relief Column departs Tien-Tsin for Peking.

Aug 5   Allied forces fight the first decisive battle at Peitsang.

Aug 6   Marines and U.S. Army and British troops lead an attack on Yang-Tsun. Generals Chaffee and Gaselee receive cipher messages from ministers in Peking.

Aug 7   Peking — The besieged Legation Quarter goes on half rations. Allied Relief Column — German, Italian, Austrian and French detachments return to Tien-Tsin because of transportation and supply problems.

Aug 8   After one day's rest, the relief column resumes its advance on Peking.

Aug 9   In Peking, the uneasy truce collapses. The Chinese attack in force. The Allied Relief Column captures Hosiwu.

Aug 10   At dawn Matou falls to the advancing relief column. Peking — the courier arrives with word that the long anticipated relief column is on the way. Expected date of arrival is August 14.

Aug 11   Changchiawan is taken by allied forces. In Peking, the Chinese attack on the Legation Quarter is constant and fierce.

Aug 12   Peking — Fierce attack continues. The Legation is shelled by a 3-inch Krupp gun from the wall of the Imperial City. Allied Relief Column — Japanese, Russian and British Indian troops sack Tungchow, fourteen miles from Peking. Forces rest one day and formulate plans for an attack on the city of Peking.

Aug 13   In Peking, the Chinese make the most terrible attack of the siege. Gunner's Mate Mitchell is badly wounded.

Aug 14   Before dawn, Allied Forces resume their advance. They arrive at the walled city of Peking and bivouac for the night.

Aug 15   In the early morning hours, the allied relief column storms the city walls of Peking. Trumpeter Calvin P. Titus, U.S. Army, plants the American flag atop Tartar Wall. Legation guard Marines and Russian sailors clear Tartar Wall west to Chien Men. British and American troops enter the Legation Quarter during the afternoon. Mm. Cuillier is wounded by a Chinese sniper and becomes the only woman wounded during the siege.

Aug 16, 1900   Legation Marine guards join Waller's Marines in support of the Ninth Infantry attack on the Imperial City. The siege is lifted. Mopping up begins.

Aug 17   Marines go into bivouac and are assigned the southeast quarter of the city to patrol.

Aug 28   Representative troops from each of the allied forces parade in the Forbidden City and a twenty-one gun salute is fired to proclaim the fall of the Forbidden City.

Oct. 3   The First Marine Regiment departs Peking for Tien-Tsin.

Oct. 10   The Marine regiment sails for Cavite, Philippine Islands, on board the USS *Brooklyn* and two naval transports, the *Zafiro* and *Indiana*. Except for a company of the Ninth Infantry, which remains in Peking as legation guards, all army units are also withdrawn.

1901   March 1—Court-martial convenes at Capt. Hall's request. He is cleared of the charge of cowardice on July 2, 1901.

1905   September 12 — One hundred Marines under Capt. Harry Lee relieve the Ninth Infantry as Legation guards in Peking.

1910   Marine band forms in Peking.

1911   A revolt occurs in South China and Sun Yat-sen is named president. Gen. Yuan Shih-ka'i betrays Sun Yat-sen and declares himself dictator. A battalion of Marines under the command of Major Phillip M. Bannon reinforces the legation guard in Peking. A Mounted Detachment is organized in Peking.

1912   The Marine legation guards' strength is reduced in May. Later, because of revolutionary incidents, the guard is increased to battalion strength. In January, the Fifteenth Infantry, U.S. Army, is deployed to Tien-Tsin. In February, the Mounted Detachment in Peking is officially recognized.

1913   The Kuomintang (Nationalist Party) revolt against Gen. Yuan fails and leaders flee to Japan.

1916   Gen. Yuan dies. Leaderless, warlords and the Nationalist Party vie for power.

1919   The Marine band in Peking introduces the saxophone to North China.

1922   Capt. Charles H. Martin and a detachment of Marines reinforce the legation guard from April 28 to May 25. A battalion of Marines under Capt. Roy C. Swank lands at Taku.

1923   Communist Russia supports the Nationalist Party with financial aid.

1924   First Lieutenant John T. Thorton and a detachment of 31 Marines from the USS *Asheville* are ashore at the International Settlement in Shanghai. The First Marine Expeditionary Force commanded by Capt. Francis S. Kierer reinforces Marines in Shanghai. In October, Capt. Kierer is ordered north to support the Marine legation guard in Peking.

1925   February 1— First Marine Expeditionary Force departs Peking on board the USS *Asheville*. On November 9, Capt. August Wilson and a detachment of 127 Marines are ashore in Tien-Tsin.

1926   November — 125 Marines from Guam on board the *Gold Star* are ashore in Chinwangtao.

1927   Generalissimo Chiang Kai-shek captures South China and turns against the communists. The Cantonese under Chiang Kai-shek threaten the International Settlement in Shanghai.

February 8 — Major Julian P. Willcox with four companies of Marines are ashore at the International Settlement, Shanghai.

February 14 — The Fourth Marine Regiment under the command of Col. Charles S. "Jumbo" Hill reinforces the Marines at the International Settlement, Shanghai.

March — The Sixth Marine Regiment with two squadrons of planes reinforce the Fourth Marine Regiment.

May 2 — Brig. Gen. Smedley D. Butler is ashore in Shanghai as commander of the Third Marine Brigade and all Marines in China.

June — Generalissimo Chiang Kai-shek's Nationalist Army moves to North China. Brig. Gen. Butler moves the Third Marine Brigade to Tien-Tsin.

December — A massive fire breaks out at the Standard Oil Plant in Tien-Tsin.

1928   Chiang Kai-shek consolidates his rule over China. Marine engineers repair bridges and a sixteen mile stretch of the Tien-Tsin-Peking highway. Grateful Chinese award Butler the "Umbrella of Blessings." Butler is awarded a second "Umbrella of Blessings" for preventing a bandit brigade from looting a village. Nationalist Forces occupy Peking. The capital is moved from Peking to Nanking. Peking is renamed Peiping.

July 25 — The United States is the first foreign power to sign a tariff treaty with Chiang Kai-shek's government in Nanking.

1929   In January, the Third Marine Brigade returns to United States.

1931   Japan seizes Manchuria.

1932   A confrontation occurs between the Chinese and Japanese armies at Shanghai. The Fourth Marine Regiment at Shanghai is reinforced by Marines from the Philippines, the USS *Houston* and the Thirty-first Infantry Regiment, U.S. Army.

June — Reinforcements in Shanghai are withdrawn.

1933   Japan withdraws from the League of Nations and succeeds in cutting off Manchuria from China.

1936   Japan dominates six provinces in North China and walks out of the Second London Conference. In November, Japan signs a treaty with Nazi Germany. Kidnapped by his military colleagues, Chiang Kai-shek agrees to end the war with Chinese Communists and fight Japan on a solid front.

1937   July 7 — Chinese and Japanese troops clash near Peiping. The invasion of China begins. Legation guards in Peiping assume a "state of preparedness." The Twenty-ninth Chinese Army abandons Peiping.
            August 3 — American nationals leave the security of the Legation Quarter and return to their homes.
            August 8 — The Japanese army under the command of General Kwabe Shozo occupies Peiping.

1938   The Marine detachment relieves the Fifteenth Infantry at Tien-Tsin and Camp Holcomb at Chinwangtao. The Marine Mounted Detachment at Peiping is disbanded.

1939   Flood waters from the Hai Po River inundate Tien-Tsin.

1940   Japan conquers most of eastern China. Chiang Kai-shek moves the capital of China from Nanking to Chungking.
            July — The amateur radio station in Peiping taken off the air by orders of the Federal Communications Commission.
            August 2 — Marine Asiatic Division Rifle and Pistol Matches are held in Peiping.
            August 12 — The East Surrey Regiment, the British legation guards, departs Peiping.
            August 14 — The combined British garrisons from Peiping and Tien-Tsin depart Tien-Tsin for Hong Kong.
            November — All dependents of United States employees are evacuated from China. The downsizing of the Marine guard detachments in North China begins.
            December 31 — An international incident occurs when Japanese and Marines are involved in cabaret row. Marines are confined in a Japanese jail.

1941   January 27 — American Ambassador Joseph C. Grew brings the incident to the attention of Japanese Minister of Foreign Affairs Matsuoka.
            March — The strength of Marine forces in Shanghai and North China are further reduced.
            May — The Marine Band in Peiping is disbanded and returns to the States.
            August — Japan imposes travel restrictions on Americans in China.
            September 21 — A second incident occurs with the Japanese in Peiping involving a Marine officer.

October 28 — Pfc. Douglas A. Bunn, a Marine guard at the entrance to the American Embassy Compound is wounded.

November 10 — Admiral Hart orders withdrawal of all Marine forces from China.

Late November — The Fourth Marine Regiment departs Shanghai for Manila, Philippine Islands. Marines in North China are scheduled to depart from Chinwangtao December 10. December 8 (Peiping time) — Pearl Harbor is bombed by the Japanese. A state of war exists between the United States and Japan.

December 8, 1300 hours, the Marine legation guards in Peiping formally surrender to the Japanese. Marine detachments in Tien-Tsin and Chinwangtao follow suit.

1942 January 8 — Marines from Peiping join the Marine detachment at Tien-Tsin. Marines from North China join Marines from Wake Island at a prisoner of war camp at Woosung near Shanghai. After some forty years, the era of Marine forces in North China ends.

Appendix B

The Legation Guard at Peking, 1900

USS *Newark*

Captain Hall, W.H.
Sergeant Fanning, I.
Private Ammann, J.C.
Private Brosi
Private Barratt
Private Carr
Private Davis
Private Daly
Private Donovan, E.J.
Private Donovan, W.F.
Private Galligher
Private Gainnie
Private Gold
Private Hall
Private Kuhn
Private Kennedy
Private Savin [Layin]
Private Martin
Private Schroeder
Private Silvia [Silver]
Private Tinkler
Private Tutcher
Private Join [Zoin]
Music Murphy

USS *Oregon*

Captain Myers, J.T.
Sergeant Walker
Corporal Dahlgren
Private Hunt
Private Butts
Private Boydston
Private Fischer
Private Greer
Private Hobbs
Private Herter [Harder]
Private Horton
Private Kehlm
Private King
Private Mullen
Private Mueller
Private Moody
Private Moore
Private O'Leary
Private Preston
Private Quinn
Private Scannell
Private Turner
Private Thomas
Private Upham
Private White
Private Young

Bluejackets at Peking

Chief Machinist T. Peterson

Colts Gun Crew

Gunner's Mate lst Cl. J. Mitchell　　Seaman S. Westermark
Seaman J. Sjorgeen

Medical Staff

Assistant Surgeon T.M. Lippett　　Hospital Apprentice R. Stanley

Casualty List

Killed	*Wounded*
Pvt. C.B. King, 24 June	Capt. J.T. Myers, July3
Sgt. Fanning, 26 June	Pvt. Gold, 25 June
Pvt. Tutcher, 30 June	Pvt. Kehm, 24 June
Pvt. R. Turner, 3 July	Pvt. Hall, 1 July
Pvt. R.E. Thomas, 3 July	Pvt. Mueller, 25 June
Pvt. Kennedy, 1 July	Pvt. Moody, 4 July
Pvt. Fischer, 16 July	Pvt. Schroeder, 30 June
	Pvt. Silvia, 1 July
	Music. Murphy, 14 July
Pvt. Shroeder died of	Dr. Lippett, 29 June
wounds 10 September	GM. J. Mitchell, 14 Aug.

APPENDIX C

Reports of Colonel Robert J. Meade and Major L.W.T. Waller

(As Reported by the New York Times, *August 18, 1900, 2-1)*

THE FIGHTING IN TIEN-TSIN
DETAILED REPORTS BY COL. MEADE
AND MAJOR WALLER.

PRAISE FOR THE AMERICANS
THEIR BRAVERY GAINS THE ADMIRATION OF
OTHER TROOPS, ALTHOUGH THEY
LOOK "LIKE FALSTAFF'S ARMY."

WASHINGTON, Aug 17. The Navy Department to-day made public the reports of Col. Robert L. Meade and Major L.W.T. Waller of the United States Marine Corps, on the fighting at Tien-Tsin. They gave not only a graphic account of the initial engagements in the Chinese campaign, but furnished the information with official exactness.

Col. Meade's report is dated Tien-Tsin, July 16. After telling of the situation around Tien-Tsin, and the decision on July 12, at a conference held at the British General's headquarters, to attack the city about day-break the next day, Col. Meade, in describing the early fighting in which the Marines and the Ninth Infantry took a gallant part, says:

"We reached the advanced position about 8 A.M. I took 180 round per man with me — 100 rounds in the belts and 80 in the haversacks. This is not sufficient for an all-day fight, and as it grew toward night I began to be apprehensive of being left in an advance position, in a fight where no prisoners were taken on either side, with only the bayonet to fight with.

"On the firing line the action was especially hot, and the enemy's fire especially rapid and accurate. At about 8:30 A.M. the enemy appeared in large numbers upon our left and among the grave mounds of the field in which we were[,] with the evident intention of flanking us. I made a turning movement to the left and rear, and we drove them away. Later in the day, about 2 P.M., they again made a flanking effort, but at this time the infantry supporting the artillery company was on the mud wall of the city and aided us by a cross fire. This company was commanded by Capt. C.G. Long. The effort of the enemy proved a failure and we drove them in.

"We remained in the trenches until about 8 P.M., when we received an order from the Brigadier General commanding to withdraw, which was probably the most difficult action of the day, since the enemy had so well covered our position that their shots struck the crest of the trenches and threw dirt in our faces, many being hit.

"The troops had had nothing whatever to eat on the 13th save the small luncheon (if it may be so called) which each man carried in his haversack. It was not expected when we started that the action would prove so long, but Gen. Dorward, knowing the situation, kindly sent to the reservation for food and other necessaries, and the bivouac proved to be a success, and the men, although very fatigued, were ready for duty.

"On the 14th inst., the south gate having been blown in, we moved into the walled city at about 6 o'clock A.M.

"We found the city filled with dead Chinamen and animals. No resistance was made to our occupation in the walled city itself, but an infantry fire was kept up by the Japanese infantry upon the enemy, who responded from the suburbs. Since then, we have had undisturbed possession of all Tien-Tsin."

Thanks from Gen. Dorward

Col. Meade inclosed the following letter from Gen. Dorward, the commander of the British forces:

"From the General Office commanding British forces in China.
To the officer commanding the United States forces:
Tien-Tsin, China, July 15, 1900.
"Sirs: I desire to express the high appreciation of the British troops of the honor done them in serving alongside their comrades

of the American Army during the long and hard fighting of the 13th inst., and the subsequent capture of Tien-Tsin, and of my appreciation of the high honour accorded me by having them under my command.

"The American troops formed part of the front line of the British attack, and so had more than their share of the fighting that took place. The ready and willing spirit of the officers and men will always make their command easy and pleasant, and when one adds to that the steady gallantry and power of holding on to exposed positions which they displayed on the 13th inst., the result is soldiers of the highest class.

"We deeply sympathize with you in the heavy losses you have suffered, especially with the Ninth Regiment in the loss of their gallant Colonel, E.H. Liscum, while at the head of his men, and with the First Regiment of Marines in the death of Capt. Davis, who met a soldier's death in the very front of the fight.

"I blame myself for the mistake made in the taking up of their position by the Ninth Regiment, not remembering that troops wholly fresh to the scene of action and hurried forward in the excitement of the attack were likely to lose their way. Still, the position they took up and gallantly stuck to all day undoubtedly prevented a large body of the enemy from turning the right of the attacking line and inflicting serious loss on the French and Japanese.

"Among many instances of personal bravery in action, I propose specially to bring to notice in dispatches the conduct of First Lieut. Smedley D. Butler, United States Marine Corps, in bring a wounded man from the front under heavy and accurate fire. Lieut. Butler was wounded while so doing, but I am glad to learn not seriously. The Regimental Adjutant, First Lieut. Henry Leonard, as Lieut. Butler was suffering severely, volunteered to carry him out of the firing line. The gallant feat he successfully accomplished, but I regret to say was very dangerously wounded in so doing.

"The Ninth Regiment were fighting somewhat outside my sphere of action, so I am to bring forward only one instance of personal gallantry in the regiment, although, circumstanced [sic] as they were, fighting for about twelve hours almost alone and unsupported, and never giving a foot of ground until directed to retire under cover of night and fire of the naval guns, such instances must have been numerous. The one I would refer to is the bringing back to me by the Acting Regimental Adjutant, Capt. Lawton, of the account of the position of the regiment across a wide fire-swept space, and returning with reinforcements to guide them to his regiment when he was severely wounded.

"The withdrawal of the regiment was a delicate military operation finely carried out, on which I congratulate Col. Coolridge and the officers and men under his command.

"I have the honor to be, Sir, your obedient servant."

"A.R.E. DORWARD
BRIGADIER GENERAL."

Col. Meade gives a list of the casualties and details the circumstances of the deaths of Col. Liscum and Capt. Davis. He also states that the allies are about to choose a president for the government of Tien-Tsin. He was informed, he says, by Gen. Dorward, that the latter expected to move on Peking in about a fortnight.

The proclamation to the inhabitants of Tien-Tsin, telling them that the bombardment was only in reply to the attacks by rebels, is also included in the report.

MAJOR WALLER'S REPORT

"At 2 in the morning (June 30) the Russian Colonel, informed me that he would push on with his 400 men, and attempt to get into Tien-Tsin and aid in the defense of the city. I objected, but was overruled in council. My reason told me that there was slim chance of passing the Chinese force with only 530 men and no guns.

"The three-inch rifle proved defective, I disabled it and rolled it into the river and followed the Russians in the twelve-mile march on Tien-Tsin. The Russian column was in advance, 400 strong, with my Colt 6 m-m [*sic*] in their front, under the command of Lieut. Powell. The advance continued until 7 A.M., without opposition when we reached the point opposite the imperial arsenal.

"There we met a small flank fire, which was quickly silenced by our sharpshooters. About ten minutes later we met a very heavy front and flank fire from 1,500 to 2,000 men intrenched. We deployed, and my line feeling the flank fire, turned to the left and rear, confronting the flank movement, our line at the time having its front advanced.

"The support of the Colt gun having dwindled to two men, and the gun having jammed several times, all the crew being shot down but one, Mr. Powell very properly decided to abandon it, which he did, after disabling the gun. Receiving notice that the Russians would retreat to a point four miles beyond our bivouac, I began my retreat, moving by the right flank and keeping up a fight for four hours with the enemy, who were in force, imperial troops and Boxers. We succeeded in falling back bringing our wounded by hand. At 2 P.M. we reached our base, having marched thirty miles and fought for four hours. I was obliged to leave the dead, but brought off the wounded. Our casualties were four killed and nine wounded.

"It was agreed that we should advance in two columns on the next day at 4 A.M., my force occupying the advance of the British column and the right of the firing line. We struck the enemy at about 7 A.M. and drove them steadily until about 12:00 P.M. when we entered Tien-Tsin, relieving the besieged Europeans, our losses being for the day one killed and three wounded."

CAPTURE OF ARSENAL

"At noon on the 27th, the Russians having attacked the arsenal, the scene of my repulse on the 22d, and which had not been captured, asked for reinforcements. I sent Second Lieut. Jolly and forty men. Mr. Harding, my Adjutant, joining as a volunteer, and placed the whole under the command of Commander Cradock, R.N. This force was about 1,800 strong and succeeded in driving the enemy from the parapets out of their fortifications and in full flight. It developed that the enemy had about 7,000 men at this point. Our men charged over the parapet with a British company, being the first in this part of the fight. Our loss here was one wounded and Lieut. Jolly overcome by heat, but not until after he had brought his men back to their quarters. Lieut. Harding acted as a volunteer and captured an imperial flag, which he gave to me.

"Having given you the bare facts, I wish to invite attention to the incidents of the busy week. Our men marched ninety-seven miles in the five days, fighting all the way. They have lived on about one meal a day for six days, but have been cheerful and willing always. They have gained the highest praise from all forces present and have earned my love and confidence. They are like Falstaff's army in appearance, but with brave hearts and bright weapons.

"I have to earnestly recommend to your notice for such reward as you may deem proper the following officers: Lieut. S.D. Butler, for the admirable control of his men in all the fights of the week; for saving a wounded man at the risk of his own life and under a very heavy fire; Lieut. A.E. Harding, for conspicuous gallantry in action; for saving wounded at the risk of his life under heavy fire; Second Lieut. W. L. Jolly for the same risk and for leading [a] fine charge over two parapets in the face of a heavy fire; First Lieut. Leonard, for saving lives under fire and for admirable control and direction of the fire; First Lieut. Powell for working and managing the Colt gun under a fierce fire without support after the crew had been shot down; First Lieut. Wynne, for his steadfast courage and encouragement of his men.

"As for the men, I feel that I cannot do them justice. I shall send you the names of special instances in their cases, hoping that a suitable reward may be given them, as far as the law allows.

"I have also to ask that you urge the department to thank the British surgeons for their care on the field and in the hospital of our wounded. Especially do I wish to recommend to the department's notice the services of Surgeon Robley H.J. Browne, R.N., H.M.S. *Alacrity*. So sure was his service and search of the field that we were able to get all the firing line with the sure knowledge that the dead and wounded would be attended to. We had no surgeon or medical supplies.

"The operations under Commander Cradock, R.N., were admirably planned and executed."

The Allies' Proclamation

The proclamation mentioned by Col. Meade is as follows:

"To the Inhabitants of the City of Tien-Tsin.

"In bombarding the city of Tien-Tsin the allied forces are only replied [*sic*] to the attacks made by the rebels on the foreign settlements.

"At present, as your authorities, forgetting their duties, have deserted their posts, the allied forces consider it their duty to establish in the city a temporary administration, which you have to obey. The administration will protect every one wishing to deal in a friendly manner with foreigners, but will punish without mercy every one who causes trouble.

"Let the bad people tremble; but the good people should feel reassured, and quietly return to their houses and began their usual work. Thus, peace will be restored. Respect this."

This was signed by the commanders of the various nationalities.

Major Waller inclosed [*sic*] a number of reports from his company commanders, giving in detail the work done by their organizations. These reports all speak highly of the conduct of officers and men. Capt. Fuller, who commanded Company F, commends the conduct of a company of British bluejackets, under command of Lieutenant from Orlando, who rendered invaluable assistance in carrying the Ninth's wounded to the rear on the retreat and in forming the rear guard.

APPENDIX D

The Letter Sir Claude MacDonald Received from "Prince Ching and Others"

The following is a translation of a letter Sir Claude MacDonald, British Foreign Minister, received from "Prince Ching and Others" on 14 July 1900, taken from Allen's *The Siege of Peking Legations,* pp. 205–206.

"For the last ten days the soldiers and militia have been fighting, and there has been no communication between us, to our great anxiety. Some time ago we hung up a board expressing our intentions, but no answer has been received, and, contrary to expectation, the foreign soldiers made renewed attacks, causing alarm and suspicion amongst soldiers and people. Yesterday the soldiers captured a convert named Chin Sau Hsi and learnt from him that all the foreign Ministers were all well, which caused us very great satisfaction. But it is the unexpected which happens. The reinforcements of foreign troops were long ago stopped and turned back by the Boxers, and if in accordance with previous agreement we were to guard your Excellencies out of the city, there are so many Boxers on the Tientsin-Taku road that we should be very apprehensive of misadventure.

"We now request your Excellencies to first take your families and the various members of your staffs and leave your Legation in detachments. We should select trustworthy officers to give close and strict protection, and you should temporarily reside in the Tsungli Yamen, pending future arrangements for your return home in order to preserve friendly relations intact from beginning to end.

"But at the time of leaving the Legations there must on no account whatever be taken any single armed foreign soldiers, in order to prevent doubt and fear on the part of the troops and people, leading to untoward incidents.

"If your Excellency is willing to show this confidence, we beg you to communicate with all the foreign Ministers in Peking, to-morrow at noon being the limit of time, and to let the original messenger deliver your reply, in order that we may settle in advance the day for leaving the Legations.

"This is the single way of preserving relations that we have been able to devise in the face of innumerable difficulties. If no reply is received by the time fixed, even now our affection will not enable us to help you.

"Compliments,
"Prince Ching and others."

APPENDIX E

U.S. Marines Who Received the Medal of Honor During the Boxer Rebellion

The Medal of Honor is the United States' highest award for military valor. During the Boxer Rebellion 33 Marines were awarded the Medal of Honor.

Name	Place	Unit
Sgt. John M. Adams (born George L. Day)	Tien-Tsin	lst Regiment
Cpl. Harry C. Adriance	Tien-Tsin	lst Regiment
Cpl. Edwin N. Appleton	Tien-Tsin	USFS *Newark*
Pvt. Erwin J. Boydston	Peking	USS *Oregon*
Pvt. James Burnes	Tien-Tsin	USFS *Newark*
Pvt. Albert R. Campbell	Tien-Tsin	lst Regiment
Pvt. William L. Carr	Peking	USFS *Newark*
Pvt. James Cooney	Tien-Tsin	lst Regiment
Cpl. John O. Dahlgren	Peking	USS *Oregon*
Pvt. Daniel J. Daly	Peking	USFS *Newark*
Pvt. Harry Fisher*	Peking	USS *Oregon*
Sgt. Alexander J. Foley	Tien-Tsin	lst Regiment
Pvt. Charles R. Francis	Tien-Tsin	lst Regiment
Pvt. Louis R. Gaiennie	Peking	USFS Newark

*Awarded posthumously.

Name	Place	Unit
Pvt. Henry W. Heisch	Tien-Tsin	USFS *Newark*
Pvt. William C. Horton	Peking	USS *Oregon*
Pvt. Martin Hunt	Peking	USS *Oregon*
Pvt. Thomas W. Kates	Tien-Tsin	lst Regiment
Pvt. Clarence E. Mathias	Tien-Tsin	lst Regiment
Pvt. Albert Moore	Peking	USS *Oregon*
Drummer John A. Murphy	Peking	USFS *Newark*
Pvt. William H. Murry (served under the name of Henry W. Davis)	Peking	USFS *Newark*
Pvt. Harry W. Orndoff	Relief Expedition	USFS *Newark*
Cpl. Reuben J. Phillips	Relief Expedition	USFS *Newark*
Pvt. Herbert I. Preston	Peking	USS *Oregon*
Pvt. David J. Scannell	Peking	USS *Oregon*
Pvt. France Silva	Peking	USFS *Newark*
Gy. Sgt. Peter Stewart	Relief Expedition	USFS *Newark*
Sgt. Clarence E. Sutton	Tien-Tsin	lst Regiment
Pvt. Oscar J. Upham	Peking	USS *Oregon*
Sgt. Edward A. Walker	Peking	USS *Oregon*
Pvt. Frank A. Young	Peking	USFS *Newark*
Pvt. William Zion	Peking	USFS *Newark*

Appendix F

Marine Officers Receiving a Brevet Commission During the Boxer Rebellion

The U.S. Congress approved the Medal of Honor in 1861 for distinguished conduct in the presence of the enemy. During the early years, officers were not eligible for the Medal of Honor. Instead, a brevet commission was conferred upon officers for distinguished conduct in the presence of the enemy. No medal, however, was authorized to denote the recipient of a brevet commission as an officer with distinguished service.

On 12 April 1921, Major General Commandant John A. Lejeune recommended to the Secretary of the Navy that the condition be rectified by authorizing an appropriate medal to be prescribed as an article of uniform to denote the possessor of a brevet commission. On 7 June 1924, a Brevet Medal was authorized as an article of uniform in the Marine Corps. Because the Brevet Medal is for distinguished service in the presence of the enemy, it ranks immediately after the Medal of Honor.

Later the brevet commission was abolished and officers became eligible to receive the Medal of Honor on the same basis as the enlisted men.

Brevet

Name	Rank	Date	Place
Butler, Smedley D.	Captain	13 June 1900	Tien-Tsin
Hall, Newt H.	Major	14 Aug. 1900	Peking

Name	Rank	Date	Place
Myers, John T.	Major	20 July 1900	Peking
Powell, William G.	Captain	21 June 1900	Tien-Tsin
Richards, George	Lt. Col.	13 July 1900	Tien-Tsin
Waller, Littleton W.T.	Lt. Col.	13 July 1900	Tien-Tsin

APPENDIX G

Appreciation from the American Missionaries for the Marine Legation Guard

LEGATION OF THE UNITED STATES OF AMERICA,
PEKING, CHINA, AUGUST 20, 1900

To: Major W. P. Biddle,
Commanding United States Marines in Peking.

Sir, — It affords me great pleasure to transmit herewith a copy of resolutions passed by the American missionaries besieged in Peking, expressing their hearty appreciation of the courage, fidelity, and patriotism of the American Marines, who so bravely and tenaciously held the key to our salvation during the whole of the trying time.

I most heartily and sincerely join in this expression, and beg you to communicate to both officers and men my personal commendation of and gratitude for their heroic and faithful services.

Yours very respectfully,
E. H. Conger

To: Hon. E. H. Conger
Minister of the United States of America.
(forwarded by Maj. Biddle, U.S.M.C., Commanding
Peking, Saturday, August 18, 1900)

Dear Sir, — At a meeting of the American missionaries held this morning at 8:30 the following resolution was unanimously adopted; and it was further voted that the resolution be drafted and presented to you:

"The Americans who have been besieged in Peking desire to express their hearty appreciation of the courage, fidelity, and patriotism of the American Marines, to whom we so largely owe our salvation.

"By their bravery in holding an almost untenable position on the city wall in the face of overwhelming numbers, and in cooperating in driving the Chinese from a position of great strength, they made all foreigners in Peking their debtors, and have gained for themselves an honorable name among the heroes of their country."

For the meeting [signed]:
Arthur H. Smith, Chairman
Charles E. Ewing, Secretary

HEADQUARTERS FIRST REGIMENT OF MARINES
PEKING, CHINA, AUGUST 23, 1900

Respectfully forwarded to the brigadier-general, commandant, United States Marine Corps Headquarters, Washington, D.C.

W.P. Biddle
Major, U.S.M.C., Commanding

Appendix H

Letters to Major Waller from British Officers Commending the Marines' Action at Tien-Tsin

On 9 July 1900, the allied forces made an attack on the Chinese Western Arsenal at Tien-Tsin. The Marines and Japanese sailors joined and entered the arsenal together. Although subject to considerable artillery fire, the Marines suffered no losses.

The following letters are from British officers.

Tien-Tsin, China, July 10, 1900

Dear Major Waller:

Sir, — The officers who were with the detachment of my regiment that were dragging the guns yesterday asked me to write and thank you for the support you gave them yesterday by keeping down the enemy's fire while they were crossing an exposed place. Their opinion is that had it not been for the action by you and your men, they would have had a good many casualties.

Please accept my sincere thanks, and believe me,

Yours sincerely,
H. Bowers

Tien-Tsin, July 9, 1900.

Dear Major Waller:

Sir, — I beg leave to thank you for having been good enough to send out a force to cooperate in the action to-day. The steadiness of your men and the manner in which they entered the arsenal were much admired. The actual command of the expedition was, as you know, under the Japanese general, with our general, Brigadier-General A. R. Dorward, D.S.O., assisting; but, as being myself present, I desire to thank you for your valuable assistance, and to assure you that we are always happy to have your officers and men associated with us.

I have the honor to be, sir,

Your obedient servant,
E. H. Seymour, Vice-Admiral

APPENDIX I

Operation Reports of the U.S. Marines in the Relief of the Besieged Legation Quarter at Peking

OPERATIONS OF U.S. MARINE CORPS,
TIEN-TSIN TO PEKING NO. 57.

Headquarters, First Regiment U.S. Marines,
China Relief Expedition,
Peking, China, August 20, 1900.

To: The Major-General Commanding
United States Forces, China
Relief Expedition, Peking, China,

Sir, — In obedience to your order of the 17th instant, I have the honor to report that the First Regiment, U.S. Marines, China Relief Expedition, left Tien-Tsin the afternoon of August 4, 1900, as part of your column. The following was the composition:

Major W.P. Biddle, commanding; Major George Richards, commissary; Captain W.B. Lemly, quartermaster; First Lieutenant D. D. Porter, regimental adjutant; Surgeon G. A. Lung, U.S.N.; P.A. Surgeon G.D. Costigan, U.S.N.; Assistant Surgeon J.C. Thompson, U.S.N.; Sergeant-Major

J.F. Lawler, regimental sergeant-major; Quartermaster-Sergeant Robt. Johnson; Hospital Apprentice Thomas Ball, U.S.N.; Hospital Apprentice G.D. Stillson, U.S.N.

First Battalion: Major L.W.T. Waller, commanding; First Lieutenant A.E. Harding, Adjutant.

Company A: First Lieutenant S.D. Butler, commanding; First Lieutenant R.F. Wynne, Second Lieutenant C.C. Carpenter, 74 enlisted.

Company C: First Lieutenant R.L. Dunlap, commanding; Second Lieutenant F.M. Wise, Second Lieutenant W.C. Harice, 74 enlisted.

Company H: Captain P.M. Bannon, commanding; First Lieutenant J.F. McGill, First Lieutenant William Hopkins, 73 enlisted.

Second Battalion: Captain F.J. Moses, commanding; First Lieutenant J.H.A. Day, adjutant.

Company D: Captain C.G. Long, commanding; First Lieutenant A.J. Matthews, Second Lieutenant W. McCreary, 73 enlisted.

Company I: Captain W.C. Neville, commanding, First Lieutenant S.A.W. Patterson, Second Lieutenant D.W. Blake, 87 enlisted.

Company F: Captain B.H. Fuller, commanding; First Lieutenant W.H. Clifford, Second Lieutenant L. McLittle, 68 enlisted.

Strength of regiment at leaving Tien-Tsin: 39 commissioned, 453 enlisted; total, 482.

In the engagement of Pei-tsang, which occurred on the 5th, the United States forces did not come under fire. On the 6th the battle of Yang-tsun took place, a report of which is hereto appended marked "A." Reports of the engagements around Peking on the 14th and 15th are also appended, marked "B" and "C," respectively. The distance marched was about eighty miles, from Tien-Tsin to Peking. On the night of the 4th the command bivouacked Shiliko, the night of the 5th at Pei-tsang, the 6th and 7th at Yang-tsun, the 8th at Tsai-tsun, the 9th to the south of Ho-si-wu, the 10th at Tshien-ping, the 11th at Chang-chai-wan, the 12th at Tung-Chow, and the 13th at Ting-fudsh. Though the distance covered daily was not great, the men suffered severely from the effects of the sun and extreme heat, but at Matow, about two-thirds of the way, when the order came to leave all men behind who were incapable of marching further, there were but four Marines who were unfit to proceed.

I wish to commend my two battalion commanders, Major L.W.T. Waller and Captain F.J. Moses, who at all times showed great judgment in handling of their respective battalions in action and had their men under excellent control. I also wish to commend my regimental adjutant, Lieutenant D. D. Porter, who was most zealous and efficient in carrying out my orders. Surgeon G. A. Lung, P.A., Surgeon G. D. Costigan, and Assistant

Surgeon J.C. Thompson were alert and zealous in caring for those overcome by heat and the wounded. The commissary and the quartermaster,
Major George Richards and Captain W.B. Lemly, worked hard and under
difficulties and succeeded most admirably in keeping supplies up with the
regiment. All officers and men performed their duties well.

The following were sent back sick, were missing, or were detached
during the march:

First Battalion

	Enlisted	Commissioned
Detached	62	1
Placed on junks	24	
Sent to hospital	6	1
Missing	4	
Total	96	2
Grand Total	98	

Second Battalion

	Enlisted	Commissioned
Detached	58	2
Placed on junks	21	1
Sent to hospital	6	
Missing	11	
Dead	1	
Total	97	3
Grand Total	100	

The strength of the regiment to-day in Peking is:

Major W. P. Biddle, commanding; Major George Richards, commissary;
Captain W.B. Lemly, quartermaster; First Lieutenant D.D. Porter, regimental
adjutant; Surgeon G.A. Lung, U.S.N.; P.A. Surgeon G.D. Costigan, U.S.N.;
Assistant Surgeon J.C. Thompson, U.S.N.; Sergeant-Major J.F. Lawler, reg-
imental sergeant-major; Quartermaster Sergeant Robert Johnson; Hospital
Apprentice Thomas Ball, U.S.N.; Hospital Apprentice G.D. Stillson, U.S.N.

First Battalion — Major L.W.T. Waller, commanding; First Lieutenant A.E. Harding, adjutant.

Company A: First Lieutenant S.D. Butler, commanding, Second Lieutenant C.C. Carpenter, 45 enlisted.

Company C: Second Lieutenant F.M. Wise, commanding, Second
Lieutenant W.C. Harlee, 40 enlisted.

Company H: Captain P.M. Bannon, commanding; First Lieutenant J.F. McGill; First Lieutenant William Hopkins, 40 enlisted.

Second Battalion: Captain F.J. Moses, commanding, First Lieutenant J.H.A. Day, adjutant.

Company D: Captain C.G. Long, commanding; First Lieutenant A.J. Matthews, Second Lieutenant L. McLittle. 69 enlisted.

Company I: Captain W.C. Neville, commanding; First Lieutenant S.A.W. Patterson, Second Lieutenant D.W. Blake, 69 enlisted.

Strength of regiment to-day in Peking: 24 commissioned, 267 enlisted; total 291.

In addition to the number that marched out with the regiment from Tien-Tsin, there were left in Tien-Tsin as guards and in the hospital: 6 commissioned, 2 surgeons, 177 enlisted, total 185.

The reports of subordinated commanders are herewith inclosed.

Very respectfully,
W. P. Biddle Major,
U. S. Marine Corps Commanding

[FIRST ENDORSEMENT]
HEADQUARTERS CHINA RELIEF EXPEDITION,
PEKING, CHINA, SEPTEMBER 1, 1900.

Respectfully forwarded to the Adjutant-General of the Army.

With special pleasure I commend the First Regiment of Marines, serving with this expedition during the march from Tien-Tsin to Peking, for fortitude shown by both officers and men during a march made most trying because of intense heat and a general absence of water suitable to drink. Without exception, the fatigue of the march was borne to the extent of physical endurance without a murmur.

The operations engaged in by this regiment on August 5th and 6th were almost entirely in fields of standing corn, and rendered alignment and the keeping of direction very difficult and marching unusually fatiguing.

The regiment was frequently under my personal observation, and I commend it highly for soldierly qualities. Particularly do I desire to invite attention to Major L.W.T. Waller and Captain F.J. Moses, the battalion commanders, whose energy, good judgment, and capacity to command their battalions I noted with pleasure.

The further operations of this regiment with the expedition, including the taking of Peking, August 14th and 15th, was exceedingly satisfactory and deserving of high praise and commendation for services well performed.

My congratulations and thanks are extended to officers and men of the regiment.

Attention is specially invited to the reports of battalion and company commanders for details of service by battalions and companies.

Anda R. Chaffee,
Major-General, U.S.V., Commanding.
No. 58.

[ENCLOSURE A]
REPORT OF THE BATTLE OF YANG-TSUN, AUGUST 6TH, 1900. HEADQUARTERS FIRST REGIMENT MARINES PEKING, CHINA, AUGUST 20, 1900

To: The Major-General,
Commanding United States Forces,
China Relief Expedition, Peking, China

Sir,-In obedience to your order of the 17th instant, I respectfully submit my report of the operations against Yang-tsun, August 6, 1900.

The Marines acted as a support to Reilly's Battery through out the day. During the early advance we came under the fire of both small-arms and artillery. At one stage of the fight the enemy's cavalry was discovered on our right front and were put to rout by several well-directed volleys. We then advanced on a village in line of skirmishers, throwing out scouts to front and taking said village with little or no opposition and without loss. After a short rest, we again advanced and drove the enemy out of another village.

Owing to frequent changes of direction, flank movements and excessive heat, many of the men were overcome. In the engagement Corporal Brophy died from heat and Private Pruitt was wounded.

Very Respectfully,
W. P. Biddle,
Major, U. S. Marine Corps,
Commanding. No. 65.

HEADQUARTERS SECOND BATTALION.
FIRST REGIMENT U.S. MARINES,
CHINA RELIEF EXPEDITION
YANG-TSUN, CHINA, AUGUST 7, 1900

To: The Commanding Officer,
First Regiment U.S. Marines, China Relief Expedition.

Sir, — In obedience to your order of this date, I have the honor to submit the following report.

About 10 A.M., August 6th, the Second Battalion followed the First over the railroad embankment and was immediately separated from it. Upon separation, we came under the fire of an enemy battery stationed on our front and right, the first shell passing over our heads and falling about twenty yards beyond. It did not explode. Marching parallel and near the railroad embankment, we took position, by your order, in a ditch in rear of the Fifth U.S. Artillery. We remained in this position for a short time, and were then ordered to support the advance of the First Battalion, which was advancing to attack a village to the east of us.

As soon as the battalion was deployed, orders were received to take position on the left of the First Battalion. Before this movement was completed the battalion was ordered well to the left to form on the left of the Fifth U.S. Artillery, which had moved its position to the left and front. While moving to this latter position, I received notice that the battery had moved to your left and was ordered to move upon a line with you and on your left. This latter movement being completed, the battery was shelled, and the battalion advanced with the First to the attack. The village was found deserted and after a short halt an advance was made to a village beyond.

The second village was not attacked by the infantry, but at 2:30 P.M. we were directed to proceed to the site selected as camp. Half of the battalion was sent to the new camp and the other half returned over the battlefield to take in those who had fallen out from heat prostration.

Owing to the intense heat and long march, one officer, First Lieutenant J.H.A. Day, adjutant, and about 40 per cent of the men, became overcome by heat, and were not able to advance beyond the first village.

During the first part of the battle the battalion was under both artillery and infantry fire, the fire of the first falling short and that of the latter going beyond us.

Where both officers and men showed, individually and collectively, such commendable fortitude and spirit, many of them just dragging themselves along in order to be in the attack, it is impossible to discriminate.

Corporal Thomas Brophy, U.S.M.C., of Company I, died at about 2:50 P.M. from heat-prostration, and Private Norman Pruitt, U.S.M.C., of Company D, was wounded in the head.

Very respectfully,
F. J. Moses, Captain, U.S. Marines,
Commanding Second Battalion.

HEADQUARTERS SECOND BATTALION
FIRST REGIMENT, U. S. M. C.,
CHINA RELIEF EXPEDITION
PEKING, CHINA, AUGUST 18, 1900.

To: The Commanding Officer,
First Regiment Marines

Sir, — In obedience to your orders of 17th instant, I have the honor to submit the following report:

About 7 A.M., August 14th, this battalion struck camp and moved forward with the regiment, and during the day remained with the regiment until about 3 P.M., when Company I joined Company D as rear guard of the pack-train. At about 10 A.M., in obedience to your order, Company D was ordered to act as guard for the pack-train. The battalion arrived in camp about 9 P.M. of that date.

On the 15th instant the battalion was under your immediate command the whole day. I inclose the report of the commanding officer of Company D.

Very respectfully,
C. F. Moses, Captain, Commanding
Second Battalion, U. S. Marine Corps.

CHINA RELIEF EXPEDITION, PEKING, CHINA

Sir, — In obedience to your order of the 17th instant, I beg leave to submit my report of operation against Peking, August 14, 1900.

The Marines advanced to a position near the north gate of the city under a slight fire, and halted while a platoon from two companies were set to the top of the wall to stop "sniping" and protect the artillery, which was successfully accomplished.

The casualties for the day were 3 wounded: Lieutenant S. D. Butler, slight wound in the chest; Private G. P. Farrell and Private F. W. Green.

We bivouacked for the night just outside the walls of the Tartar City.

Very respectfully,
W. P. Biddle, Major, U. S.
Marine Corps, Commanding.

No. 68.
Headquarters Second Battalion
First Regiment U.S. Marines,
Peking, China, August 20, 1900.

To: Major W. P. Biddle, U.S.M.C., Commanding
First Regiment U. S. Marine Corps

Sir, — In obedience to your order of the 17th instant, I have to report that during the actions of August 14th and 15th, Company I, which I have the honor to command, was always with the regiment in the advance on and entrance into Peking.

Very respectfully,
W. C. Neville,
Captain, U. S. Marine Corps,
Commanding Company J.

APPENDIX J

Roster of Marine Personnel in North China on December 8, 1941

Colonel
ASHURST, William W.

Majors
BROWN, Luther A.
MCCAULLEY, Edwin P.

Captains
CLIMIE, James F.
HESTER, James R.
WHITE, John A.

First Lieutenants
NEWTON, George R.
WEBER, Richard D.

Second Lieutenants
HUIZENGA, Richard M.
MCBRAYER, James D., Jr.

Chief Warrant Officer
LEE, William A.

Quartermaster Clerk
CARLSON, August W.

Pay Clerk
WILLIAMS, Robert L.

Sergeant Majors
DAVIS, Jack
DIETZ, Cecil M.

Master Technical Sergeant
FOSTER, Abner E.

Quartermaster Sergeant
REHM, Orville E.

First Sergeants
MILLER, Frank
NEWHOUSE, Gerald A.

Gunnery Sergeant
ELLIS, CliffOrd L.

Technical Sergeant
PIERCE, Charles D., Jr.

Supply Sergeants
CALLIS, James A.
SCHICK, Michael J.
STOWERS, Henry B.

Platoon Sergeants
BISHOP, Jack H.

CARPENTER, Thomas R.
CASH, Holland

Staff Sergeants

ECCLES, Raymond E.W.
ELVESTAD, Henry A.
JARRETT, Elmer P. (Mess)
SMITH, Raymond E. (Mess)

Sergeants

BERG, Norman J.
CIARRACHI, Victor F.
CLARK, Russell P.
DOBSON, Roy A.
HAUGO, Morris F.
HOWARD, William H.
KAHL, William A.
KILLEBREW, William F., Jr.
KOSSYTA, Frank J.
MACDONALD, Edward L.
MOHL, Frederick F.
REILLY, Walter J.
SMITH, Robert A.
STONE, George B., Jr.
STROMSTAD, Eric
SYDOW, Alan A.D.
WARSHAFSKY, Jack
WOLF, Herman

Chief Cooks

DARR, Charles H.
LEON, Antonio
MILLER, Orin R.

Corporals

AKERS, Irving M.
ANDERSON, Willis W.
ANDREESEN, Arnold
ARMSTRONG, Robert L.
BATTLES, Connie G.
BEEMAN, Gerald L.
BLAHAUTA, Alvin H.
BRADSHAW, "A Z"
BRIMMER, Charles M.

BROWN, Harold P.
CHITTENDEN, William H.
CRAFTS, Glenn F.
CREWS, "T G"
DAVIDSON, Arthur C.
DEDMON, Theodore R.
ELLISON, John H.
ENGLER, Irvin J.
FOUCHE, Chandle E.
GAFF, Max "S"
HARDWAY, James E.
HOFFMAN, Harold A.
JONES, Joel
KEITH, Robert V.
KELLY, Bernard F.
KIRK, Terence S.
KIRKPATRICK, Edward L.
LADY, Dennis G.
LAREAU, Robert A.
LINDSEY, George D.
MCFARLAND, George W.
MCLEOD, Winfred N.
MARSHALL, Donald R.
MELTON, Oliver S.
NOVAK, Frank J.
O'NEAL, Elza S.
PARR, Charles W.
PITNER, John D.
RETZKE, Harold L.
RIDER, Richard
ROARK, Clyde E.
SAWYER, Alvin E.
SCHNEIDER, Jacob V.
SERRA, Miguel
SOMMERS, James M.
STORY, Jerald B.
TIMPANY, David A.
WRATHALL, John C.

Field Cooks

BENSON, Benjamin R.
PARR, George W.

Field Music Corporals
    BUCHER, Carroll W.
    GRAY, Martin L.

Privates First Class
    ADAMS, William L.
    ALLEN, Walter C.
    ANDERSON, Allison L.
    ARMSTRONG, Wade H., Jr.
    BEAVERS, John
    BECKER, Robert C.
    BEESON, Darrel M.
    BENNETT, Raymond O.
    BENNISON, Elroy L.
    BENTON, Willie L.
    BIGGS, Chester M., Jr.
    BOYDEN, William H., Jr.
    BRIGHAM, William J.
    BROWN, Fred H.
    BUNN, Douglas "A"
    CARSON, Morris A.
    CASTOR, Melvin H.
    CHAMBERS, Philip S.
    CLARK, Kenneth R.
    COLE, James H.
    CROTEAU, Edgar A.
    DAVIS, Kenneth W.
    DAWSON, Jasper F.
    DEES, William J.
    DITEWIG, Wilbur E.
    ESTEP, Norman R.
    EVANS, Glenn "G"
    FITZGERALD, Bernard J.
    FREHR, Joseph J.
    FREIBERGER, Walter E.
    GENTRY, Mark N.
    GESSNER, Maurice E.
    GLAZE, James E.
    GOLDMAN, Luther E.
    GOUDY, Ralph H.
    GRIFFIN, Earl D., Jr.
    GUYNN, Marion

HABERMAN, Robert R.
HALL, Richard T.
HARBISON, Leonard S.
HARMON, Jack B.
HINKLE, James E.
HIRSCHKAMP, George
HORNSBY, Jack C.
HUMPHREY, Thomas S.
JESSE, John H.
LEASE, Raymond E.
LEPPERT, Roy W.
LITZ, Eugene H.
LOGAN, Emit F.
LUDLOW, Charles C.
LUSK, Thomas V.
MCCARTHY, Roy E.
MCMAHON, Ronald O.
MCSHANE, George L.
MATTHEWS, Raymond L.
NAHAS, Richard
NEUSE, Max H.
ORR, Herbert J.
PARRISH, Lloyd "G"
PERMETER, Calvin L.
PLOG, Francis L.
PRATER, Frank P.
PRATTE, Ralph
PRUETT, Johnnie M.
RAMSEY, Marvin C.
READER, William D.
RIDER, Neil O.
RODRIGUEZ, Fernando C.
SALAY, Steve A.
SEDENERG, Leslie
SHEETS, Fremont F.
SIMO, Marino J.
SMITH, Dick R.
SOUSEK, Merlyn J.
SPARKMAN, Orville R.
STEWART, Charles A., Jr.
STEWART, Jimmie L.

STOCKMAN, Frank D.
STOHLMAN, Matthew H.
THOMAS, William H.
TROTH, Leslie R.
WELSH, Thomas P.
WHIPPLE, John W.
WILSON, James C.

Field Music First Class
LARSON, Ernest T., Jr.

Field Music
BRAWDY, Ira M.

U.S. Navy Medical Corps
Commander
THYSON, Leo C., Sr.(Dr.)

Lieutenants, jg
FOLEY, William T.(Dr.)
POLLARD, Eric G.F.(Dc)

Chief Pharmacist's Mate
HALL, Ellison K.

Pharmacist's Mates First Class
BLACK, Loy J.
CASTLETON, John V.
FOX, Edwin J.
HUNT, William S.
RILEY, William E.
WALMER, Dan

Pharmacist's Mates Third Class
DAVIS, Herman
RYAN, John F.
SCHRADER, Arthur H.

Hospital Apprentice First Class
JOHNSON, Earl R.

Appendix K

Knights of the Round Table Roster

As explained in Chapter 11, the so-called "Round Table" was a gathering place for certain Marines on liberty in Peiping. The Round Table sat in the back of Hemple's Restaurant on Hataman Street, and those who gathered there called themselves "the Knights of the Round Table." Following World War II, Clem Russell of El Paso, Texas, an old China hand from the 1930s, recovered the actual Round Table and now has it in his home.

M. Ogdan	K. Kakansan
A. C. Mandel '30	E. Litke
Chief Bender	Detcil Dyson
J. T. Lawrence '30	F. F. Gowen '30
Jimmy Burch '32	S. Bonner
Frank Beal '39	Doc Spring '31
F. E. Grimm	Jack Fliey
E. J. Lewis	A. D. Smith '39
Swede Gagner	H. Malcolm
M. Cooper	Harry Bryan '30
W. L. Tracy	W. F. Kromp '30
J. Greer	R. Leard
Bull Blasi	R. Chaumeron
Pop Parsons '31	Kinel
H. L. Wilkinson	C. Anner 1937
W. Meeks	Garrison
A. J. Herrick	C. P. Rabe

R. Johnson
Otto Miller
R. W. Johnson '30
G. Personius
Joe Crousen
J. G. Coyle
Paddy Boyd '39
Pa Hempel
W. Henry
J. J. McGarth '31
Leo Hein
C. F. Creswell '30
C. J. Meyers
Ludvigson
Lord Howard
Frank Miller
Joe Beckett '31
Pop Niblo
Pappy Teel
Pop Peal
W. L Williams '31

J. Golden '30
J. H. Griffin '31
G. T. O'Brien '31
O. Hempl
Karl '31
P. B. Cowles
Fredie Milam '31
T. C. Burton
R. Jameson
S. E. Johnsen
Bill Dyer
Ballon Walters '30
C. F. H. Noll
W. S. Smith '31
J. Jaroszewski
John Anderson
C. E. Douglas '30
Gus
Soapy Smith
A. E. Foster
"Ajax" Roberts '31
G. Davidson '31

Notes

Prologue

1. Although the United States fully agreed with the "Open Door" Policy, it declined to participate in any kind of demonstrations that would menace in any way the integrity of the Chinese Empire. While the United States wanted to protect American lives, property, and trade and commercial interests, it was not willing to form any alliances with the Western Powers to do so. During the Boxer Rebellion this policy posed a problem for Admiral Kempff when it came to carrying out his orders, while cooperating with the allied powers, to protect American lives and property. The allied powers were critical of the United States, claiming the United States was benefiting from their fighting, without actually engaging in the same.

Chapter 1

1. *New York Times,* 2-13-1895 (5–4), "China Settled Method; Reminiscences of the English French Experience in Their Invasion of Thirty-five Years Ago."

Chapter 2

1. Elliott later became the 11th Commandant of the of the Marine Corps and the first permanent major general commandant of the Marine Corps.
2. Conger, Sara Pike, *Letters from China,* Hodder and Stoughton, 1909, 24–29.
3. Conger, *op. cit.* 207.
4. *Ibid.*

Chapter 3

1. *New York Times*, 4-15-1900 (21–5).

2. Coltman, Robert, Jr., M.D., *Beleaguered in Peking; The Boxer War Against the Foreigners*, F.A. Davis Company, Publishers, 1901, 40–41.

3. Coltman, *op. cit.*, 41.

4. *Ibid.*

5. *New York Times*, 4-14-1900 (5–2).

6. *New York Times*, 4-15-1900 (21–5).

7. *New York Times*, 5-31-1900 (1–5).

8. *Ibid.*

9. *New York Times*, 4-15-1900 (21–5).

10. *Ibid.*

11. *Ibid.*

12. *Ibid.*

13. *Ibid.*

14. "The Chinese lunar year is divided into twelve months of 29 or 30 days (compensating for the lunar months means [a] duration of 29 days, 12 hours, 44.05 minutes). The calendar is synchronized with the solar year by the addition of extra days at regular intervals. The years are arranged in major cycles of 60 years. Each successive year is named after an animal: rat, ox, tiger, hare (rabbit), dragon, snake, horse, sheep, (goat), monkey, rooster, dog and pig. These twelve-year cycles are continuously repeated. The Chinese New Year is celebrated at the second new moon after the winter solstice and falls between January 31 and February 19, on the Gregorian Calendar." *Times Almanac 2001*, Family Education Co., Boston, MA. The Boxer Rebellion in 1900 was in the year of the rat.

15. "Planchette — a small three cornered device, often having as one of its supports a pencil, that is supposed to write out a message or, as with a Ouija board, point to letters or words, as it moves with the fingers resting lightly on it." *Webster's New World Dictionary of the American Language*, Simon & Schuster, 1972.

16. Coltman, *op. cit.* 42.

17. Coltman, *op. cit.* 42–43.

18. Coltman, *op. cit.* 43–44.

Chapter 4

1. New York Times, May 26, 1900, 5-2. "United States Government Declares They Must Be Suppressed and Americans Protected."

2. *Ibid.*

3. *New York Times*, April 8, 1900, 7–1. "Boxers Society Demand Their Suppression."

4. Brown, the Rev. Frederick, *From Tientsin to Peking with the Allied Forces*, Longmans, Green and Company, London, 1902, 33.

5. Hoover, Herbert, *The Memoirs of Herbert Hoover, Years of Adventure, 1874–1920*, The Macmillan Company, New York, 1951, 52.

6. Conger, Sarah Pike (Mrs. E. H. Conger, wife of American foreign minister), Hodder and Stoughton, London, (1909), 15.

7. Hooker, Mary, *Behind the Scenes in Peking*, Brentano's, New York, 1910, 24–29.

Chapter 5

1. Clements, Paul H., *The Boxer Rebellion*, New York, 1961, 132.

2. Capt. J. K. Taussing, USN, *Experiences During the Boxer Rebellion*, U.S. Naval Institute Proceedings, 1927.

3. *New York Times*, 6-30-1900 (1–7), "Seymour's Story of His Struggles."

4. *Ibid.*

5. Heinl, Robert Debs, Jr., Col., USMC, *Soldiers of the Sea*, National Nautical and Aviation Publishing Company of America, Baltimore, Maryland, 1991, 131.

6. Clements, *op. cit.*, 133.

Chapter 6

1. American Minister Conger's dispatch to Secretary of State, 15 June 1900, in Foreign Relations of the United States, 1900, Washington, 1902, 154.

2. Daggett, Aaron Simon, Brig. Gen., USA, Retired, *America in the China Relief Expedition*, Hudson-Kimberly Publishing Company, Kansas City, 1903, 10.

3. Thomas, Lowell, *Old Gimlet Eye: The Adventures of Smedly D. Butler,* Farrar & Rinehart, Inc., New York, 1933, 48.

4. *Ibid.*

5. Daggett, *op. cit.* 25–26.

6. Thomas, *op. cit.* 50–51, and Schuan, Karl, editor, *The Leatherneck*, Franklin Watts, Inc., New York, 1963, "Old Gimlet Eye," Polete, Harry, 101.

7. *Correspondence Relating to the War with Spain Including the Insurrection in the Philippine Islands, and China Relief Expedition.* April 15, 1896 to July 30, 1900. Vol. I. and II, Washington, D.C., Printing Office, 1902, 477.

8. *Ibid.*

9. Thomas, *op. cit.*, 53–54.

10. *New York Times*, Aug. 8, 1900 (2–3).

11. Major L.W.T. Waller's Report to CinC, Asiatic Station, 22 June 1900. See Major Waller's Report of 26 Sep.

12. *Ibid.*

13. Adm. Louis Kempff, commanding the China Squadron, forwarding endorsement to CinC, Asiatic Station, 4 July 1900.

14. Daggett, *op. cit.*, 21.

Chapter 7

1. Brown, The Rev. Frederick, *From Tien-Tsin to Peking with the Allied Forces,* Longmans, Green and Company, London, 1902, 33.

2. *New York Times* 6-25-1900 (1–7), "Allied Troops at Tien-Tsin in Peril."

3. *New York Times* 6-26-1900 (1–7), "The Relief Forces Enter Tien-Tsin."

4. Second Lieutenant Frederick M. Wise, USMC, who served with Meade's First Marine regiment during the attack on Tien-Tsin and the march to Peking, was his son.

5. Wise, Frederick M., Col., USMC, *Tell It to the Marines,* J.H. Sears & Co., Inc., 1929, 27.

6. *New York Times* 6-20-1900 (1–1), "Taku Battle."

7. Fleming, Peter, *The Siege at Peking,* Harper & Brothers, New York, 1959, 80.

8. *Ibid.*

9. *New York Times* 6-20-1900 (3–3), "Kempff Has Wide Powers."

10. *Ibid.*

11. *Ibid.*

12. *Ibid.*

13. *Ibid.*

14. *Correspondence Relating to the War with Spain Including the Insurrection in the Philippine Islands and the China Relief Expedition,* April 15, 1898 to July 30, 1902, Volumes I and II, Washington, D.C., Government Printing Office, 1902, 422.

15. *New York Times* 6-19-1900 (1–1), "China Is at War with the World."

16. The USS *Brooklyn* was the largest cruiser in the Asiatic Squadron.

17. Wise, *op. cit.* 26–27.

18. Wise, *op. cit.* 29.

19. *Ibid.*

20. *Ibid.*

21. Wise, *op. cit.* 31.

22. Daggett, Aaron Simon, Brig. Gen., USA, Ret., *America in the China Expedition,* Hudson-Kimberly Publishing Co., Kansas City 1903, 26–27.

23. Herbert Hoover, *The Memoirs of Herbert Hoover: Years of Adventure 1874–1920,* Vol. II, The Macmillan Company, New York, 1951, 53.

24. *Ibid.*

25. "Marines in the 1900 defense of Peking Legations and the China Relief Expedition — known popularly as the Boxer Rebellion — carried a mixed bag of rifles. The Legation Guard, made up of two ship's detachments, used the 6mm Winchester-Lee. The First Marine Regiment, from the Philippines, had the .30 caliber Krag-Jorgensen made at the Springfield armory. Ship's detachments, organized into a Second Marine Regiment, used the older .45 caliber trapdoor Springfield and Lees. Ammunition resupply was a quartermaster headache." From Simmons, Edward Howard, and J. Robert Moskin, *The Marine,* The Marine Corps Heritage Foundation, Hugh Lauter Levin Associates, Inc., Hong Kong, 1998, 158.

26. The gingals were Chinese rifles with seven-foot barrels and breech-loading stocks. They fire a one-pound projectile. It took three men to handle the gingal. The weapon was sighted over the shoulders of two and fired by a third. They

could be sighted accurately to a very long range. They gave terrific wounds. Wise, *op. cit.* 34.

27. Fleming, *op. cit.* 98.

28. Enfiladed — gun fire directed from either flank along the length of a column or line of troops.

29. Action Report by CO, Ninth Infantry, 25 July 1900.

30. Thomas Lowell, *Old Gimlet Eye*, Farrar & Rinehart, Inc., New York, 1933, 65.

31. Heinl, Robert Debs, Jr., Col., USMC, *Soldiers of the Sea*, The Nautical & Aviation Publishing Company of America, Baltimore, 1991, 65.

32. Hoover, *op. cit.* 53.

33. Wise, *op. cit.* 38.

34. Daggett, *op. cit.* 28.

35. *Correspondence Relating to the War with Spain*, *op. cit.* 438.

36. *Correspondence Relating to the War with Spain*, *op. cit.* 440.

37. *China Marine Association*, Turner Publishing Co., Paducah, KY, 1995. 11.

38. Heinl, *op. cit.* 137.

39. Moskin, J. Robert, *The U.S. Marine Corps Story*, McGraw-Hill Book Company, New York, 1997, 111.

Chapter 8

1. Myers, John T., Personal Papers Collection, Marine Corps University Archives, Quantico, Va.

2. Tuttle, A.H., *Mary Gamewell And Her Story of the Siege of Peking*, Eaton and Mains, New York, 1907, 195.

3. *Ibid.*, 199.

4. *Ibid.*, 204.

5. *Ibid.*, 205.

6. Conger, Sara Pike, *Letters from Peking*, Hodder and Stoughton, London, 1909, 126.

7. Hooker, Mary, *Behind the Scenes in Peking*, Brentano's, London, 1910, 36.

8. Myers, John T., "Military Operations and Defense of Peking," United States Naval Institute Proceedings, September 1902, 544.

9. Heinl, Robert Debs, Jr., Col., USMC, Ret., *Soldiers of the Sea: The United States Marine Corps, 1775–1963*, The Nautical & Aviation Publishing Co., Baltimore, Maryland, 1991, 137.

10. Hooker, *op. cit.* 98.

11. Lord, Walter, *The Good Years, From 1900 to the First World War*, Harper & Row, Publishers, New York, 1960, 22.

12. It should be noted that the Russians shared the breastworks on the west end of Legation Street and not the Wall. The two Russians were in the Legation Street breastworks and not the Wall barricade.

13. Hooker, *op. cit.* 72.

14. Hooker, *op. cit.* 127.

15. Tuttle, *op. cit.* 248.

16. Tuttle, *op. cit.* 249.

17. Fleming, Peter, *The Siege at Peking,* Harper & Brothers, New York, 1959, 145.

18. Hooker, *op. cit.* 115.

19. Hooker, *op. cit.* 96.

20. Coltman, Robert, Jr., M.D., *Beleaguered in Peking; The Boxers' War Against the Foreigners,* F.A. Davis Company, Publishers, Philadelphia, 1901, 172.

21. Hooker, *op. cit.* 96.

22. Hooker, *op. cit.* 95.

23. Oliphant, Nigel, *Siege of the Legations of Peking,* London, 1901, 59.

24. Diary of Oscar J. Upham, Personal Papers Collection, Marine Corps University Archives, Quantico, Va.

25. *Ibid.*

26. Note by Sir Claude MacDonald contained in notes of an investigation by Captain William Crosier, USA, of conduct of Captain Newt Hall at Peking, in files of Judge Advocate General, case of Captain Newt Hall.

27. Coltman, *op. cit.* 216.

28. Coltman, *op. cit.* 97.

29. Moskin, J. Robert, *The U.S. Marine Corps History,* McGraw-Hill Book Company, New York, 1997, 328.

30. Millett, Alban R., *Semper Fidelis, The History of the United States Marine Corps,* Macmillan Publishing Co., Inc., New York, 1980, 158.

31. Lord, *op. cit.* 28.

32. Miller, Mitchell, "Battle Atop Tartar Wall, Boxer Rebellion," *Leatherneck,* Magazine for Marines, August 2000, Volume LXXXII, 29.

33. Hooker, *op. cit.* 56.

34. Tuttle, *op. cit.* 227.

35. Hooker, *op. cit.* 65.

36. Giles, Lancelot, *The Siege of the Peking Legations,* University of Western Australia Press, Nedland, Western Australia, 1970, 144.

37. *Ibid.,* 144.

38. Before the American forces were withdrawn from North China in 1900, General Chaffee shipped "Old International" to West Point where she is now on display.

39. Upham Diary, *op. cit.*

40. Hooker, *op. cit.* 91.

41. Upham Diary, *op. cit.*

42. *Ibid.*

43. Coltman, *op. cit.* 107.

44. Allen, the Rev. Roland, *The Siege of the Peking Legations,* Smith, Elder, & Co., London, 1901, 206.

45. Lord, *op. cit.* 32.

46. Hooker, *op. cit.* 136.

47. *Ibid.,* 136

48. *Ibid.,* 137

49. Upham Diary, *op. cit.*
50. Coltman, *op. cit.* 120
51. Lord, *op. cit.* 33.
52. Oliphant, *op. cit.* 136
53. Lord, *op. cit.* 33.
54. Coltman, *op. cit.* 129–130.
55. *Ibid.*, 131.
56. *Ibid.*, 133.
57. *Ibid.*, 134.
58. *Ibid.*, 131.
59. *Ibid.*, 134.
60. Lord, *op. cit.* 34.
61. *Ibid.*, 34.
62. *Ibid.*, 34.
63. *Ibid.*, 35.
64. Coltman, *op. cit.* 140.
65. *Ibid.*, 140.
66. Lord, *op. cit.* 37.
67. *Ibid.*, 37.
68. Russell, S.M., *The Story of the Siege of Peking*, Elliott Stock, 62 Paternoster Row, E.C., London, 1901, 29.
69. Brown, the Rev. Frederick, *From Tien-Tsin to Peking with the Allied Forces*, Longman, Green & Co., London, 1902, 113. Brown was appointed correspondent for the *New York Times* after his first report on the fall of the Taku Forts.
70. Hooker, *op. cit.* 187.
71. Quoted in Heinl, *op. cit.* 141.
72. Heinl, *op. cit.* 142.
73. *Ibid.*, 142.
74. *Ibid.*, 142.

Chapter 9

1. Thomas, *op. cit.* 67.
2. Major Biddle was nicknamed "Sitting Bull" by his junior officers because of his love for a comfortable chair. Wise, *op. cit.* 42.
3. Thomas, *op. cit.* 66.
4. Heinl, *op. cit.* 144.
5. Scuttlebutt — In the days of sailing ships, a butt (cask) of water was lashed in place on deck near a small hatch called the scuttle. Men could get a drink of water with a dipper through a small opening in the lid. The butt was called scuttlebutt because of its location. Men who met at the scuttlebutt would exchange news, information, gossip and rumors. Any information picked up at the scuttlebutt was called scuttlebutt. In the naval service today, any information circulating in a command, whether true or untrue, is called scuttlebutt. Incidentally, all water fountains in the naval service today are known as scuttlebutts.

6. Wise, *op. cit.* 43.

7. Thomas, *op. cit.* 69–70.

8. Brown, the Rev. Frederick, *From Tien-Tsin to Peking with the Allied Forces,* Arno Press & The New York Times, New York, 1970. 57. After his dispatches first reported the fall of the Taku Forts, Brown was appointed correspondent for the *New York Journal.*

9. Brown, *op. cit.* 58

10. Wise, *op. cit.* 44.

11. Wise, *op. cit.* 52–53.

12. Wise, *op. cit.* 53.

13. Fleming, Peter, *The Siege at Peking,* Harper & Brothers, New York, 1959. 186.

14. Fleming, *op. cit.* 183.

15. Thomas, *op. cit.* 71.

16. Thomas, *op. cit.* 69.

17. Fleming, *op. cit.* 189.

18. "In 1937, the Second Battalion, Royal Fusiliers once more lay alongside the Marines in China during the crisis in Shanghai. In 1957, the Corps and the regiment exchanged trophies dating back to, and commemorating their first encounter before the walls of Tien-Tsin." Fleming, *op. cit.* 191.

19. Fleming, *op. cit.* 193.

20. Butler was convinced that a Marine was not complete unless he had a tattoo. "His belief was reinforced when Colonels George F. Elliott and Robert L. Meade had themselves tattooed. Butler was sure that this was one of the things necessary to become a real Marine." Harry Polete, "Old Gimlet Eye," in Schuon, Karl, *The Leatherneck,* Franklin Watts, Inc., New York, 1963, 100. While Butler was stationed in the Philippines, a Japanese tattoo artist, after several hours, covered eighteen-year-old Butler's chest with a huge Marine Corps emblem.

21. Thomas, *op. cit.* 73–74.

22. Fleming, *op. cit.* 208.

23. Thomas, *op. cit.* 75.

24. Wise, *op. cit.* 63.

25. *New York Times,* Dec. 27, 1900 (7-1).

26. Wise, *op. cit.* 64–65.

27. Wise, *op. cit.* 2–3.

28. Thomas, *op. cit.* 78.

29. Wise, *op. cit.* 70–71.

30. Thomas, *op. cit.* 76.

31. Millett, Alban R., *Semper Fidelis: The History of the United States Marine Corps,* Macmillan Publishing Co., Inc., New York, 1980, 162.

Chapter 10

1. Heinl, *op. cit.* 145.

2. *China Marine Scuttlebutt,* Hodgson, Robert A., Editor, June 1997. "The Horse Marines and Other Adventures, 1925–1929," Burnside, Wayne, 12.

3. *The Leatherneck* magazine, April 1938, 64.

4. American Legation Guard Annual, Peiping, China, 1934, 170–173.

5. Davis, Burke, *Marine! The Life of Chesty Puller*, Bantam Books, New York, 1962, 78.

6. *China Marine Scuttlebutt, op. cit.* 12.

7. Davis, *op. cit.* 78.

8. *The Leatherneck* magazine, *op. cit.* 64.

9. Peiping Marine, Volume Number 5, May 1941, 9.

10. *New York Times*, Oct. 17, 1911, 7:1–3.

11. The Fourth Marine Regiment had been activated on 16 April 1914, and had fought in the Dominican Republic from 1916 to 1924. The Regiment would stay in Shanghai for the next 15 years without even firing a shot and were known as the "China Marines." "Seven of its China-duty members eventually became Commandant of the Marine Corps. Alexander A. Vandergrift (who commanded the Third Battalion in 1927); Clifton. B. Cates; Lemuel C. Shepherd, Jr.; Randolph McC. Pate; David M. Shoup; Wallace M. Green, Jr.; and Robert E. Cushman, Jr. China was the nursery for the Marine Corps leadership in World War II." Moskin, *op. cit.* 452.

12. Metcalf, *op. cit.* 532.

13. Thomas, *op. cit.* 238.

14. *The Annals*, Volume CXLLIV, July 1929. "American Marine in China," An informal address by Brig. Gen. Smedley D. Butler.

15. Thomas, *op. cit.* 389.

16. *Ibid.*, 289.

17. *Ibid.*, 290.

18. *Ibid.*, 290.

19. Finney, Charles G., *The Old China Hands*, Greenwood Press, Westport, Connecticut, 1959, 154.

20. *Ibid.*, 156.

21. *Ibid.*, 154.

22. *Ibid.*, 165.

23. Thomas, *op. cit.* 294.

24. *The Annals, op. cit.*

25. *Ibid.*

26. Moskin, *op. cit.* 453.

27. Heinl, *op. cit.* 292.

28. *New York Times*, Dec. 26, 1927 (1-4).

29. Thomas, *op. cit.* 295–296.

30. *New York Times*, Dec. 26, 1927 (1-4).

31. Thomas, *op. cit.* 296.

32. *New York Times*, Oct. 21, 1928, X (7-2).

33. Thomas, *op. cit.* 298.

34. When the Chinese Nationalists captured Peking (Northern Capital) from the warlords in 1928, the name of the city was changed to Peiping (Northern Peace). The capital of China was moved to Nanking. In 1949, the Chinese Communists restored the name of Peking to the City when it once again became the capital. Later, however, the name of the city was changed to Beijing.

35. Thomas, *op. cit.* 294.

36. *Ibid.*, 298.

Chapter 11

1. *Leatherneck* magazine, January 1938, p. 14.

2. *Leatherneck* magazine, *op. cit.* p. 14–15.

3. Skittles is a game of nine pins that the British enjoy. In this phrase "beer and skittles" means pure pleasure and enjoyment.

4. *Leatherneck* magazine, *op. cit.* p. 53.

5. *New York Times*, July 28, 1937, 4 (1-3).

6. *Leatherneck* magazine, *op. cit.* p. 53.

7. *New York Times*, February 23, 1938 (14-4).

8. *New York Times*, February 28, 1938 (14-4). Another article appeared in February 27, 1938, IV (2-6).

9. Taken from the *Tien-Tsin Marine 1940 Annal*, p. 80.

10. The account of the Tien-Tsin flood was taken from Col. Hawthorne's "Record of Events During the Tientsin Flood–1939." Frank Prater's Personal Papers.

11. *New York Times*, August 10, 1940.

12. *Ibid.*

13. *Ibid.*

14. *The Peking Chronicle*, December 31, 1940. News clippings from the author's personal papers.

15. *The Peking Chronicle*, December 31, 1940, and succeeding issues in June 1941. News clippings from the author's personal papers.

16. *New York Times*, January 4, 1941.

17. American Ambassador Grew in Japan presented this account in an oral statement to Matsuoka, the Japanese minister of foreign affairs, on Jan. 17, 1941. It appeared in Vol. 1 of *Papers Relating to the Foreign Affairs of the United States and Japan 1931–1941*, Washington, D.C.: Government Printing Office, 1943, pp. 707–9.

18. *New York Times*, May 31, 1941. Under the Protocol of 1901 and other agreements, American citizens traveling and conducting business in China, for the most part, came under U.S. Laws and cases involving them were heard by federal judges. Therefore, Hull's statement not only involved the diplomatic corps but also all Americans. By removing the Marines, he felt that the extraterritorial rights for Americans would be endangered.

19. Statement of First Lieutenant George R. Newton, Sept. 22, 1941, on Marine-Japanese incident of Night of Sept. 21, 1941. Author's personal papers.

20. *New York Times*, August 3, 1941.

21. Statement of Chief Marine Gunner William A. Lee, October 28, 1941, on the shooting of Pfc. Douglas A. Bunn. Author's personal papers.

22. *The Peking Chronicle*, October 29, 1941. Author's personal papers.

23. *New York Times*, October 29, 1941.

24. James H. Herzog, *Closing the Open Door: American-Japanese Relations 1936–1941*, Annapolis, Md.: Naval Institute Press, 1973. p. 179.

25. *New York Times*, May 13, 1941; *Herzog, Closing the Open Door.* p. 187.

26. Col. Luther A. Brown papers. Personal Papers Section, Marine Corps Historical Archive, Quantico, Va.

27. White, John A. Col., USMC, Ret., *The United States Marines in North China*, published privately, 1974. p. 15.

28. *Ibid.*

Bibliography

Published Works

Allen, Roland, the Rev., *The Siege of Peking Legations*, Smith, Elder & Co., London, 1901.

Biggs, Chester M., Jr., MSgt., USMC, Ret., *Behind the Barbed Wire*, McFarland & Company, Inc., Publishers, Jefferson, NC, 1995.

Blakeney, Jane, *Heroes, U.S. Marine Corps, 1861–1955*, Guthrie Lithograph Co., Inc., Washington, D.C., 1957.

Brown, Frederick, the Rev., *From Tien-Tsin to Peking with the Allied Forces*, Arno Press & The New York Times, New York, 1970, 57.

Butler, Smedley D., Brig. Gen., USMC, "American Marines in China," An extract from *The Annals*, Vol. CXLIX, July 1929.

China Marine Association, Turner Publishing Co., Paducah, KY., 1995.

Clements, Paul H., *The Boxer Rebellion*, AMS Press, New York, 1967.

Coltman, Robert, Jr., M.D., *Beleaguered in Peking: The Boxer War Against the Foreigners*, F.A. Davis Company, Publishers, Philadelphia, 1901.

Conger, Sarah Pike, *Letters from China*, Hodder and Stoughton, London, 1909.

Correspondence Relating to the War with Spain Including the *Insurrection in the Philippine Islands and the China Relief Expedition*, April 15, 1898 to July 30, 1902, Vol. I and II, Government Printing Office, Washington, D.C., 1902.

Daggett, Aaron Simon, Brig. Gen., USA, Ret., *America in the China Relief Expedition*, Hudson-Kimberly Publishing Co., Kansas City, 1903.

Davis, Burke, *Marine! Life of Chesty Puller*, Bantam Books, New York, 1962.

Finney, Charles G., *The Old China Hands*, Greenwood Press, Publishers, Westport, Connecticut, 1959.

Fleming, Peter, *The Siege at Peking*, Harper & Brothers, New York, 1959.

Giles, Lancelot, *The Siege of the Peking Legations*, University of Western Australia Press, Nedlands, Western Australia, 1970.

Heinl, Robert Debs, Jr., Col., USMC., *Soldiers of the Sea: The United States Marine Corps, 1775–1963*, The Nautical & Aviation Publishing Company of America, Baltimore, MD, 1991.

Herzog, James H., *Closing the Open Door: American-Japanese Relations 1936–1941.* (Annapolis, MD: Naval Institute Press, 1973.

Hooker, Mary, (Polly Condit Smith), *Behind the Scenes in Peking*, Brentano's, New York, 1910.

Hoover, Herbert, *The Memoirs of Herbert Hoover: Years of Adventure 1874–1920*, Vol. II, The Macmillan Company, New York, 1951.

Letcher, John Seymour, Capt., USMC., *Good-Bye to Old Peking*, Ohio University Press, Athens, Ohio, 1998.

Lord, Walter, *The Good Years, From 1900 to the First World War*, Harper and Row, Publishers, New York, 1960.

Metcalf, Clyde H., Lt. Col., USMC, *A History of the United States Marine Corps*, G.W. Putman's Sons, New York.1939.

Millett, Alban R., *Semper Fidelis: The History of the United States Marine Corps*, Macmillan Publishing Co., New York, 1980.

Moskin, J. Robert, *The U. S. Marine Corps Story*, McGraw-Hill Book Company, New York, 1997.

Oliphant, Nigel, *Siege of the Legations of Peking*, Longmans, Green and Company, London, 1901.

Papers Relating to the Foreign Affairs of the United States. *Japan 1931–1941.* 2 vols. Washington, D.C.: Government Printing Office, 1943.

Polete, Harry, "Old Gimlet Eye," article taken from Schuon, Karl, editor, *The Leatherneck*, Franklin Watts, Inc., New York, 1963.

Purcell, Victor, *The Boxer Uprising*, Cambridge University Press, London, 1963.

Russell, S.M., *The Story of the Siege of Peking*, Elliot Stocks, London, 1901.

Shoup, David M., *The Marines in China — 1927–1928*, Archon Books, Hamden, CT, 1987.

Simmons, Edwin H. *The United States Marines, 1775–1975*, The Viking Press, New York, 1974.

Thomas, Lowell, *Old Gimlet Eye: The Adventures of Smedley D. Butler*, Farrar & Rinehart Inc., New York, 1933.

Tuttle, A.H., *Mary Gamewell and Her Story of the Siege of Peking*, Eaton & Mains, New York, 1907.

White, John A., Col. USMC, Ret., *The United States Marines in North China*, published privately, 1974.

Williams, Robert Hugh, Brig. Gen., USMC, Ret., *The Old Corps: A Portrait of the U.S. Marine Corps Between the Wars*, Naval Institute Press, Annapolis, MD, 1982.

Wise, Frederick M., Col., USMC, *Tell It to the Marines*, as Told to Meigs O. Frost, J.H. Sears & Co., Inc., New York, 1929.

Wu, Chao-Chu, Chinese Minister, "Chinese-American Relations," An extract from: *The Annals*, Vol. CLXIX, July 1929.

Periodicals, Newspapers, and Annuals

The American Legation Guard Annual, Peiping, China, 1934.
China Marine Scuttlebutt, June 1997, China Marine Association, Jamestown, PA, June 1997.
Fortitudine, Newsletter of the Marine Corps Historical Program, issues: Summer & Fall of 1983, Fall of 1985, Fall of 1986.
Leatherneck, Magazine of the Marines, Marine Corps Association, Quantico, VA, issues: September 1987 January, April, June, October 1938; October, November, December 1999; March, June 2000
New York Times, years 1895, 1900, 1911, 1926, 1927, 1928, 1937, 1938, 1940, 1941.
North China Marine, Monthly Magazine, June 1941 through November 1941. (Successor to *Peiping Marine* and *Tientsin Marine.*)
Peiping Chronicle, Clippings covering period Dec. 31, 1940, through October 29, 1941.
Peiping Marine, Monthly Magazine, June 1940 through May 1941.
The Tientsin Marine 1940 Annual, Marine Guard Detachment, 1940.

Personal Papers Collection, Marine Corps University Research Archives, Quantico, Virginia

Boxer Rebellion.
Brown, Luther A., Col. USMC (Ret).
Butler, Smedley D., Maj. Gen.
Fuller, Ben H.
Hawthorne, William Gillman, Col. USMC.
Myers, John T.
Russell, Clem D.
Snyder, Harold C.
Upham, Oscar J.—Diary/Journal
Waller, Jr., Littleton W.I.
Wortan, William Arthur

Personal Papers

Biggs, Chester M., Jr., MSgt, USMC, Ret.
Marshall, Joe K., MSgt, USMC, Ret.
Prater, Frank P., Marine in China, circa 1940–45

Index

Abarenda, US naval collier 151
Adams, J.M., Sgt., USMC 59
Adriance, H.C., Cpl., USMC 59
Akira, Sugiyama, Japanese Chancellor
  see Sugiyama
Alacrity, HMS, British warship 227
Albany, USS 149
Allen, Walter G., Pfc., USMC 198
American forces in China 140
Amherst, Lord, British officer 8
Andressen, Cpl., USMC 196
Ankron, Merlin W., Pfc., USMC 198
Anping, North China city 50
Armstrong, Miss, sister of Lady Mac-
  Donald 66
Armstrong, Wade H., Pfc., USMC 204
Asheville, USS 150
Ashurst, William W., Col., USMC 205,
  206, 207
Aurora, HMS, British warship 53

Ball, Thomas, Hospital Apprentice,
  USN 239, 240
Baltimore, USS 11, 13
Bannon, Phillip M., Capt., (Maj.),
  USMC 130, 140, 329, 241
Barber, Francis A., Cpl., USMC 198
Bayly, S., Capt. HMS *Aurora* 53
Beadle, Roger W., lstLt., USMC 180
Bean, Fred, Capt., USMC 180
Beavers, Pfc., USMC 196
Bengal Lancers, British Army Unit 54
Berger, American consul Tientsin 190

Biddle, William P., Maj., USMC, CO,
  lstMarReg. 118, 119, 134, 234, 238,
  240, 242, 245
Bitten, USS 188
Blackhawk, USS 188, 190
Blake, D.W., 2dLt., USMC 239, 241
Bowers, H., British Commander 236
Boxer Bill *see* "Old International"
Boxer Rebellion 15
Boxers 15, 16, 18, 19, 20, 21, 26, 63, 72
Brazier, Mr., British Commissioner of
  Custons 105
British Concessions 7
Brooklyn, USS 49, 52, 52, 135
Brooks, the Reverend, British, 20
Brophy, Cpl., USMC 244
Brown, Luther A., Maj., USMC 205,
  206, 207
Browne, Robley H. J., Surgeon, Royal
  Navy 227
Bucher, Carroll W., Field Music Cpl.,
  USMC 207
Bunn, Douglas A., Pfc., USMC 203
Burns, 1stSgt., USMC 141
Burnside, Wayne, Pvt., USMC 147
Butler, Smedley D., lstLt. (Capt.–
  BrigGen.), USMC 40, 42, 43, 44, 57,
  53, 59, 119, 126, 130, 134, 135, 153,
  154, 155, 157, 158, 159, 160, 161, 162,
  165, 166, 224, 226, 239, 240
Butterfield & Swire British tugboat
  189, 191
Butts, Pvt., USMC 108

Camp Barrows 141, 178, 182
Camp Burrough *see* Camp Barrows
Camp Holcomb 182
"Can Do" Regiment 140, 158, 183
Canton, treaty port south China 6, 10
Captain Jinks, legendary Marine 182
Carpenter, Charles C., RAdm., USN 11, 239, 240
Carr, William L., Pvt., Bugler, USMC 117, 130
Carter, Pvt., USMC 42
Carving Knife Brigade, Volunteers, Legations, Peking, 100
Castner, Joseph, Gen., 15th Infantry, USA 158, 159
Cathay (China) 5
Chaffee, Adan R., MajGen., USA, Commanding American Forces 114, 116, 117, 118, 119, 120, 123, 130, 131, 132, 133, 134, 138, 242
Chamot, Auguste M., Swiss proprietor of Hotel de Pekin 65, 78, 80, 91
Chamot, Mrs., American wife of M. Auguste Chamot 77, 78, 80
Chang Foo Shiang, Chinese General 39
Chang Hsin Tien, Town 16 miles from Peking, battle site 65
Chang Tsu-lin, Gen., Chinese warlord 155, 168
Changchiawan, battle site 127, 239
Chaumont, USS 152, 188, 191
Cheefoo, treaty port North China 11, 188
Cheshire, F.D., American Legation Interpreter 89
Chia Ching, 1796–1820 Emporer 15
Chiang Kai-shek, Chinese Generalissimo 138, 151, 162, 165, 171
Chidester, lstLt., USMC 180
Chien men watch tower (pagoda) 67, 68, 80, 81, 82, 130, 131, 132, 133, 153, 181, 201
Chih Hua Men, gate in Tartar Wall Peking, Japanese objective 128, 129, 131
China Expedition 140
Chinwangtao, port of entry, North China 189
Chou En-lai, Chinese communist leader 171
Chungking Riots of July 1886 73

Clifford, W.H., lstLt., USMC 59, 239
Cochrane, Henry Clay, Col., USMC 134
Coldstream Guards, British Regiment 154, 157
Collins, B. B., Pvt., USMC 180
Coltman, Robert, Jr., British missionary doctor 23, 24, 85, 92, 96, 110
Concessions 7, 44
Conger, E.H., American Minister 13, 14, 20, 21, 26, 27, 31, 40, 72, 88, 94, 95, 99, 108, 110, 116, 117, 234, 235
Conger, Sarah Pike, wife of American Minister 13, 14, 30, 74, 99
Conoley, Odell M., lstLt., USMC 180
Coolidge, Calvin, 30th president 153
Coolridge, Col., 9th Infantry USA 224
Cordes, Herr Heinrick, German interpreter 76
Cossacks, Russian army unit 47, 65, 91, 127
Costigan, G.D., P.A. Surgeon, USN 238, 239, 240
Cradock, Christopher, Commander, RN 43, 45, 226, 227
Crozier, William, Capt., U.S. Army 116
Crusades 5
Cuillier, Mme., French, only woman wounded 114
Custom's Mess 86

Daggett. Aaron S., BrigGen., USA, 14thInf. 46, 11
Dahlgren, Cpl., USMC 70
Daly, Dan, Pvt., USMC 107
Davis, Pvt., USMC 108
Davis, A.R., Capt., USMC 59, 224, 225
Day, J.H.A., lstLt., USMC 239, 241, 243
Dees, William J., Pfc., USMC 204
Dehn, Carl von, Sub-Lieutenant, Russian officer 91
Denby, Col., British, 44
Denby, Charles, Col., USA, American Minister 11
Denham, James L., Maj., USMC 174
Dewey, George, Adm., USN 14
Dorward, A.R.F., BrigGen., British Army 54, 56, 57, 59, 223, 225, 237
Duncan, John, MajGen., British 152
Dunlap, R.L., lstLt., USMC 124, 239

Dutton, Robert McN., Capt, USMC 13
Duysberg, M., Missionary 74

East Arsenal, Tientsin 45, 46
East Surry Regiment, British 194
Elgin, Lord, British officer 8, 9, 15, 17
Elliott, George F., Capt., USMC 11, 13, 139
Empress Dowager 20, 21, 23, 24, 25, 30, 38, 52, 76, 109
Empress Dowager's Carriage Park 88
Ewing, Charles E., Missionary 235
Extraterritorial Treaty Rights 6, 8, 202

Fang, Wu Ting *see* Wu
Fanning, John, Sgt., USMC 77, 89, 220
Fargo, Son of Mr. Squires 79
Farrell, G. P., Pvt., USMC 245
Favier, Bishop, Peitang Cathedral 71, 115
Fengtai Railway 65
Fenn, M., Missionary 79
Fifteenth Infantry Regiment, USA 140, 155, 157, 158, 178, 180
Finch, USS 188
Finney, Charles G., Pvt., 15th Infantry 155
First Expeditionary Force, USMC 150
First Marine Division 209
First Marine Regiment 52, 55, 56, 57, 58, 59, 118, 133, 135
Fischer, Pvt., USMC 108
Fist of Righteous Harmony 15
Flame, British gunboat 50
Flemming, Peter, British volunteer 90, 126, 127
Fliszar, Julius F., Pvt., USMC 173
Foochow, treaty port 6
Foote, Capt., Ninth Infantry, USA 60
Fourteenth Infantry, US Army Regiment 118, 124, 130, 132
Fourth Marine Regiment 151, 155, 169, 171, 192, 206
French Concession 7, 188, 195
Frey, Gen., French Army 125, 128
Frieburger, Walter F., Pfc., USMC 204
Fu Chiang, Chinese Marshall 162
Fuller, Ben H., Capt., USMC 56, 57, 58, 59, 118, 119, 227, 239

Gamewell, Frank Dunlap, American Missionary doctor and engineer 69, 73, 83, 106
Gamewell, Mary Porter, wife of Dr. Gamewell 90, 100
Garris, Jim., PltSgt., USMC 180
Gassell, British General commanding International Force 111, 113, 114, 128, 131
Gibson, John, Lt., USN 14
Giers, M., Russian Minister 115
Gingals, Chinese weapon 57, 59, 86
Glorified Tigers, Chinese army unit, CO Prince Tuan 85
Goen, lstLt., USMC 180
Gold, Harry, Pvt., USMC 89
Gold Star, US naval collier 151
Gowan, Frank F., part owner Hemple's 170
Graf, W.F., Lt., USN 188, 189
Grant, SS President, oceanliner 153
Green, F.W., Pvt., USMC 245
Gregory, Cpl., British Royal Marine 98
Grew, Joseph C., Amer Ambassador to Japan 199
Gros, Baron, French officer 8, 9, 15, 17
Gulf of Pe-Chi-Li 48
Gurkhas, British troops 54
Gutzlaff, Karl, German missionary 8

Hai-Ho River 183
Hall, Newt, Capt., USMC 27, 29, 31, 69, 73, 77, 95, 99, 106, 107, 113, 116, 117, 220
Hall, Thomas F., Pvt., USMC 95
Halliday, Capt., CO British Royal Marines 88
Hamlin Academy, Chinese Library 80, 87, 88
"Handsome Jack" *see* Myers, John T.
Hardee, W.C., 2dLt., USMC 240
Harding, A.E., lstLt., USMC 40, 42, 43, 226, 239, 240
Harice, W.C., 2dLt., USMC 239
Harrick, A. J. Part owner of Hemples 170
Harrison, SS 206
Hart, Sir Robert, Chief of Customs, British 89
Hart, Thomas C., Adm., USN 205, 298

Hawthorne, William C., LtCol., USMC 183, 187, 189, 191
Hayes, John, American Sec. of State 6
The Heavenly Ford 7
Heinl, Robert Debs, Jr., Col., USMD, Author 116, 117
Helms, Herman, Pvt., USMC 81
Hemple, Frank, proprietor of Hemple's 170
Hemple's Hotel and Restaurant 170
Henderson, USS 150, 153
Henderson, lstSgt.; USMC 170, 180
Hester, James R., Capt., USMC 203
Heywood, Charles, MajGen, Commandant of the Marine Corps 116, 132, 136, 138
Hill, Charles S., "Jumbo," Col., USMC 151
Hiller, S.D., lstLt., USMC 59
Hisku Arsenal, Tientsin 122
Holcomb, Thomas, lstLt., USMC 139
Holly Lands 5
Homma, LtGen., Japanese 188
Hong Kong, treaty port 10
Hooker, Mary, American missionary 72, 86, 92, 99, 100
Hoover, Herbert, American engineer, 31st President 28, 47, 56, 59, 62
Hopkins, William, lstLt., USMC 239, 241
Horse Marines see Mounted Detachment
Hosiwu, town in North China, battle site 127, 239
Hotel de Pekin 77, 78, 80
Hough, John F., Capt., USMC 176
Houston, USS 169
Hsia Kuo Men, gate in Tartar Wall, Peking, British objective 131
Hsiki Arsenal 38, 44, 46
Huizenger, Richard, 2dLt., USMC 206, 207
Hull, Cordell, American Sec. of State 202
Hunt, Martin, Cpl., USMC 98

I Ho Ch'uan see Boxers
Imperial Bannerman, Chinese army unit 389
Imperial Hiski Arsenal at Tientsin 38
Inbecks, Foreign Food Store in Peking 79, 90

Indiana, USS 135
Ingles, Dr., Missionary 85

James, Heberty, missionary professor 78
James, William C., LtCol., USMC 180
Japanese Concession 7
Jewett, H.E., Paymaster, USN 28
Johnson, Maj., British 39
Johnson, Robert, Quartermaster Sgt., USMC 240
Jolly, Wade L., 2dLt., USMC 40, 58, 226
Jung Lu, CO Peking Field Force 85

Kailan Mining Administration 182
Kang-Yi, Pres. of Chinese Ministry of War 50
Kempff, Louis, RAdm., USN 28, 43, 45, 51, 85
Kennedy, John, Pvt., USMC 95
Ketteler, Klemens, Baron von, German Minister 68, 76, 77
Kierer, Francis S., Capt., USMC 150
Kierfuff, Foreign Food Store in Peking 79, 90
King, Charles B., Pvt., USMC 81
Kirk, Capt., USMC 180
Knights of the Round Table 170–171
Korietz, Russian heavy cruiser 5
Krag-Jorgensen Rifle 57, 128
Krupp Gun 48, 58, 100, 113
Ku Ku Beach 189, 190
Kuomintang, Chinese Nationalist Party 137, 148, 150, 151
Kwang Has, Chinese emperor 20

Lady MacDonald, wife of British minister 66, 73
Lady MacDonald's Mess 85
Lambert, Miss, missionary nurse 84
Lang-Fang, city in North China, site of engagement 36, 38, 72
Lawler, J.F., SgtMaj., USMC 239, 240
Lawton, Capt., 9th Infantry 224
Lay, Harry, Col., USMC 159
Lee, Harry, Capt., USMC 139
Lee, William A., Chief Marine Gunner, USMC 204, 206
Lee Rifle 128

Lejeune, John A., MajGen., USMC 152
Lemly, W.B., Capt., USMC 59, 238, 239, 240
Leonard, Henry, lstLt., USMC 40, 42, 58, 59, 224, 226
Lineivitch, Gen., Russian Army 120, 131
Lippett, T.M., Assistant Surgeon, USN 27, 29, 31, 72, 99
Liscum, E,H., Col., CO Ninth Infantry, USA 52, 54, 59, 224, 225
Little, L.M., 2dLt., USMC 58
Logan, USS, army transport 139
Long, C.G., Capt., USMC 56, 59, 132, 239, 241
Lowery, missionary doctor 85, 99
Lowery, E.K., missionary in Tientsin 110
Lukouchow, town near Peiping 171
Lung, G.A., surgeon, USN 238, 239, 240

MacDonald, Sir Claude, British Minister 34, 82, 87, 91, 94, 110, 115, 128, 228
Machiapu Railroad Station, Peking 65
MacMurry, John V.A., American Minister to China 154, 160
Macao, Portuguese colony, 6
Madame Paula von Rosthorn, wife of Austrian Chargé d'Affaires 77
Madison, SS ocean liner 206
Mallory, J.S., LtCol., Fourteenth Infantry, USA 110
Manchukuo Province 168
Manchuria 168
Mao Tse-tung, Leader, Chinese Communist Party 138
Marco Polo, Italian explorer 5
Marco Polo Bridge 171
Marston, John, Col., USMC 172
Martin, Charles H., Capt., USMC 149
Matou, city North China, battle site 127, 239
Matson, GySgt., USMC 141
Matthews, A.J., lstLt., USMC 239, 241
Mauser Rifle 48
McCalla, Bowman H., Capt., USN 28, 29, 30, 31, 33, 34, 35, 39, 44, 46, 72, 117, 120
McCartney, Lord, British officer 7

McCaughtry, Walter E., Capt., USMC 151
McClellan Saddle 143
McCreary, Wirt, 2dLt., USMC 120, 123, 125, 239
McDonald, Cpl., USMC 144
McGill, J.F., lstLt., USMC 239, 241
McHugh, J., 2dLt., USMC 141
McLeod, K.F., lstLt., USMC 239, 241
McLittle, L., 2dLt., USMC 329, 241
Meade, Robert L., Col., USMC 52, 54, 56, 58, 61, 119, 222, 223, 225, 227
Merchant, Gerald C., Pvt., USMC 145
Merz, Carl F., Capt., USMC 151
Methodist Mission, Peking 67, 68, 69, 71, 73, 77
Miller, PlSgt., USMC 141
Miller, C.M.C., agent for J.P. Morgan 61
Ming Dynasty 7, 48
Mission Mess 85
Mitchell, Joseph, Gunner's Mate lst Class, USN 88, 100, 101, 102, 103, 104, 105, 112, 113
Mongol Market, Peking 92, 93, 111
Monocacy, USS 11, 13, 41, 45, 50, 51, 52, 53
Montaubaun, Gen., British officer 9
Moody, Fred D., Pvt., USMC 99
Morgan, J.P., American financier 61
Morrison, C.E., missionary doctor 65, 78, 116,
Moses, Frank J., Capt., USMC 118, 239, 241, 244
Mounted Detachment 141, 142, 173, 180, 181
Mueller, Martin L., Pvt., USMC 89
Munson, Maj., USA, military attaché 203
Murphy, Sgt., Royal British Marines 97
Muslims 5
Myers, John Twiggs, Capt., USMC 27, 29, 31, 65, 67, 68, 70, 71, 72, 73, 75, 81, 82, 83, 88, 89, 92, 96, 97, 98, 99, 101, 110, 116, 117, 131, 220

Nagasaki, Japan 13, 27, 52
Nan-T'ang, Catholic Mission, Peking 14, 74
Nashville, USS 41, 49

Neville, Wendell C., Capt., USMC 119, 239, 241, 245
New Chwang, treaty port, 10
Newark, USS 27, 33, 49, 117
Newton, George R., lstLt., USMC 203
Niccoli, lst Marine band leader in Peking 147
Nieh, Gen., Chinese army 35, 36
Ningpo, treaty port, 6
Ninth Infantry Regiment, USA 52, 56, 59, 124, 135, 136, 138, 139, 222, 224

Olaguez, August, MSgt., USMC 148
Old Betsy *see* "Old International"
Old Crock *see* "Old International"
"Old International," American artillery piece 102, 103, 104, 109, 112, 113
Oliphant, Nigel, volunteer, British Legation 93, 97
Open Door Policy 6, 9
Opium War 6, 8
Oregon, USS 27, 49, 104
Orlando, Lt., USN 227
Orr, William W., Capt., USMC 180

Palmer, Mars W., Chief Radio Electrician USN 176
Paomachang Race Track 197
Parker, Lt., USMC 58
Partridge, Pvt., USMC 58
Patterson, S.A.W., lstLt., USMC 239, 241
Pei-Ho River 7, 8, 11, 15, 27, 35
Pei-tsang, town in North China, site of battle, 123, 239
Peitang Cathedral, Peking 67, 71, 115
Peking 1, 7
Peking-Tientsin Railroad 27, 177, 183
Pethick, W.N., missionar 74, 117
Petroff, George, Cpl, USMC 198
Piet-Lang, North China city
Pittner, Pfc., USMC 196
Poole, missionary doctor 84
Poole, Capt., USN 31
Porter, Dave D, Capt., USMC 118, 134, 238, 239, 240
Powell, W.G., lstLt., USMC 40, 41, 42, 225, 226
Prince Chia Ch'ing 24, 108, 109, 228–229
Prince Chia Shui 24
Prince Liao Shou Heng 24

Prince Na T'ung 24
Prince Tuan 19, 24
Protocol 1901 10, 172
Pruitt, Cpl., USMC 244
P'u Chun, boy emporer, 20, 108
Puller, Lewis B. "Chesty," Capt., USMC 146, 147

Ragsdale, American consul in Tientsin 110
Rahden, Baron von, Lt., CO Russian guards 68, 91, 96, 98
Raleigh, USS 13
Randall, David F., lstLt., USMC 182
Reid, George C., lstLt., USMC 40
Reilly, Capt., USA 131, 132, 133
Reilly's Battery, Fifth Artillery, USA 118, 124, 131
Remey, George C., RAdm., USN, CinC Asiatic Squadron 61, 117, 119
Richards, George, Maj., USMC 238, 239, 240
Righteous Harmonious Fist *see* Boxers
Rixey, Presley M., Col, USMC 168
Rockhill, W.W., American Minister to Peking 136, 139
Roman Catholic Church 16
Roosevelt, Franklin D. 197
Roosevelt, Theodore 118, 139
Root, Elihu, U.S. Sec. of War and Sec. of State 130, 138
Royal Welsh Fusiliers, British regiment 54, 56, 57, 62, 118

Schatzel, DeWolf, 2dLt., USMC 182
Schroeder, John, Pvt., USMC 94
Scuttlebutt 119, 120
Seventh Rajputs, British Regiment 114
Seymour, Edward H, VAdm. British Naval officer 34, 35, 37, 39, 44, 45, 46, 72, 117, 120, 237
Shanghai 6, 10, 154
Sheets, Fremont F., Pfc. USMC 204
Shiba, Col., CO Japanese Marines 110
Shozo, Kawabe, Japanese General 197
Sikhs, British regiment 54, 118
Silva, Joseph, Pvt., USMC 95
Sixth Cavalry Regiment, USA 118, 119
Sixth Marine Division 209

Sixth Marine Regiment 152
Smith, Arthur H., missionary 235
Snyder, Harold C., Col., USMC 152
Soden, Graf Alfred von, CO German marines 81, 94
Solace, USS 40
Soldiers' Mess 85
Sousa, John Phillip, American Composer & band leader 62
Squires, Herbert, American First Secretary 32, 65, 79, 90
Squires, Mrs., wife of American First Secretary 65, 91
Stahl, George W., Chief Pay Clerk USMC 174
Standard Oil Company fire, Tientsin 162
Stanley, R., Hospital Apprentice, USN 28
Stillson, G.D., Hospital Apprentice, USN 239, 240
Strouts,B.M., Capt., Royal British Marines 68
Sugiyama, Japanese Chancellor, Peking 70
Summer Palace 9
Sun Cheh-Yan, Chinese General 172
Sun Yat-sen, Pres. of Chinese Republic 137
Sutton, Clarence E., Sgt., USMC 59
Swank, Roy C., Capt., USMC 150

Taku Forts, Chinese forts on Pei-Ho River 8
Tangku, river port on Pei-Ho River 7, 8, 28, 41, 188
Tehsheng, British liner 194
Tenth Marine Artillery Regiment 161
The Fu, Chinese princes' palace 78, 80, 84, 90, 105, 111
Third Marine Brigade 153, 155, 157, 158, 161, 165
Thirty-first Infantry Regiment, USA 169
Thomann, Capt., Austrian navy 86, 87
Thomas, Welshman, helped Mitchell build Old Betsy 102
Thomas, Robert E., Pvt., USMC 98
Thompson, J.C., Assistant Surgeon, USN 238, 239, 240
Thornhill's Toughs, British volunteers 100

Thornton, John T., Capt., USMC 150
Tia-ping Rebellion 55
Tiencienwey (Tientsin) 7
Tientsin Flood 183
Tientsin-Peking Railway 27, 177, 183
Titus, Calvin P., Trumpter, 14thInf. USA 130
Tominogo Kyoju, LtGen., Japanese 206
Trachita, Lt., USMC 180
Treaty of Nanking 6
Treaty of Nertchinah of 1680 65
Treaty of Tientsin 8, 10, 15
Treaty of Whampoa 6
T'set Sun, Chinese rebel leader 137, 140
Tsumlgi Yamen, Chinese Imperial Foreign Office 20, 24, 26, 63, 76
T.T. Wang's Emporium 182
Tung Chih Men, gate in Tartar Wall, Peking, Russian objective 128, 131
Tung Fu-Hsiang, Chinese Gen., CO Fierce Khansu 23, 25, 73, 85, 92
Tung Pien Men, gate in Tartar Wall, Peking, American objective 128, 129, 130, 131
Tungchow, North China city battle site 9, 128, 239
Turnage, Allen H., Col., USMC 191
Turner, Albert, Pvt., USMC 97, 98
Turner, Thomas C., LtCol., USMC 152
Tutcher, John W., Pvt., USMC 94
Twenty-ninth Chinese Army 172

Umbrella of Blessing, Chinese award 163, 164, 165, 166
Unequal Treaties 6
Upham, Oscar J., Pvt., USMC 77, 94, 104, 106, 109
U.S. Army Forces in China 140

Vandergrift, Alexander H., Col., USMC 172
Vasco da Gama, Portuguese explorer 5
Velde, Dr., German Surgeon 84
Vroome, R.L., 2dLt., USMC 182

Waller, Littleton W.T., Maj., USMC 40, 41, 42, 43, 45, 53, 56, 57, 60, 61, 62, 115, 118, 119, 132, 133, 222, 227, 236, 237, 239, 240, 241
Wallis, C.O., Capt., British 194
Warren, Col., USMC 110

Water Gate, gate in Tartar Wall, Peking
     130, 131
Watson, Adm., USN 27
Watts, James, English civilian 47
Wells, Summer, American Sec. of State
     195
West Arsenal, Tientsin 56
Wheeling, USS 27, 49
Whiting, British gunboat 50
Willcox, Julian, Maj., USMC 151
Williams, Clarence S., Adm., USN 154
Williams, Dion., Col., USMC 142
Wilson, August, Capt., USMC 150
Wise, Frederick M., Comdr., USN 45,
     50, 51, 53
Wise, Frederick M., Jr., lstLt., USMC
     53, 57, 119, 121, 124, 125, l33, 239, 240
Woosung Prisoner of War Camp–Japa-
     nese 209

Worton, W. A., Capt., USMC 141
Wu, Chinese minister to Washington,
     D.C. 108
Wynne, R.F., lstLt., USMC 40, 58, 226,
     239

Yamen *see* Tsumgli Yamen
Yang-Tsun, North China city and battle
     site 37, 38, 124, 125, 126
Yiksang, coastal steamer 11
Yu Hien, Boxer leader 20
Yu Hsien, Governor of Shantung 18, 21
Yuam Shih-kai, Chinese dictator 137
Yuan, Gen., military governor 20
Yuan Shih K'ai, Chinese general 21, 140
Yung Lo, Chinese Emperor 1421 7

Zafiro, USS 135
Zanta, Austrian cruiser 86